MODERNISTS BOHEMIANS MAVERICKS

MODERNISTS
BOHEMIANS
MAVERICKS

JIM BURNS

PENNILESS PRESS PUBLICATIONS
www.pennilesspress.co.uk

Published by

Penniless Press Publications 2021

ISBN 978-1-913144-24-1

Cover: Some books reviewed

CONTENTS

ACKNOWLEDGEMENTS

Many of these reviews and essays were written for the on-line *Northern Review of Books*. The appropriate details are listed below:

The Deep End: The Literary Scene in the Great Depression. September, 2020

Charles Reznikoff. September, 2020

Dawn Powell in Greenwich Village. July, 2020

Tess Slesinger. May, 2020

Denys Val Baker. April, 2020

Norman Levine. May, 2020

The Beats. May, 2020

Little Magazines of the Beat Era. April, 2020

Henry Harland in Bohemia. May, 2020

Circles and Squares: The Hampstead Modernists. June, 2020

Bill Butler and the Unicorn Bookshop. August, 2020

Sherlock's Sisters. October, 2020

Broadway and the Blacklist. January, 2020

William Faulkner in Hollywood. April, 2020

John Dos Passos and John Howard Lawson. June, 2020

John Nash. December, 2019

The Poster: 200 Years of Art and History. July, 2020

Modigliani. November, 2020

The Scottish Colourists. November. 2019

Burning the Books. October, 2020

The Secret War Against the Arts. October, 2020

Labour's Mind. April, 2020

The King Over the Water. June, 2020

The Irish War of Independence. July, 2020

Down in the Valley. August, 2020

The Streets of Europe. October, 2020

Fighting for Spain. October, 2020

British Music Hall. June, 2020

Dave Brubeck. March, 2020

Jazz from Detroit. January, 2020

Other acknowledgements are listed below:

A Soho State of Mind. Previously unpublished, but adapted from a review of *Shot in Soho* (Prestel, London, 2019) in the *Northern Review of Books,* January, 2020

Bohemia. *Oasis* 16, London, 1976. A shortened version of the original

Crystal Eastman. *Palantir* 14, Preston, April, 1980

Early Modernists. *Tribune,* London, 24th April, 1970 and 5th March, 1971

James Wright. *Ambit* 132, London, 1993

Paul Potts. *Palantir* 14, Preston, April, 1980

Gary Snyder and the Wobblies. *Beat Scene* 98, Coventry, Late-summer, 2020

South of the Border. *Beat Scene* 97, Coventry, Early-summer, 2020

The Day I Met Jack Kerouac. *The Kerouac Connection* 8, Bristol, October, 1985. And in *Kerouac at the "Wild Boar"* edited by John Montgomery. Fels & Firn Press, San Anselmo, 1986

Woody Guthrie/Joe Hill. *Tribune,* London, 27th March, 1981

Sacco and Vanzetti. *Tribune,* London, 12th February, 1982

Fooling Around. *Cells*, Grosseteste Press, Lincoln, 1967; *The Honest Ulsterman* 7, Belfast, November, 1968; *For Bill Butler,* Wallrich Books, London, 1970; *Notes From a Greasy Spoon,* University College Cardiff Press, Cardiff, 1980

The Girl. *Chelsea* 22/23, New York, 1968

The Salesmen. *Workshop* 4, London, Autumn, 1968

Lunchtime O'Booze. *Notes from a Greasy Spoon,* University College Cardiff Press, Cardiff, 1980

The Swinger. *For Bill Butler*, Wallrich Books, London, 1970

My thanks to the editors concerned and to Ken Clay and Joan Mottram

INTRODUCTION

This twelfth selection of reviews and essays kicks off with a couple of personal pieces which, taken together, might provide a pointer to some of my concerns over the years. I've always been fascinated by the history of bohemia, in both its social and literary/artistic manifestations. There's a long catalogue of novels, stories, poems, memoirs, and social histories dealing with bohemian centres such as Greenwich Village, Montparnasse, Montmartre, Soho, and other urban locations, together with artists' colonies like St Ives, Pont-Aven and numerous additional places where painters congregated.

There are people who dismiss the whole notion of bohemia as simply a distraction from the work of a few geniuses who kept themselves apart from all the supposed frivolities and created the works that are really worthy of our attention. It seems to me that to stick to the main avenues of literature or art, and ignore all the side-streets, minor roads, and even the cul-de-sacs, is to miss a lot that can be entertaining. I've often tried to delve into areas of activity that have been overlooked or forgotten, and in doing so have come across numerous interesting books and fine paintings.

I suspect that much of the literature of the 1930s is little-known these days. A a handful of major novels have survived, but many more have been consigned to the attentions of a few academics. The book *Deep End* by Jason Boog, does draw attention to at least certain obscure authors of the Depression Days. The essays about Dawn Powell, Charles Reznikoff, and Tess Slesinger might say some things of value with relevance to a few books of the period.

I referred to artists' colonies, and the most-famous one in the British Isles has usually been identified as being in St Ives. I've written about it, and some of the painters associated with it, in earlier collections. The present one has essays looking at the connections between St Ives and Denys Val Baker and Norman Levine. Baker was a lively character, editing *The Cornish Review,* writing novels, short stories, and books about Cornwall. I've singled out some of the novels and stories that deal specifically with St Ives and its artistic community. I've done something similar with Norman Levine, a Canadian who lived in St Ives for a number of years. His *From a Seaside Town* seems to me a first-rate novel and not only for the light it shines on St Ives.

The actual painters covered in this book do not include any St Ives artists. John Nash, the brother of, and often overshadowed by, the more-celebrated Paul Nash, produced some excellent landscapes. The Scottish Colourists – Peploe, Caddel, Fergusson, and Hunter – were adventurous artists, influenced by what was happening on the Continent, and their work is attractive to look at. As for Modigliani, there is the combination of talent and bohemianism, and the fact of his being in Paris at a time of enthusiastic activity in painting and sculpture.

There are, as always, some pieces about the Beats. Their years in the limelight seemed to be an exciting period for little magazines, and the essay on them attempts to draw attention to their existence. It was, for me, always a pleasure to get the magazines through the post, or find them in the London bookshops I frequented. I first came across Gary Snyder's work in a little magazine, and I write about the early days and the references, in his poetry, to the militant organisation, The Industrial Workers of the World. There are some Beat associations in the essay about two novels on the lives of American expatriates in Mexico. As for "The Day I Met Jack Kerouac", readers must make up their own minds.

The cinema is touched on in pieces about William Faulkner in Hollywood, and the fictional portrait by John Dos Passos of the blacklisted screenwriter John Howard Lawson. The blacklist also crops up in a review of a book about how it affected Broadway. Writers and artists being investigated by MI5 and Special Branch in Britain are looked at. And the review of *Burning the Books* points to what happens when culture and knowledge are under different forms of attack. The review of a book about Bill Butler, a bookseller hounded by the police, perhaps comes into this category?

In three essays I look at different aspects of Scottish, Welsh, and Irish history. There is a review of a book about the role of the International Brigades in the Spanish Civil War. Some characters from American radical history are referred to in reviews of books about Woody Guthrie, Joe Hill, and Sacco and Vanzetti. They are admittedly short pieces, written for the left-wing weekly, *Tribune,* but reviving them here might trigger some readers into looking a little further into their lives.

There are several musical items. A review of a lively book about the heyday of British music-hall, another about the jazz scene in Detroit in the 1940s and 1950s, and one about Dave Brubeck. I hope that, together with the other pieces, they'll indicate that variety is indeed the spice of life.

A SOHO STATE OF MIND

Someone once said that Soho is a state of mind. I take it to mean that you don't necessarily need to live there to share its culture. It perhaps represents something that people aspire to in terms of its creativity, freedom of expression, and indulgences in types of behaviour which would be frowned on elsewhere. People have been drawn to Soho for these reasons, some permanently, others just as occasional visitors who feel the need to break away for a time from their more-settled daily lives. A period spent in Soho can help to rejuvenate the creative impulses. It can also just be fun.

I suppose I'd place myself in the "occasional visitor" category. I first ventured into Soho in 1952 as a sixteen-year old fan who was there in search of bebop, the then-dominant form of modern jazz. My contact with it until then had been of hearing snatches of it on the radio (the BBC ran a tight ship in the 1950s so didn't broadcast a lot of jazz) and on the few records I could afford to buy. Life in a drab Northern industrial town was brightened by the sounds of bebop, though the nature of the music meant that I could only play my records when other members of the family were absent. But the music of Dizzy Gillespie, Charlie Parker, Howard McGhee, and the few British musicians playing bebop, or something close to it, were, along with the cinema, my early entrance into the general world of culture. I read the weekly *Melody Maker* avidly and eventually persuaded my parents that a trip to London was essential. I had the addresses of a couple of clubs where I hoped to experience some live examples of the music.

One of the clubs was called the Studio '51 and was located in Great Newport Street, just off Charing Cross Road and a few steps away from the area known as Soho. I'm not sure what I expected to discover at the bottom of some stairs. What I did find was a basement with a low bandstand at one end on which were gathered a small group of mostly casually-dressed musicians. Thinking back almost seventy years, I recall there were two groups performing that night, one of which seemed to feature a couple of musicians from the Johnny Dankworth Seven – trumpeter Eddie Blair and trombonist Eddie Harvey – and the other with tenor saxophonist Kenny Graham and the Jamaican trumpeter Dizzy Reece. The alto player Johnny Rogers was also there. The one thing that sticks in my mind about that evening is Dizzy Reece, smart-suited in contrast to the others, leaning back against the piano, smoke from a cigarette curling in the air, as he blew smooth bop lines with

11

ease and confidence.

A year or so later I made a longer trip, this time to Dublin, to hear the Stan Kenton Orchestra. Because of a Ministry of Labour and Musicians' Union ban on American musicians appearing in Britain, Dublin was the nearest location for many British fans. Kenton at that time had musicians like Lee Konitz, Zoot Sims, Frank Rosolino, and Conte Candoli featured as soloists, and I knew their names from records and reports in the *Melody Maker* and *Jazz Journal*. I'm mentioning this because, although the American musicians were clearly superior to their British counterparts when it came to playing modern jazz, there was something about that earlier experience in the cramped Studio '51 that has lingered in my mind over the years. It may not have been more than a routine night for the musicians, but it left its mark on me. It was, perhaps, something akin to one's first love affair in its impact. It's something you never forget.

London was still quite shabby in 1952, with the effects of the war years and post-war austerity still lingering, and I wandered through Soho which seemed to have a different atmosphere to other parts of the city. Or was it just my imagination adding a little light and colour to streets which were untidy but livelier? I was too young to go into pubs like the French, and in any case I was unaware of its reputation as a gathering-place for writers and artists.

I suppose I could be like the old man who once saw Shelley plain, or the man who was fanatical about Beau Brummel and, by a series of coincidences, persuaded himself that, when he was a child, he must have passed the famous dandy on a street in Brighton. But I won't pretend that I saw Julian Maclaren-Ross, or the two Roberts (the Scottish painters, Colquhoun and MacBryde), or anyone else like them. I wouldn't have known them even if I had. I think my notions of Soho at that time had, the jazz angle apart, largely been influenced by newspaper articles about vice and crime more than culture. Even the jazz was, to many people, suspect, with memories of the police raid on the Club Eleven when several musicians, including Ronnie Scott, were charged with drugs offences, continuing to linger in the public mind. People in my home town looked askance at me when I told them I'd roamed around Soho in the dark at the age of sixteen.

A couple of years later I went into the army for three years, and when stationed not too far from London used to go into the city if I had a free weekend. I was still looking for jazz (Dobell's record shop on Charing Cross Road was a regular stop on my travels), and being eighteen could go into pubs without any questions. I remember hearing the Johnny Dankworth big-band, just before I was posted to Germany, though where has disappeared from my memory. And the army, being what might be called the second stage of my entry into culture, had given me time to start reading more widely than I had been doing. I still have the old copy of Julian Maclaren-Ross's *The Nine Men of Soho* that I'd found in a second-hand bookshop on Charing Cross Road.

When I came out of the army in 1957 I began a cycle of regular visits to London that has continued until the present, going into the jazz clubs, including Ronnie Scott's original club in Gerrard Street. It's in my mind that it wasn't much of an improvement on the Studio '51 basement, but I heard Dexter Gordon there on his first trip to Britain in 1960. There was another club where Joe Harriott, like Dizzy Reece an immigrant of what is now referred to as the Windrush Generation, had a quintet with Hank Shaw on trumpet. Shaw was one of the few British jazzmen who successfully handled the bebop style with ease. And he was reputed to be somewhat eccentric in his personal habits. The musician and writer, Benny Green, later wrote a short-story, "Goggles in the Dust", which was about an oddball character based on Shaw.

By the late-1950s and into the early-1960s I'd gravitated into the cultural scene, writing for jazz magazines, publishing poetry, and contributing articles and book reviews to *The Guardian* and especially the left-wing weekly *Tribune*. My political interests often took me into Collett's on Charing Cross Road. I got to know Reg Groves, an old Trotskyist from the 1930s associated with the Balham Group. And my curiosity about anarchism took me to the anarchist bookshop in Whitechapel, and at some point I met Arthur Moyse, a talkative type who contributed sometimes bawdy drawings to little magazines. He also wrote short stories, one of which I published in a magazine I edited in the 1970s. As for my jazz interests, they continued and I occasionally met up with Albert McCarthy, editor of *Jazz Monthly*, and someone who had been around Soho since the 1940s. He'd take me to after-hours drinking clubs when the pubs closed.

My visits to London, sometimes to take part in poetry readings in various places, brought me into contact with writers, little-magazine editors, and some artists. I was in and out of the French regularly, and have memories of chatting with Bobby Hunt, who had been around the Soho scene since the early-1950s and had his portrait painted by the ill-fated John Minton. I tried to hold a conversation with Paul Potts, author of the once-popular *Dante Called You Beatrice*, because I wanted to tell him how much I liked the poems in *Instead of a Sonnet*, published

13

in 1944, but he had obviously been drinking heavily and didn't really register what I was saying. There were other encounters in the French, with Jay Landesman and others, and I once saw an inebriated Jeffrey Bernard being evicted from the premises by the landlord, Gaston Berlemont. It was a great pleasure for me some years later when I gave a reading in an upstairs room at the French. I felt that I was in the presence of the ghosts of old bohemians.

I suppose that in some ways it was inevitable that Soho, and especially certain periods in its history, would become the stuff of legends. The same happened with many of the old bohemian centres in Europe and America. The Left Bank in Paris is no longer the haunt of many writers, artists, and radicals, and seems a different place to the one I first visited in 1962. Shakespeare and Company has been smartened up, and George Whitman is no longer around to preside over his chaotic bookshop and its equally chaotic and motley crew of customers. It was pleasant to walk through Greenwich Village when I was in New York in the 1980s, but even then it was no longer the haunt of impoverished bohemians. The affluent have taken over. I hear reports from other countries about the decline of artistic enclaves in city centres. Few people, and certainly not the working-class or the bohemians, can afford to live there and are driven to the outskirts.

Bohemia, of course, was always yesterday, and a book like Julian Maclaren-Ross's *Memoirs of the Forties* deserves to be read. There's an obscure novel, Julian Horwitz's, *Can I Get There by Candlelight,* that provides a portrait of wartime London, with its blackout curtains and darkened streets. The painter Nina Hamnett, by the 1940s an alcoholic veteran of bohemia, appears in the book. In 1973 there was an exhibition at the Parkin Gallery called *Fitzrovia and the Road to the York Minster* which, as the title indicates, was the real name of the French. Ruthven Todd wrote the text for the catalogue of the exhibition and colourfully evoked the characters and the atmosphere of Fitzrovia and Soho in the Thirties and Forties. Anecdotes about Dylan Thomas, Augustus John, and others who liked to live it up in the pubs and clubs, abound. It's a collector's item now and hard to find.

There's plenty about the 1950s Soho scene, leaving aside biographies of individuals like Francis Bacon and John Minton. A couple of novels spring to mind – Colin Wilson's *Adrift in Soho* and Terry Taylor's *Baron's Court, All Change* – along with Daniel Farson's memoir, *Soho in the Fifties.* Farson was a photographer as well as a writer, and his book is sprinkled with pictures of Soho characters. Another photographer who can be referred to for his Soho portraits was the notorious

John Deakin, who nobody seemed to like: "A nasty, detestable person" was one of the kinder descriptions of him. He was often a fixture at the Colony Room Club, an establishment I never got to, though that may have been a blessing. I doubt that Muriel Belcher, who often denied people entrance to the club on the whim of a moment, would have wanted me there, and in any case I would have been a fish out of water in the hard-drinking, verbally aggressive atmosphere of the club. To get a flavour of it read Sophie Parkin's *The Colony Room Club 1948-2008: A History of Bohemian Soho.*

I have to admit that Soho today doesn't impress me as much as the Soho I read about and experienced in the 1950s and 1960s. There doesn't appear to be as much literary and artistic talent in the area, and unexpected encounters are less frequent, though that may be because so many of the people I knew are no longer around for one reason or another. Old age takes its toll. But I still venture off Charing Cross Road and into Soho whenever I'm in London. It's changed, and so have I. And yet, I suspect that, in some ways, I still have a Soho state of mind.

BACK TO BOHEMIA (1976)

We are about to become involved in another period of bohemianism. Those of you who read a wide variety of little magazines will, I hope, excuse me for embarking on a voyage into a subject I've admittedly touched on elsewhere. But it has different aspects to it and I'll try not to cover too much ground I've already been over.

My own personal opinion is that such a period may not be too bad a thing. There is always a load of nonsense surrounding bohemianism, of course, and human nature is such that the genuine types are swamped by the phoneys and bandwagoners. But it does usually give a fillip to activity in and around the arts. Purists will probably suggest that it's the kind of fillip the arts can well do without (and it's true that any dedicated artist or writer carries on regardless of the distractions) but purists usually lack a sense of humour and mortality and can't see bohemianism as a little part of life's rich panorama.

The politicals, too, will condemn a resurgence of bohemia as "bourgeois irrelevance or opportunism". Something like that. I was never very good at trotting out those sort of clichés, despite being a veteran of political and union meetings and all that. In fact, I decided a sense of proportion was necessary years ago. And it struck me that many of the political people I knew were like the purists and lacked a sense of humour. But it is possible to be both bohemian and political. There were lots of people in Greenwich Village and Chicago's bohemia during the first quarter of the Twentieth Century who managed it pretty well. We haven't had many books on the subject in recent years, but if you can locate copies, Allen Churchill's *The Improper Bohemians* (Cassel, 1961) and Albert Parry's *Garrets and Pretenders* (Dover, 1960) are worth investigating.

I could ramble on about bohemianism from a sociological point of view and why I think it's on the way back, but I'm writing this piece for a literary magazine so I'll keep my comments in context. The last big bout of bohemianism happened during the Beat years, and it did stimulate quite a few people into writing, editing little magazines, and starting small presses. I can hear the purists asking if it was all worthwhile, and where are the poets now, has their work survived, are the now-defunct magazines and pamphlets of any real interest other than to literary historians? They're fair questions, but could be asked of any literary period, whether bohemia-inspired or not. As a collector and occasional historian of little magazines I know how they and their contribu-

tors can easily slip from sight. But I like to be positive and the magazines and little presses helped worthwhile writers into print. They
weren't all going to be major poets and novelists, but they often had
something worthwhile to say.

I've never been a devotee of the argument that says that only a few
great writers matter, or that longevity and volume denote quality. A
man may have only one book in him, but it could be worth as much as
the output of a prolific writer. One of the inviting aspects of bohemia is
that it gives ephemera a chance. When I think back to the Beat years
the names of some aspiring writers spring to mind, despite the fact that
they produced very little and later disappeared. But I remember their
poems and stories, whereas I've forgotten a lot of the work of so-called
established writers. Had it not been for the little magazines and off-beat
presses I doubt that some poets and others would ever have seen their
work in print. No great loss, say the purists and those who only admire
the famous, but I disagree. The obscure and forgotten are always of
interest.

Can the idea of Bohemia as a location, as with Greenwich Village,
Montparnasse, Soho, still have some relevance? Perhaps not. But as a
state of mind it may continue to inspire works of art.

THE DEEP END: THE LITERARY SCENE IN THE GREAT DEPRESSION AND TODAY

Writers are having a hard time in the current climate of economic uncertainty, cutbacks, Covid-19, and major changes in the ways that information and entertainment in the form of literature is disseminated. Libraries are either closing down or limiting their activities. Jason Boog says that "San Francisco Library pulped 250,000 forgotten books to make way for computers and reading spaces". And bookshops have been seeing a steady decline for decades. As someone who has spent well over sixty years prowling around bookshops old and new, market bookstalls, book fairs, and any other kind of location where books might be sold, I can testify to their disappearance. Towns that once had several bookshops now have only one, and that often part of a commercial chain. Any independent shops that are still open struggle to survive. As for attention to books in the press, an editor at *The Guardian* newspaper announced the closure of the weekly book-review supplement and said she wanted to focus on "lifestyle journalism".

Boog, thanks to his own situation of suddenly finding himself losing a steady job as a writer, and retreating to a library to study what had happened in the 1930s, has come up with the idea of selecting several writers from that period and looking at their experiences at a time when it seemed as if the capitalist system in the United States was about to collapse. He also discusses the current problems facing writers generally, though occasionally he seems to be focusing mostly on opportunities and outlets for journalists. It might be argued that, even at the best of times, uncertainty for novelists in terms of being published is a way of life. And even if their work does appear in print there's no guarantee it will sell. I'd guess that most creative writers have other jobs. And when it comes to poets, a regular job, often not directly linked to literature, is usually a necessity.

Things are bad now, and were even worse in the 1930s. But writers still wrote and their work was published. Edward Newhouse's *You Can't Sleep Here,* appeared in 1934 and told the tale of an out-of-work journalist who drifts into the shanty towns set up by the unemployed and unfortunate. He sees himself as part of the "crisis generation", educated to a level where he should have been able to find professional employment, but suddenly having to come to terms with a bleak future. Boog doesn't mention him, but another Thirties writer, Alfred Hayes, caught the mood of such people in the poem, "In a Coffee Pot", where the narrator says that "I brood upon myself. I rot/Night after night in this cheap Coffee Pot", and reflects on what has happened to a friend who seemingly had bright prospects, but is now a "bus boy in an eat-quick joint/At seven per week twelve hours a day", and another who is "on the bum".

Newhouse wrote a second novel, *This is Your Day*, which pointed to his links to the Communist Party, but later drifted away from radical politics and became a staff writer for the *New Yorker*, where he published numerous short stories. His 1949 novel, *The Hollow of the Wave*, was satirical about communists in New York. It's interesting to note that Alfred Hayes, who had appeared widely in left-wing publications, likewise cast off his radical roots. After service as a war correspondent he wrote novels, worked in Hollywood and for TV and, it's said, tended to dismiss his earlier inclinations as youthful follies.

Boog praises Maxwell Bodenheim for an act which, he claims, drew attention to injustices in the way that relief funds were dispensed. Bodenheim, because of his past escapades as a bohemian poet who attracted many female admirers, could always get the attention of journalists. He's perhaps a difficult case to deal with when it comes to a question of his political leanings. He wrote two novels, *Run, Sheep, Run* and *Slow Vision*, which have a place in studies of American radical literature, and some of his poems ("To a Revolutionary Girl" and "Southern Labour Organiser", are two examples) point to left-wing tendencies. But when he's remembered now it's largely because his 1920s affairs made headlines in newspapers across America, and for his slow decline into the poverty and alcoholism of the late-1930s and 1940s which led to his murder in 1954. The fact that he wrote twelve novels and nearly as many poetry collections, as well as contributing poetry and prose to most of the leading magazines of the day, is overlooked. Or if it's acknowledged it's usually with the comment that his work was often flawed. But there are passages in the novels deserving of attention, and some of his poems can still be read with pleasure.

Something that crops up in connection with Bodenheim is his involvement with the Raven Poetry Circle. This group of mostly lesser-known poets met regularly in Washington Square Park and pinned their poems for sale on fencing. Boog writes sympathetically about them instead of adopting the usual patronising line of commentary, when dealing with such groups, which says that the poems vary wildly in quality, and some of the poets are eccentric in their dress and behaviour. One of them, Anca Vrbovska, was perhaps more-talented than many of the others, and did establish something of a minor reputation as a poet. And

May Swenson, who became a leading poet in America, had exhibited with the Raven Circle when she was young.

Poetry then and now was and is often printed by little press publishers and magazines. And in some ways it's perhaps easier than it was in the 1930s to publish a small book or a magazine. Or just put poetry on-line. But even in the depths of the Depression there were people prepared to commit themselves to producing magazines and pamphlets, especially if what was in them had a radical edge. I've got in front of me a copy of *When the Sirens Blow*, a collection of poems by Leonard Spier, published by B.C. Hagglund (based in Holt, Minnesota) in 1933. A glance at the acknowledgements will indicate where both Spier and Hagglund resided in political terms: *Daily Worker, Left, The Industrial Democrat.*

Another publication on my desk as I write is a slim book, *We Gather Strength,* published by the Liberal Press in 1933. It features four poets, Edwin Rolfe, Joseph Kalar, Herman Spector, and Sol Funaroff, all of them from the Left. Neither this nor the Spiers book received subsidies from government sources. Both the poems and the lives of the four named poets continue to be worthy of note. Rolfe wrote movingly about his time in Spain during the Civil War. Funaroff died young from poverty and tuberculosis. His poem, "What the Thunder Said: A Fire Sermon", was sometimes declaimed by the folk-singer and political activist, Ewan MacColl during his street-agitation days in Salford and other places in the 1930s. Spector referred to himself as "the bastard in the ragged suit", and wrote dark, bitter poems. Kalar lived in Minnesota and worked in sawmills when there was work. His poems created a "landscape of shut-down factories, peopled by hard-drinking, down-on-their-luck workers".

Kenneth Fearing's work has survived better than that of Spiers, though I suspect it's largely known mainly by academics curious about the 1930s and a few individuals who like to look outside the usual sources for what was of value in the past. I would guess he might retain some interest for readers of crime fiction. His *The Big Clock* is still in print. Boog says that Fearing's poems "blasted the bankers, fat cats, and politicians who plunged the country into an economic dark age". Like a lot of poets on the Left he was probably too idiosyncratic to ever fit neatly into a fixed political category. There's an anecdote about him being asked by an FBI investigator if he was a member of the Communist Party and replying "Not yet". He was, perhaps, the kind of communist who, as Ben Hecht said of Maxwell Bodenheim, "would have been booted out of Moscow, overnight".

Fearing had, like many other writers, been hired to work for the Federal Writers Project (FWP), a branch of the Works Progress Administration (WPA), part of President Roosevelt's New Deal. Boog writes favourably about the FWP, seeing it as giving struggling novelists, poets, and others a basic income in return for carrying out surveys, compiling guide books and similar activities. In some cases it allowed writers to focus on their own creative work. It didn't always function smoothly. There were strikes and other actions that disrupted the smooth running of the organisation. And not everyone classified as a writer turned out to have any literary skills. It was as if some people were directed to the FWP when they were unsuited for anything else. There's a passage in a novel by Eric Ambler where a police chief, examining someone's documents, says, "Your passport describes you as a writer but that is a most elastic term".

A 1941 novel by Jack Balch, *Lamps at High Noon,* is based on events surrounding a 1930s strike at the St Louis office of the Missouri branch of the FWP. Politics often became a central part of dissension in the FWP, with pro and anti-communist elements competing for influence. And attracting attention from politicians who were hostile to the whole idea of funding writers in any form, especially if they seemed to be left-wing. Boog writes about Orrick Johns, a one-legged poet, and one-time poetry editor for the communist *New Masses,* who was appointed Director of the New York branch of the FWP and struggled to maintain control in the face of recalcitrant writers, suspicious politicians, lack of funds, and general disorder, not to mention personal problems with alcohol. Congressman Dies and his supporters attacked the FWP as "a school for Communist writers" in ways that were forerunners of what the House Un-American Activities Committee (HUAC) would later employ to demonise left-wing screenwriters, novelists and poets.

A writer some people might see as a curious inclusion among a group of left-wing authors is Cornell Woolrich, best-known for his crime novels and stories, and as a leading light in the world of pulp magazines and books. Prior to 1934, when his first pulp story appeared, Woolrich had written six novels, all of which were published, but might best be described as conventional and were none of them best-sellers. Boog says that he "wanted to be the next F. Scott Fitzgerald". I've read only one of the early Woolrich novels, *Manhattan Love Song,* and it didn't strike me as being in the Fitzgerald class or having any distinguishing features that might have enabled it to stand out on its own merits. When Woolrich turned to pulp fiction he was much more interesting as a writer. Books like *Phantom Lady, Deadline at Dawn,* and

The Black Angel, to name just three of my own favourites, are examples of popular writing at its best. And they might be seen as good illustrations of how writers need to adapt to changing circumstances.

There are some passages in Boog's book where he discusses responses to an article by a journalist, Mark I.Pinsky, which advocated the setting up something similar to the FWP. Boog says that many of the responses questioned the assumptions that lay behind this idea: "Go and develop new skills that are in demand in the market-place and get yourself another job…..You don't have any kind of 'right' to a job in journalism and any kind of 'right' to be paid to write a single word". I think a lot of people would agree with those comments. And I have to admit that I've always had an uneasy suspicion about state funding for writers.

I have perhaps been a minor beneficiary of such aid, some of the poetry readings I've done, and magazines I've contributed to, having been subsidised by government-funded arts associations and the like. I've also had one or two commissions to write reports for the Arts Council and similar bodies. But I've done lots of readings for groups that paid what little they could, and contributed to many miniscule literary and political publications that paid nothing at all. I never thought I had a "right" to be paid for anything I've done. It was my choice to do it. If I'd wanted to make money I'd have done something else. I have knocked out pulp fiction and popular writing for newspapers and magazines now and then. And worked part-time in adult education establishments and at other jobs in industry and local government. It did amuse me that a left-wing weekly that I contributed poems, reviews, and articles to for around thirty years was said to have received money from Russia. The thought that the small payments I got might have been partly "Moscow gold" had its lighter side.

Other writers from the 1930s that Boog refers to include Muriel Rukeyser, Nathanael West, and Richard Wright. They're all of interest, though I suspect that Rukeyser is a poet little-known in Britain. Looking at her poems from the Depression decade shows that she had a firm sense of commitment to left and liberal causes. She went to Spain in 1936 and was there when the Civil War started. Her novel, *Savage Coast*, was about that experience, but only appeared in print in 2013 after being discovered in the Rukeyser archives and published by the Feminist Press in New York. Should anyone want to read her poetry the *Muriel Rukeyser Reader*, published by Norton in 1994, is recommended.

Nathanael West's *The Day of the Locust* is a classic novel about Hollywood, and came out of his experiences there as a screenwriter. But before deciding to move to California West had published other books, none of which had sold well. One of them, *Miss Lonelyhearts*, had the misfortune to have only just appeared when the publisher went bankrupt. It was something that affected more than one writer. Boog draws a comparison between what happened in the 1930s and the situation during the 2008 financial crisis: "At the height of the Great Depression Franklin Roosevelt chastised our entire nation for abusing credit and mounted a massive national bailout that put everybody – from farmers to construction workers to clerks to writers – back to work. We bailed out the banks and left everybody else to fend for themselves". West's adventures before Hollywood had included working as a hotel clerk in New York, and inviting his impoverished friends like Edmund Wilson, James T.Farrell, and Dashiell Hammett to stay for free in any empty rooms that were available.

The black author Richard Wright had been a supporter of the John Reed Clubs set up by the Communist Party to provide encouragement for working class and black writers. He was a member of the Communist Party and attended the First American Writers Congress in New York in 1935. A glance at the Contents page of the published record of the Conference indicates that it attracted what Boog refers to as "the leaders of the radical literary world". They included Malcolm Cowley, Granville Hicks, Joseph Freeman, John Dos Passos, and the proletarian novelist, Jack Conroy.

When Farrell some years later wrote his fictional account of the Conference in *Yet Other Waters* he satirised Conroy as a rather blustering and foolish speaker. It wasn't a totally fair description and Conroy's actual talk on "The Worker as Writer" did have some relevant points to make. But the Party was beginning to move away from its support for proletarian writing and coming out in favour of a Popular Front which would have a range of opinions represented with middle-class liberals and anyone else who was anti-fascist made welcome. The Party wanted names for its propaganda purposes. Proletarians like Conroy then tended to be pushed into the background.

Wright's account of his days among the communists can be found in *American Hunger* and in his contribution to *The God That Failed,* a 1950 anthology that put him alongside Arthur Koestler, Stephen Spender, and others, with their stories of how they became disillusioned with communism.

What is notable in Boog's story is that the Communist Party, or a gen-

23

eral commitment to left-wing values in one form or another, is in evidence at all times. Can the same be said of today? Liberal ideas may be prevalent among many writers, but there isn't the sense of solidarity that seems to have been present in the 1930s. And certainly no sense of identification with the industrial working-class. That group itself has been decimated over the years by the decline in labour-intensive industries, as automation, computerisation, and other factors came into play. And it has moved towards conservatism instead of socialism in response to hard times.

Miners, dockworkers, shopworkers, and many others, have all had to retrain for different work, sometimes at lower rates of pay, or accept long-term unemployment as a fact of life. I've been through redundancy and early-retirement situations myself. I'm not saying that what has happened has been a good thing. But it is what happens, and writers are no more immune to it than anyone else. It would be ideal if a united front could be formed to oppose many of the worst aspects of capitalism, but is it likely? Union membership is at an all-time low. The lack of strong unions has led to a worsening of working conditions. Reading about the way in which staff at Amazon have to work at speed made me think of Albert Halper's 1937 novel, *The Chute,* where they race around on roller-skates desperate to meet their quotas at the mail-order company they're employed by. The supervisor is always watching and ready to dismiss anyone not keeping up. And "there are plenty of people waiting to take your job if you don't like it here".

Jason Boog has written a useful and provocative book. It's useful because it draws attention to some writers of the 1930s who deserve better than to be consigned to the dustbin of history. In his own small way he joins literary historians like Walter B. Rideout (*The Radical Novel in the United States 1900-1954*), Daniel Aaron (*Writers on the Left: Episodes in American Literary Communism)*, Cary Nelson (*Repression and Recovery: Modern American Poetry and the Politics of Cultural Memory 1910-1945* and *Revolutionary Memory: Rediscovering the* Poetry *of the American Left*), and Alan Wald (*Exiles From a Future Time; The Forging of the Mid-Twentieth Century Literary Left; Trinity of Passion: The Literary Left & the Anti-Fascist Crusade* and *American Night: The Literary Left in the Era of the Cold War*) in chronicling the publications and experiences of often unjustly-neglected poets and novelists. All the books listed obviously deal with American writers, but Andy Croft's *Red Letter Days: British Fiction in the 1930s* should additionally be mentioned.

And Boog is provocative because he raises questions relating to the contemporary situation to which there are no easy answers, but which need to be asked.

THE DEEP END: THE LITERARY SCENE IN THE GREAT DEPRESSION AND TODAY

By Jason Boog

OR Books. 241 pages. £16. ISBN 978-1-935928-91-1

CHARLES REZNIKOFF: A POET'S PROSE

How many people in Britain will be familiar with Charles Reznikoff's work? I'm thinking of people outside university American Studies departments. Or, perhaps, those not particularly interested in Jewish matters. I doubt that too many readers of poetry will have come across his books, few of which have had a wide circulation in the United Kingdom. And it may be that if his name is known it will be because of his links to the Objectivist poets (George Oppen, Carl Rakosi, and others) of the 1930s.

I'm not intending to offer an examination of Reznikoff's poetry. There is a substantial body of it, and it includes many fine individual poems, though I've always thought of him writing what was essentially one long poem throughout his lifetime. The continuity is always evident. And there are two book-length works, *Testimony* and *Holocaust*, which can be seen as standing outside what might be called the general run of things because of their nature. Both are works described as "documentary poems", and primarily created by extracting from court records and shaping actual accounts into a poetic form. There may be a danger of being accused of simply using chopped-up prose to establish the story, but if the poet is skilful enough it is possible to create an impression of some sort of cadence sufficiently sustained to maintain the impetus.

My own view is that they are powerful works. *Testimony: The United States 1885-1915* is a history compiled from court sources, and *Holocaust* likewise used transcripts of the Nuremberg Trials and the Eichman trial to provide material for the poet to transform into a poem. It has to be said that these works have been criticised because they don't do any more than repeat what is in the records. The poet doesn't offer any commentary, nor add to the words to give them any extra resonance. They are just statements of what people had seen and experienced. An unsympathetic reader might say that they achieve their effect by playing on the emotions and disarming questions about their qualities as poetry. That may be the case. But I recall reading *Holocaust* years ago and finding its harrowing narrative completely compelling. There are times when facts speak for themselves and don't need any additional commentary to make their impact on the reader. It's enough to set down what happened. The personality of the writer is put aside, and he or she becomes only responsible for the selection and shaping of the basic material. That might indicate some partiality, but it's not intrusive if handled properly.

26

What I want to do in this short essay is look at three prose works, two published in his lifetime, and one posthumously, that Reznikoff wrote in addition to his poetry. Two of them primarily deal with the lives of his parents in Russia and America, and his own younger days. He was born in Brooklyn in 1894, his parents having emigrated from Russia some years before. Their story is told in *Family Chronicle*, which was, as far as I know, the one book by Reznikoff published in Britain. I reviewed it for *Tribune* in 1969, and I have a notion that it was one of the few notices, possibly even the only one, that it received. I do recall someone saying to me that the book had sold a limited number of copies.

Family Chronicle is divided into three sections, each one of which tells the story of the early lives of Sarah (mother), Nathan (father), and Charles (son) Reznikoff. There is inevitably a certain amount of overlap within the sections, though not to the point where the narrative becomes repetitious. Sarah's and Nathan's lives prior to arriving in America bring in different aspects of the experiences of Russian Jews in small-town and village communities. It was not an easy existence, and women were especially hard done by in terms of the opportunities available to them. Sarah grows up struggling to assert her individuality and obtain some sort of education. Convention works against her, with many of her fellow-Jews of the opinion that, "If women could read they would not do their household duties". There is also built into her character a fear of being thought too radical and so inviting the attentions of the police: "You must be satisfied with things as they are. Work and be content", she is told. When she sees some well-to-do people riding comfortable in carriages and reflects bitterly on their prosperity, while she works long hours and earns little, she is afraid to speak out: "She would be thought a Nihilist".

She finds a way to get to America, where she meets Nathan who, like her, could see no future in the world of Russian Jews, with its numerous social, economic, political and religious restrictions, imposed by both the Russian state and Jewish social hierarchy. And the ever-present threat of arranged marriages, pogroms, compulsory military service, and limitations on the capacity to widen one's ambitions. He is not particularly radical in his views, and always plans to inch his way up the ladder of success, if in a modest fashion. Sarah, too, generally adopts a moderate approach to life in America. Looking for work she soon learns to say "yes" to everything. And gets an inkling of how things stand in general between employers and employees when a "union lady" says of a seemingly-liberal manager, "A boss is a boss. He'll work himself up and be like the rest".

There is an irony here because, in due course and after various mishaps, Sarah and Nathan, who have married, become employers and operate, for a time, a thriving millinery business. There are some fascinating passages on the manner in which businesses operated in New York in the late-1890s and early-1900s. It was, in many ways, a highly-competitive world, with Jews conniving to outdo each other and exploit their fellow-Jews, and working conditions in the sweat shops unhealthy and dangerous. It isn't referred to by Reznikoff, but the tragic Triangle Shirt Waist Company fire of 1911 when 146 young girls and women, mostly either Jewish or Italian, lost their lives, led to reforms in safety laws and an increase in membership of the International Ladies Garment Workers Union (ILGWU) which fought to raise standards for workers in the needle trades.

I'm moving across *Family Chronicle* and *By the Waters of Manhattan* because parts of them essentially cover much of the same ground. The first section of *By the Waters of Manhattan* (originally published in 1930) was used by Reznikoff in only slightly-amended form to open *Family Chronicle*. It's worth noting that *Manhattan* was highly-praised by Lionel Trilling who said that Reznikoff's prose style had enabled him to write "the first story of Jewish immigrants that is not false. The book has charm and force which is marked by a soft liveliness and warmth". Other critics have compared it to Michael Gold's *Jews Without Money*, also published in 1930, and which had a definite socially-committed content and language. Gold, a stalwart of the American Communist Party, needed to make his book relevant to the growing radicalism of the 1930s, though it's about an earlier period. For the record, his book was more critically and commercially successful than Reznikoff's.

What is additionally interesting in *Manhattan* is the portrait of the son of Sarah and Saul. Named Ezekiel, he's averse to working in the traditional Jewish jobs which are mostly in and around the needle trades. He's literary-minded – he remembers "No hope can have no fear" from James Thomson's *City of Dreadful Night* when faced with the possibility of having a business proposition rejected – and is determined to open a bookshop in Greenwich Village. He does, though not without difficulty, and through it meets a lady called Jane Dauthendey who is only partly Jewish.

In this it's possible to see a move towards the assimilation that marked the lives of later generations of intellectually-inclined Jews, and is accorded attention in a novel like Isaac Rosenfeld's *Passage From Home*, where the gap that opened up between the older Yiddish-speaking parents and the newer Americanised sons is explored. Reznikoff's novel doesn't make a claim to have any kind of solution to the problems Ezekiel is likely to face either in his personal life or in relation to the bookshop. It has an open-ended final chapter that leaves matters hanging in the balance. Readers wanting a story that would tidy everything up neatly at the end were destined to have experienced disappointment. They were more likely to have been satisfied with Gold's conclusion in *Jews Without Money*: "A man on an East Side soapbox, one night, proclaimed that, out of the despair, melancholy and helpless rage of millions, a world movement had been born to abolish poverty".

The third book by Reznikoff is *The Manner Music*, a novel that turned up in his papers after his death in 1976. It moves away from the pre-1917 world of the sweat shops and other aspects of Jewish life in New York. With this In mind it may be useful to sketch in a few details about Reznikoff's life. He attended the University of Missouri for a short time, but left to work as a salesman for his parent's millinery business. He was undecided about what to do next, but "settled on the study of law……and was admitted to the bar in 1916 at the age of twenty-two". He practised only briefly, and instead used his knowledge to work for *Corpus Juris*, "an encyclopaedia of law for lawyers".

He also, at various times, functioned "as a salesman, an editor of a small magazine, a translator, and - for a few years in Hollywood – as a general factotum to a friend of his, Albert Lewin, who was a successful producer at Paramount Pictures". Lewin is probably now best known for a series of imaginative films he directed in the 1940s and early-1950s, including *The Moon and Sixpence, The Picture of Dorian Gray,The Private Affairs of Bel Ami*, and *Pandora and The Flying Dutchman*. He appears in Reznikoff's novel, *The Manner Music,* as Paul Pasha.

The story centres around Jude Dalsimer, a musician and budding composer, but is told through the words of an old friend who encounters him twenty years after they had grown up together and shared a passion for poetry. The friend now works as a salesman, touring the country, and gradually pieces together what has happened to Dalsimer's hopes and ambitions. As he says, "Jude Dalsimer may have been a great musician. I can't say for I know little about music. I know the great names, of course, that everybody knows and listen to their music with respect and sometimes with pleasure. But Jude Dalsimer's music just puzzled me".

The problem is that it seems to puzzle everyone. His employment with Paul Pasha in Hollywood comes to an end (Reznikoff clearly used some of his own experiences to give substance to this section) and he moves back to New York. Whatever he does in terms of compositions which are intended to have a degree of popular appeal turn out to be failures. And he's unable to hold down jobs which might at least provide some sort of financial support. It's a difficult time to be looking for any kind of work, even the most menial. As the narrator says: "in New York itself I had never seen the Depression so bad, seen so many beggars, so many worried and hurried. Conditions were much worse than I had imagined". Jude's mental state declines, and he's found wandering in Central Park and committed to Bellevue Hospital. The narrator meets Jude's wife and asks her about his music. It turns out that Jude has burnt everything.

I've briefly outlined the basic structure of *The Manner Music*, and there is more to it than I've indicated. What is particularly significant is the way in which a variety of encounters by both Jude and the narrator are inserted into the narrative to illustrate the temper of the times. References to Huey Long, populist Governor of Louisiana, and the rabble-rousing Catholic priest Father Coughlin, crop up. Anti-Jewish sentiments are seen and heard. Refugees from the rise of fascism in Europe arrive in the city. A man passes through a subway train selling a communist newspaper.

And there are fragments of overheard conversation which don't appear to have any direct reference to the lives of either Jude or the narrator, but provide a background to their actions. I was put in mind of Joe Gould's legendary *Oral History of Our Time*, a work which may or may not have existed. It was Gould's contention that real history could be constructed from mundane details, everyday exchanges (think of Yeats and "The history of a nation is not in/parliaments and battle field,/but in what people say to each other"), and other forms of seemingly-irrelevant detail. It was believed that he'd secreted dozens of notebooks in places around New York, but they've never been discovered. And possibly never existed in bulk form, though some fragments were published in magazines in the 1920s.

The three prose works by Charles Reznikoff that I've looked at seem to me to be worth remembering. *Family Chronicle* and *By the Waters of Manhattan* have great value as documents of Jewish life in Russia and New York in the late-nineteenth and early-twentieth century. But they have more than that in terms of their clarity and what Lionel Trilling referred to as the "charm and force" of the writing. As for *The Manner*

Music, its qualities as a broad account of an artistic temperament collapsing in the face of everyday adversities seem to me impressive. It does leave the reader wondering whether someone like Jude was ever likely to succeed, and that only he could ever hear the music he wanted to compose. Would his world, and his mind, have fallen apart whatever social and economic circumstances he encountered?

BIBLIOGRAPHICAL NOTE

Family Chronicle by Charles Reznikoff. Norton Bailey, London, 1969.

By the Waters of Manhattan by Charles Reznikoff. Markus Wiener Publishing, New York, 1986. Originally published in 1930.

The Manner Music by Charles Reznikoff. Black Sparrow Press, Santa Barbara, 1977.

Poems 1918-1975: The Complete Poems of Charles Reznikoff. Black Sparrow Press, Santa Barbara, 1996.

Holocaust by Charles Reznikoff. Black Sparrow Press, Santa Barbara, 1977.

Testimony: The United States 1885-1915 by Charles Reznikoff. Black Sparrow Press, Santa Barbara, 2015.

Jews Without Money by Michael Gold. Carroll & Graf, New York, 1984. Originally published in 1930.

Passage From Home by Isaac Rosenfeld. Markus Wiener Publishing, New York, 1988. Originally published in 1946.

World of our Fathers: The Journey of the East European Jews to America and the Life They Found and Made by Irving Howe. Harcourt Brace Jovanovich, New York, 1976.

Joe Gould's Teeth by Jill Lepore. Vintage Books, New York, 2017.

The Objectivists edited by Andrew McAllister. Bloodaxe Books, Newcastle, 1996.

Botticelli in Hollywood: The Films of Albert Lewin by Susan Felleman. Twayne Publishers, New York, 1997.

DAWN POWELL AND GREENWICH VILLAGE

I wonder how many readers in the United Kingdom will have heard of Dawn Powell ? She was born in 1897 and died in 1965. In her lifetime she published fifteen novels, two dozen short stories, had three plays performed, and wrote articles for various publications such as *The New Yorker* and *Harper's Bazaar*. If Gore Vidal is to be believed, one of her plays was turned into a movie, and another staged by the Group Theatre in 1933. Among those who spoke highly of her work were Gore Vidal, Edmund Wilson, John Updike, John Dos Passos, and E.E. Cummings. A long-time resident of Greenwich Village, Powell attracted some notoriety for living in a ménage à trois with Joseph Gusha and Coburn Gilman. Wilson described her novels as "among the most amusing being written" and Vidal, commenting on a dismissive review of one of them by Diana Trilling, mockingly said: "Apparently to be serious a novel must be about very serious – even solemn - people rendered in a very solemn – even serious – manner".

Powell did not only write about Greenwich Village and its characters, but the two novels I want to look at are more or less set in that environment and have some relationship to the bohemian idea. *The Wicked Pavilion* was published in 1954, and *The Golden Spur* in 1962. Both are what might be called "conventional" novels in terms of their structure and overall intention, i.e. to tell a story in a witty and entertaining manner while casting a perceptive eye on the sometimes wayward behaviour of the personalities involved.

Much of the action in *The Wicked Pavilion* takes place in the Café Julien which is based on the café at the Lafayette Hotel, "off Washington Square at University Place and Ninth Street". At one point in the novel, Dalzell Sloane, an artist, reflects on the nature of cafés and why he goes to them: "One came here because one couldn't decide where to dine, whom to telephone, what to do". And there was a possibility of meeting other people: "Someone barely known might come into the café bringing marvellous strangers from Rome, London, Hollywood, anyplace at all, and one joined forces, went places after the café closed that one had never heard of before and never would again, talked strange talk, perhaps kissed strange lips to be forgotten next day". Dalzell is clearly someone who has lost his bearings, especially since his friends had gone: "Marius dead, Ben lost for years".

With Marius dead, dealers are desperate to locate any of his work, his sudden demise having pushed up prices and increased the demand for it. When Ben re-appears, he and Dalzell hunt for Marius, who they be-lieve may still be alive, and discover a stack of his unfinished canvases at a house in a suburb of New York. Both of them are broke and can't find buyers for their own work. They decide to finish the paintings, and paint a few more, and market them as by Marius, claiming that he left them to Ben. After all, they reason, Marius wouldn't have minded, had he still been around: "he had to die to make a living, but the fact was he never even tried to get anywhere. He didn't want to be anybody. All he wanted to do was paint what he liked when he liked, have the dames he liked, get as drunk as he liked".

They find out that Marius really is alive and, in effect, hiding out at a lady friend's farm. The story about his death arose from him being bad-ly hurt in an accident in Mexico, and he realised that he was happy to be "dead": "Creditors, fights, dames, then borrowing this guy's car – that is, without his knowing it – Well, I had about every bone in my body broken when I wrecked it". Ben and Dalzell try to encourage Marius to come back to New York to take advantage of his new-found fame. He refuses and tells them to carry on their work of forgery with his paintings. He doesn't even want the money they offer him. But he asks them never to tell anyone that he didn't actually die.

I've outlined just one story from the several that intertwine throughout *The Wicked Pavilion*, and there are others that are similarly entertain-ing. The café setting provides for people coming and going, and mix-ing. It also allows Dawn Powell to introduce characters who have a close resemblance to real people. A rich gallery-owner named Cynthia is more or less based on Peggy Guggenheim, well-known for support-ing certain artists and also having affairs with them. A sequence enti-tled "We all go up to Cynthia's house" brings in the inevitable party which often seems to be a hallmark of novels about bohemia (Dachine Rainer's *The Uncomfortable Inn*, to take just one example), and which brings together many oddballs, including Hoff Bemans, "a middle-aged, beery fellow in black beret, black flannel shirt and plaid jacket". He's a survivor from the 1920s and with his companions talks with scorn of so-called bohemians who wallow in the "middle-class eupho-ria of neo-modern furnishings, TV rooms, Sunday roasts, blended Scotch, and Howdy Doody".

The last few pages of *The Wicked Pavilion* describe how the Lafayette Hotel was demolished in 1957 (it had been closed since 1949, which suggests that the novel is set between 1945 – there is a reference to someone returning at the end of the war – and that date), and with it the premises that provided the inspiration for Dawn Powell's Café Julien.

The book has a nostalgic final paragraph: "The Café Julien was gone and a reign was over. Those who had been bound by it fell apart like straws when the baling cord is cut and remembered each other's name and face as part of a dream that would never come back".

Gore Vidal described *The Golden Spur* as Dawn Powell's "last and perhaps most appealing novel". In it, a young man, Jonathan Jaimison arrives in New York in the early-1950s. He's looking for information about his mother who, in 1927, had spent some time in the city, and had returned pregnant to her home-town in Ohio. She married a local man who later left her and her son, and Jonathan grew up never knowing who his real father was. He has a notebook in which his mother had jotted down a few names of people she'd known in Greenwich Village. His intention is to trace them, if they're still alive.

Along the way he encounters some of the residents of Greenwich Village, among them a couple of young women who invite him to stay with them. They've both been involved with a painter called Hugow, a bawdy Jackson Pollock-like figure, but he's left his studio in their possession and gone to live with Cassie Bender, a rich gallery-owner and patron of the arts (another version of Peggy Guggenheim) who enjoys the company of artists in more ways than one.

Many of the people Jonathan meets drift in and out of the Golden Spur, a bar where artists in particular congregate to drink, argue, and sometimes fight. It's based on the Cedar Tavern, in the 1950s a well-known gathering-place for the abstract-expressionists. A couple of other bars do get passing mentions. There's the White Horse, where Dylan Thomas was said to have downed his final, fatal drinks. And the San Remo where the New York Beats hung out. You can get an idea of the period from the fact that when Jonathan enters the Golden Spur one of the first things he notices is a man reading *Encounter*. There may be a clue, too, to some of Powell's own feelings about new trends in the arts when Jonathan asks the bartender if Hugow is any good as a painter, and the man cryptically replies, "He gets away with it". Later in the book one of the old bohemians Jonathan has met refers to "West Coast bums" moving in, which may be a reference to the Beats and the mistaken notion that the movement started there.

Among the people from his mother's past that Jonathan wants to meet is a lady called Claire Van Orphen, whose name is in his mother's notebook. She had been a popular writer in the 1920s – garden and travel articles and love stories for family magazines - but has since fallen on hard times and struggles to survive. But the fact that Jonathan persuades her to meet him at the Golden Spur leads to her being introduced to Earl Turner who, twenty or so years ago, had edited a short-lived little magazine called *The Sphere*. He's since scuffled to make a living from writing. When asked by a more-successful writer what he's done recently, he replies: "Nothing new, now and then - a review — eight bucks for fifteen hundred words of new criticism in a little magazine, or forty for six hundred words of old criticism in the Sunday book sections. A pulp rewrite of a De Maupassant".

Turner talks to Claire about her writing and explains to her that in the "old days the career girl who supported the family was the heroine, and the idle wife was the baddie......and now it's the other way round. In the soap opera, the career girl is the baddie, the wife is the goodie because she's better for *business*". He helps her rewrite some of her old stories and she later tells him: "Well, you were right. CBS has bought the two you fixed, and Hollywood is interested". She has a deal with him to share the money she makes on a fifty-fifty basis, and the fact of a relatively steady income for a time, at least, persuades Turner to abandon plans he was making to move to Mexico. Powell was writing in the early-1950s when TV and advertising were advocating the virtues of domesticity, bright furniture, washing machines, and stay-at-home mums.

There is also Alvin Hardshawe, a successful novelist with problems who Jonathan thinks might be his father, and Professor Kellsey, a hard-drinking academic who had met his mother and could be another candidate for the role. And George Terrence, a prominent and wealthy lawyer, is someone else who might fit the bill. Jonathan is beginning to realise that his mother had more adventures during her short stay in New York than she'd ever admitted to.

Jonathan suddenly comes into a large inheritance from a surprising source, and is soon being pursued by a number of people anxious to help him spend it. Cassie Bender, entices him into investing money in her venture, and he becomes Associate Director of the Bender Gallery. He seems set for success, but the role doesn't suit him. They have an exhibition of Hugow's paintings and the opening is attended by the kind of people Cassie knows and likes, the rich and influential.

Jonathan realises that he's ill-suited to such a setting, and leaves the gallery: "He thought wistfully of the pack of gallery-flies prowling through the night, battering on doors to be let in, brawling and bruising down to the Golden Spur, and he thought those were the real backers of art, those were the providers, the blood donors, and Cassie's salon of critics, guides, and millionaires were the freeloaders, freeloading on other people's genius, other people's broken hearts, and when it came to that, other people's money".

By chance he runs into Hugow and a young woman named Iris who Jonathan has taken a liking to. Hugow has left Cassie: "He wanted to throw up the whole scene, the fine yellow gin, the perfect studio Cassie had fixed for him, the successful authors and actors and art-lovers and Bennington girls – "the cream of the Cape", as Cassie said – their Good Conversation; Christ, how sick you could get of Good Conversation. "Good Talk".There was no such thing as Good Talk. Talk was Talk and worse than marijuana for getting you high and nowhere.......he wanted "to get back to a slum full of overturned ashcans, Bowery bums sprawling over the doorstep........he wanted to get back to a studio that had no comforts, just light and nobody in it".

Jonathan gets in the car with them and though initially he doesn't know where they are going, "He was very glad that Hugow had turned back downtown, perhaps to the Spur, where they could begin all over".

I haven't read everything that Dawn Powell wrote, so I can't say whether or not Gore Vidal was right in calling *The Golden Spur* her "most appealing novel". But it's certainly one that I thought was funny, well-written, astute in its portrayal of different characters, and certainly appealing in the way that it deals with people who, for all their faults, have a certain kind of adherence to a way of life that isn't likely to lead to always being comfortable, but has its compensations in terms of lively company and provocative experiences.

BIBLIOGRAPHICAL NOTE

The Wicked Pavilion by Dawn Powell. Vintage Books, New York, 1990.

The Golden Spur by Dawn Powell. Virago Press, London, 1991.

Turn, Magic Wheel by Dawn Powell. Steerforth Press, South Royalton, 1999. Originally published in 1936 this novel, while not set in Greenwich Village, offers a satire of the New York literary scene.

Republic of Dreams, Greenwich Village: The American Bohemia, 1910-1960 by Ross Wetzsteon, Simon & Schuster, New York, 2002. Includes an informative chapter on Dawn Powell.

TESS SLESINGER : NEW YORK IN THE 1930s

Tess Slesinger's novel *The Unpossessed* was published in 1934. It doesn't rate a place in two early studies of left-wing American writing, Walter B. Rideout's *The Radical Novel in the United States, 1900-1954* (1956) and Daniel Aaron's *Writers on the Left* (1961), though the book was later "rediscovered" and reprinted. And Alan Wald has placed Slesinger firmly in the context of 1930s New York intellectual activity, and discussed her work in his *The New York Intellectuals* (1987). She is probably still only something of a fringe figure and little-known beyond the bounds of the academy, and possibly even then only where there is a focus on 1930s radicalism, or Jewish writers in America. In that context, it might be of interest to note that a large anthology, *A Treasury of American Jewish Stories* (1952), failed to acknowledge Slesinger. She had died in 1945, and her books were out-of-print, so was a forgotten figure by 1952.

She was born in 1905 into a comfortable Jewish family. Her father was a businessman and her mother a social worker who became a successful psychoanalyst. One of Slesinger's brothers also practised as a psychoanalyst. She was educated at Swarthmore College and the Columbia School of Journalism. She had always nursed ambitions to be a writer, and started publishing short stories in the late-1920s and early-1930s, including in such publications as *Scribner's,* the *New Yorker*, and *Vanity Fair,* as well as in little magazines like *Pagany* and *This Quarter.*

In 1928 she married the journalist and editor Herbert Solow. He was connected to the *Menorah Journal*, a predominantly Jewish publication edited by Solow and Elliot Cohen. A couple of her stories were published in the magazine. Her marriage to Solow failed in the early-1930s, and some of the reasons for that may be suggested by the story "Missis Flinders", which revolves around an abortion that a woman undergoes at the insistence of her husband. Did Slesinger have to face up to a similar situation? The story had been rejected by some American magazines because of the nature of the subject-matter, but was accepted by the editors of *Story* who were then operating from Spain. It was later used by Slesinger as the final chapter of *The Unpossessed*. It might also be worth considering that there could have been political differences between Solow and Slesinger. He had started as a fellow-traveller with the communists, but switched his allegiances to the Trotskyists, whereas she seems to have remained closer to the Communist Party, insofar as she was politically active. Solow's deviations eventually took him towards conservatism and a job as an editor at *Fortune*.

It's generally accepted that the novel, satirical in its intentions, uses aspects of Slesinger's experiences among the *Menorah Journal* group of left-wing writers as its basis. Some of the originals for the book's characters have been identified, though Slesinger had not in any way written straightforward descriptions of the persons concerned. Her husband, Herbert Solow, may have had some of the habits of thought of Miles Flinders, but the latter was not Jewish, whereas Solow was. And Margaret Flinders may have corresponded to Slesinger in part, but it has also been suggested that Elizabeth, an artist who has been living in Europe and returns to New York half-way through the story, could represent some of Slesinger's state of mind in the 1920s, if not necessarily her actions.

A couple of other characters – Bruno Leonard and Jeffrey Blake – are based on Elliot Cohen and Max Eastman, with whom, Alan Wald says, "Slesinger had an affair at the time". But, as he is quick to stress, "the characters in *The Unpossessed* are essentially composites designed to express a variety of themes emanating from the milieu" in which the originals functioned. Wald says that Lionel Trilling thought "Slesinger's book was an act of passing judgement upon and separation from the very 'contemporaries' to whom the book was dedicated". One other significant difference between the originals and their fictional versions is that Cohen and Solow were involved with an existing magazine, whereas in the novel, Leonard, Blake, and Flinders, not to mention some others, are planning to launch one, if they can raise enough money. The money aspect leads to some amusing consequences. It's rather reminiscent of Irving Howe's comment that, "when intellectuals can do nothing else, they start a magazine". But it's a mistake to assume that the book is a documentary account of the group that came together in the pages of the *Menorah Journal*. It is, first and foremost, a novel.

It's not my intention to provide a detailed analysis of the plot of *The Unpossessed*. It essentially concerns itself with the relationships between the people I've mentioned, and several additional men and women who pop in and out of the narrative. Leonard is beset by a group of young radicals anxious to have a platform for their ideas in the new magazine. They're of the opinion that poetry is "propaganda for sitting on your ass reading it", while "forgetting what's wrong with the world". At the same time, Leonard's mind keeps returning to Elizabeth, his childhood sweetheart, who is due to arrive from Paris. Blake is busy seducing a wealthy woman into funding the magazine, and keeping one or two other women, including his placid wife, happy. Flinders is trying to bring his gloomy New England temperament into line with his communist beliefs, while his marriage to Margaret appears to be floundering. In between, like all intellectuals, they talk and argue about what the magazine should aim for. As one of the participants dryly remarks: "We talk and talk like an old Russian novel. I'd like to know what any of us *do*?". And, of course, a Manifesto has to be drawn up.

Comrade Fisher, a plain-looking activist, appears and impresses Blake with her radical accreditations. She's been to Russia, slept with a working-class strike leader and a couple of officials from the Communist Party, and spent a night in jail after being arrested on a picket line. She's bitter, though, because she's been rejected as not ready for proper Party membership. He beds her in her dingy room with a poster of Lenin looking down on their activities. Later, he discards her and begins to chase after Elizabeth, the hard-drinking artist who supposedly has come to link up with Leonard.

The high-point of the book is a party the foolish wealthy woman insists on having to raise funds for the Hunger Marchers heading to Washington, and for the new magazine. One of the more-engaging characters at the event is the woman's husband, a self-made man who takes a surprisingly relaxed view of the fact that it's his money that is being used to provide food and drink for the party and, in due course, the magazine. He's humorous and mildly mocks the supposed revolutionaries and their antics, but without ever losing his temper or becoming unduly concerned. It's as if he knows that ultimately they will never present a real threat to him or his kind, so why take them seriously?

The party ends in chaos when Bruno, whose speech to promote the magazine has been sabotaged by a young admirer who has become disillusioned, gets drunk and improvises an address that appears to pull down the supposed lofty ideals of the intellectuals. Murray Kempton, looking back at the novel in his *Part of Our Time,* described Leonard's speech as "a haunted exposition of the desperation of some intellectuals in the year 1932". At one point he ridicules his young followers, and says, "Run, Sheep, Run", and it raises the question of whether or not the phrase had been picked up by Slesinger from Maxwell Bodenheim's 1932 pro-Communist novel of that name?

It's interesting that a party given by a similarly silly wealthy woman is also the subject of one of Slesinger's short stories. "After the Party", was included in her collection, *Time: The Present,* published in 1935. The woman in question has divorced her husband after he's turned into a committed socialist and decided to give away all his money. She has her own income so isn't affected by his actions. Following the divorce her doctor advises her to find a new interest in life. After rejecting several suggestions which might involve some discomfort she settles on becoming a party-giver, but of a specific kind. She'll host parties at which a noted literary celebrity will be the special guest. But she doesn't want "certain critics, who should not be brought face to face with certain writers".

The satirical approach is obvious and one of the invited novelists is a young woman called Regina Sawyer who has written a book called *The Undecided* which has had some success. It's not difficult to decipher that she may be Tess Slesinger in fictional form and perhaps capitalising on her experiences attending literary events. It's not a major story, but has a light touch and neatly makes fun of the woman and her guests. Another party-story, "Mr Palmer's Party", from the *New Yorker* in 1935, seems light-weight but has an edge as Mr Palmer finds himself side-lined by his aggressive wife and the guests he has invited. He's either ignored or derided when he tries to make conversation. It's funny, but sad, and one somehow feels sorry for Mr Palmer, an essentially kind-hearted, mild-mannered man, treated contemptuously by the indifferent in spirit.

There were at least three stories in *Time: The Present* which can be said to have been directly concerned with social, economic and political matters in the 1930s. "The Times So Unsettled Are" is about a young Viennese woman whose boyfriend, an ardent communist, is killed during the 1934 uprising in the city when the Karl Marx Hof (specially constructed workers' accommodation) was attacked by the military and police during a left-wing uprising. She had previously met a couple from America who seemed to exemplify everything about personal relationships that she desired. Hearing of her predicament they invite her to New York. When she arrives they whisk her away to a café and she senses that something is not quite right. Finally, the man gets up to leave. The couple no longer live together - "here in America, too – the times unsettled are".

"Jobs in the Sky" more directly comments on the effects of the Depression. It is Christmas Eve in a large department store, and a young man has obtained a temporary job after being unemployed for eight months. He's in charge of a section in the book-hall and anxious to impress the supervisor in the hope that he'll be offered a more-permanent position. He's also fantasising that if he is, he'll ask one of the other assistants, an attractive young woman, for a date. In the end he's told that he's no longer required, and he slinks out, knowing that he has nothing to offer anyone in the harsh economic climate of 1930s New York, a place where his father had always told him he would be sure to succeed. He's not the only one dismissed. A middle-aged woman who has lost her job as a teacher, and is desperate to find alternative employment, is also sent on her way. The title of the story plays on the old Wobbly (IWW – Industrial Workers of the World) song, "The Preacher and the Slave", with its line, "You'll get pie in the sky when you die".

Another story, "The Mouse Trap", sees a smooth-talking boss defusing a potential strike situation when he reduces the wage of one of the workers and the others try to rally in her support. He's assisted by his good-looking secretary who considers herself a cut above the others, dreams about marrying the boss, and has told him what is about to happen. He isolates individuals, preying on their fears about unemployment in a city with 400,000 families on relief, and pointing to their domestic situations and other factors that might cause hardship should they lose their jobs. As he says to them, there are lots of people looking for employment and they can easily be replaced: "I can get college professors to write copy, and debutantes to sell it – while you people will have a hard time finding work anywhere else". The initial defiance of the potential strikers slowly fades away until only three or four of the most militant employees are left isolated. There is something of an ironic ending when the boss, high on his success, attempts to seduce his secretary only to be rebuffed when she, realising what he really wants from her, flees from his office.

There are a couple of other stories deserving of attention, though they aren't specifically set in a 1930s context. "On Being Told that her Second Husband has taken his First Lover" is an interior monologue using a stream of consciousness technique as a woman contemplates her situation. "A Life in the Day of a Writer" interestingly takes on the thoughts of a male author as he struggles to overcome a temporary block and get a short-story underway while his wife fumes at his behaviour: "He had spoken to no-one all the morning since Louise – shouting that she could put up with being the wife of a non-best-seller, or even the wife of a chronic drunk with a fetish for carrying away coat hangers for souvenirs, but not by God the duenna of a conceited adolescent flirt – had slammed the door and gone off cursing to her office". It's essentially a story about the creative process as the writer slowly constructs a story out of the fragments of memory, imagination, and his wife's assertions swirling around in his mind.

I think it's fair to say that Slesinger did try to move her writing in the novel and several of her stories beyond a straightforward narrative account. Alan Wald comments: *"The Unpossessed* is a highly original novel. Slesinger adapts some of the modernist techniques of Joyce, Proust, and the early Hemingway to her purposes, but the book is also closely shaped by her close reading of Katherine Mansfield, Dorothy Parker, and Virginia Woolf. The book anticipates both Saul Bellow's novels about frustrated Jewish intellectuals such as *Herzog* (1964) and Mary McCarthy's political satires such as *The Oasis* (1949)".

Slesinger's last published story appeared in 1936 and *The Unpossessed* was her only novel. It's difficult to know if she intended to write more fiction or had decided to call it a day. She moved to Hollywood, married a producer and screenwriter named Frank Davis, had two children, and was hired for work on a number of films, only a couple of which might be said to have survived the years. *The Good Earth* (1937) was based on a novel by Pearl S. Buck, and *A Tree Grows in Brooklyn* (1945) on a novel by Betty Smith. Another film that Slesinger worked on, *Dance, Girl, Dance* (1940) has aroused interest among feminists in more-recent years. It was directed by Dorothy Arzner, one of the few women functioning in that role in the Hollywood of the 1930s and 1940s.

A Tree Grows in Brooklyn was directed by Elia Kazan, a member of the Hollywood left-community at the time. Slesinger herself seems to have become part of it and sustained her commitments to left-wing causes, but it isn't clear if she ever became a member of the Communist Party. Both she and Frank Davis belonged to the Hollywood chapter of The League of American Writers, an organisation which included numerous socially-committed writers and was considered by the FBI to be a Communist front. Slesinger appears to have aligned herself with the Party line on certain subjects as, for example, when her name appeared on a Communist Party document attacking the Dewey Commission for its investigation of the Moscow trials. She died in 1945 from cancer, so escaped the HUAC hearings which divided Hollywood in 1947 and again in 1951. Had she still been alive and called to testify, her involvements with communism might have been made public. It has been indicated that she may have become disillusioned with the Party because of the 1939 Nazi-Soviet Pact, but remained pro-Russia throughout the war years.

BIBLIOGRAPHICAL NOTE

The Unpossessed by Tess Slesinger. Simon and Schuster, New York, 1934.

Time: The Present by Tess Slesinger. Simon and Schuster, New York, 1935.

"A Life in the Day of a Writer" by Tess Slesinger. *Story*, New York, November, 1935.

"Mr Palmer's Party" by Tess Slesinger. *The New Yorker*, New York, April, 1935. Also in *Short Stories from The New Yorker,* Victor Gollancz, London, 1951.

The New York Intellectuals: The Rise and Decline of the Anti-Stalinist Left from the 1930s to the 1980s by Alan Wald. The University of North Carolina Press, Chapel Hill, 1987.

Daughters of the Great Depression: Women, Work, and Fiction in the in the American 1930s by Laura Hapke. The University of Georgia Press, Athens, 1995. There is an excellent discussion of *The Unpossessed* and several of the short stories, plus some useful information about Slesinger's activities, in this book.

Writing Red: An Anthology of American Women Writers, 1930-1940 edited by Charlotte Nekola and Paula Rabinowitz. The Feminist Press, New York, 1987. Contains Slesinger's short-story, "The Mouse-Trap".

James T, Farrell: The Revolutionary Socialist Years by Alan Wald. New York University Press, New York, 1978.

Part of Our Time by Murray Kempton. Simon and Schuster, New York, 1955.

Days of Anger, Days of Hope: A Memoir of the League of American Writers, 1937-1942 by Franklin Folsom. University Press of Colorado, Niwot, 1994.

The Beginning of the Journey: The Marriage of Diana and Lionel Trilling by Diana Trilling. Harcourt Brace, New York, 1991. Useful for her comments about Slesinger and *The Unpossessed.*

Script Girls: Women Screenwriters in Hollywood by Lizzie Francke. British Film Institute, London, 1994.

Sam Holman by James T.Farrell. Prometheus Books, New York, 1983. Farrell's novel was published posthumously. Sam Holman is clearly based on Herbert Solow and Frances Dunsky on Tess Slesinger. Farrell only lightly disguised them and most of the other characters can easily be identified (see Alan Wald's book about the New York intellectuals referred to above). And Frances Dunsky publishes a novel called *Uncommitted Young Men* in which Holman is made to seem "powerless and ineffectual in his aim to change the world" and not only "a little naïve but also a little ridiculous".

There have been reprints of *The Unpossessed* and *Time: The Present* in recent years. An edition of the novel, with an introduction by Elizabeth Hardwick, was published by New York Review Books in 2002. The short stories, with the addition of the previously uncollected "A Life in the Day of a Writer", have been reprinted under the title, *On Being Told that Her Second Husband has taken His First Lover*.

DENYS VAL BAKER AND ST IVES

My main purpose in writing this essay about Denys Val Baker is to direct attention to two novels and half-a-dozen short stories in which he drew on aspects of the artists' colony in and around the one-time, small Cornish fishing town of St Ives. I say "one-time" because tourism is now largely its main source of income. However, as I looked at the material referred to, it increasingly occurred to me that it would be necessary to provide some relevant background to Val Baker's activities before and during his time in Cornwall.

He was born in England in 1917. His parents were Welsh, but his father was then serving with the Royal Flying Corps at an aerodrome not far from York. He grew up wanting to be a writer, and started working-life as a junior reporter on the *Derby Evening Telegraph*. He moved to London and worked for various publications. His first short story to be published appeared in *Weldon's Ladies Journal* in 1941.

Val Baker was a conscientious objector during the Second World War, and seems to have been active around literary London. He started a little magazine called *Opus* (it later changed its name to *Voices*), believing that, in the words of his biographer, Tim Scott, "the format of the little magazines was the standard-bearer of contemporary literature". It should be remembered that the 1940s were boom years for magazines, perhaps because the fragmentary and transient nature of life during wartime lent itself to the production of poetry, short stories, essays, and other written work that could be achieved while on active service or working long hours in factories and offices.

That Val Baker had more than a passing interest in little magazines was demonstrated by the publication of his first book in 1943. Titled *Little Reviews 1914-1943*, it provided a fifty-three page summary of significant publications in the period concerned. As Val Baker himself pointed out, it was "an apparently unexplored field" in terms of trying to document developments and differences in magazine publishing. To follow up on his small book, Val Baker was chosen to edit an annual selection of material from current little magazines which continued from 1943 to 1948. I should add that a glance at a Val Baker bibliography will show that he was also involved with several other publications, such as *Writing Today, Modern Short Stories,* and *Voyage*. As well as editing, he was also working on his own novels and stories. His first novel was published in 1945, with two more appearing before the end of the decade.

45

Cornwall had always attracted Val Baker and after several short visits he more or less settled there in 1948. There had, of course, always been artists' colonies in Cornwall, primarily in Newlyn and St Ives, but the post-war years saw an influx of young, restless artists who, in due course, would attract international attention and establish St Ives as a beacon not only for creativity, but also a noticeable bohemianism. It was a factor that did not always sit well with the serious, working painters and sculptors, or many of the locals. The non-productive beat-niks of the late-1950s and early-1960s were, in particular, to become a nuisance.

Val Baker would easily fit into the bohemian category, but could never be accused of being non-productive. Once situated in Cornwall, he started a magazine, *The Cornish Review*, which survived for ten issues from 1949 to 1952. An anthology compiled from this publication and published many years later has work by W.S. Graham, Jack Clemo, Peter Lanyon, Sven Berlin, Charles Causley, Arthur Caddick, Guido Morris, Norman Levine, and others, not to mention an informative in-troductory essay by Martin Val Baker. The magazine was revived by Denys Val Baker in 1966 and there were twenty-seven issues before it came to an end in 1974.

Val Baker was clearly aware of the presence of artists in Cornwall, and in 1950 he wrote the introduction to *Paintings from Cornwall,* pub-lished by Cornwall Libraries. But his main efforts in promoting the notion that St Ives had something special to offer, both in terms of its physical location and as a centre for artistic activity, went into *Britain's Art Colony by the Sea*, which appeared in 1959. It has been described as a fairly lightweight survey of the subject, and it's true that it doesn't pretend to provide a deeply critical analysis of what was being pro-duced in and around St Ives in the late-1950s. It offers a broad, liberal-ly-illustrated account that sums up the history of the town as a haven for artists, and gives some information about Val Baker's contemporar-ies like Peter Lanyon, Wilhelmina Barns-Graham, Bryan Wynter, John Wells, and Barbara Hepworth. It mentions pottery, too, and it's inter-esting to note that Val Baker's wife, Jess, worked as a potter and that he later wrote books on the subject.

I've hopefully managed to impart the idea that he was an established member of the St Ives artistic community, so was in a position to ob-serve its personalities, absorb its atmosphere, and create fictional in-terpretations of life there. A constant theme appears to be to indicate that moving to live in Cornwall did not always lead to contentment. Very few of the artists, writers, and others who were in St Ives or nearby had been born in Cornwall. Peter Lanyon was an exception. The others had arrived for one reason or another and often carried their economic and emotional baggage with them. As few of them were financially independent, they often led somewhat impoverished lives, a fact that could grate hard on their partners, if they had them. They'd frequently come to Cornwall with expectations of fulfilling dreams of escaping from unwelcome work and finding the freedom to create as they wanted to.

In Val Baker's novel, *A Journey with Love,* published in 1955 (see Bibliographical Notes), Martin works in an advertising agency but really wants to abandon commercial work and paint for his own satisfaction. Lesley in an actress. They decide to quit London and head for Cornwall. It all seems idyllic, though Martin has to continue doing some commercial work to earn money for the basics. As with so many artists he can't make enough from his creative productions to support himself and his wife, And soon they have a child. Then Martin is badly injured in a boating accident. Like the hero of Ernest Hemingway's *The Sun Also Rises,* the accident leaves him unable to have sexual intercourse. He sinks into depression, his work suffers, as does his relationship with his wife and son. There is eventually a resolution to his problems, but only after a period of doubt and anguish.

It might be worth mentioning that *A Journey with Love* was originally published in the USA in 1955, with a paperback edition in 1956. British publishers had been reluctant to handle it because it was considered too explicit in its sexual themes. It's difficult to now see why they thought that way, but it was before the *Lady Chatterley's Lover* trial and the near-collapse of censorship in the 1960s. Val Baker later published the novel in Britain under two different titles. *The Faces of Love* came out as a Sabre paperback in 1967. I've never seen a copy of this title, so don't know if it has the full text of the American edition. When Val Baker published it again in 1974, this time as *As the River Flows*, he omitted around thirty of the opening pages and re-shaped some other parts. My own feeling is that the American edition is the best one to read. It gives the characters of Martin and Lesley a greater substance.

There are references to St Ives and its colony of artists. Martin visits a sculptor (probably based on Sven Berlin) in the town. He goes into the Castle Inn on Fore Street, where, in the 1950s, the landlord was Endell Mitchell, brother of the sculptor, Denis Mitchell, and where paintings by St Ives artists were displayed on the walls. And there is a section where Martin thinks about three of the "small 'ginger' group of younger artists who shared his own desire to penetrate into the hidden depths and meanings of Cornwall". One of them is, from the description of his work, Peter Lanyon. Another could be Bryan Wynter.

A second Val Baker novel, *Company of Three,* appeared in 1974, though the events it was partly based on took place in the 1950s. It has some quite obvious autobiographical elements, as for example in the character of Stanley, a writer who edits a small, short-story magazine and whose wife is a potter. They have previously lived in Cornwall, but are now in London. One day they receive a note from Vivian, one of their Cornish contacts, someone who had lodged in their old house near Penzance, inviting them to visit for the weekend. They drive down to the South West, but the trip revives memories of their earlier days in Cornwall and why they left. Nell, the wife, had become obsessed with Vivian and had an affair with him.

The weekend develops, with Vivian who is now, as one of his friends points out, "Drinking like a fish, never eating, never sleeping......", and still in love with Nell. It all ends in tragedy when Vivian drives off in his battered old van after shouting to Stanley, "you and your swanky new car. Race you to Penzance!". There is inevitably a crash in which Vivian is badly injured and later dies in hospital.

It would seem that there was an incident like this when the potter Len Missen was killed and that Val Baker had been present and driving on the same road as Missen. There doesn't appear to have been any evidence that they were racing and, in fact, Val Baker's vehicle was in far better condition than Missen's and a competition would have been a non-starter. It's probable that Missen had been drinking and was driving too fast, anyway. The noteworthy thing about *Company of Three* is that the originals for most of the characters are easily recognisable.

The two novels referred to seem to be the only ones in which Val Baker dealt directly with art and artists. But he also wrote several short stories which revolved around painters and others. In "A Work of Art", a writer "discovers" the work of an artist he initially knows nothing about. His comments on how he reacts to the paintings are enlightening: "I am a writer, not a painter or an art critic and no doubt my attitude to painting would be what is called literary, i.e. rather on the romantic side; indeed, I must confess I did not know then and have never bothered to ascertain since, exactly what standards of technical abilities lay behind the painting I now gazed upon in that gallery window". It's the "vivid scattered combinations – colours and shapes, lines and shadows, sea and land and sky all concentrated into some cohesive whole –" that draw his attention to the painting.

He finds out who the artist is, sees more of her work, meets her in person, and he begins to be attracted to her. But when he realises that she is probably in love with someone else he starts out on a campaign to destroy her work, commencing with the paintings by her that he owns, proceeding to attack canvases hung in galleries, and finally invading her studio and disfiguring what he finds there. The story ends in a bizarre way and with the writer aware that whatever he has done he is still a "superficial observer". She has told him at one point that "Words are really inadequate, aren't they?", and it suggests that he will never be able to break through to either her or her work.

Although Val Baker put the words into the mouth of his fictional female artist they are actually from an interview with the painter Margo Mackleberghe that he included in his non-fiction survey of the creative spirit in Cornwall, *The Timeless Land*. (see Bibliographical Notes). This doesn't in any way indicate that he based his fictional character on her.

The suggestion that an encounter with artists and their work might not always be beneficial is also to be found in "Testament of a Green-Eyed Man". A young couple move to Cornwall and begin to mix with the artists there. They meet Veronica, an older woman who is a well-known sculptor, and she asks the wife, Danny, to model for her. The husband is suspicious of Veronica, and is soon jealous of the way in which Danny is spending more and more time with her. It's obvious to him that some sort of relationship has developed between his wife and Veronica, and that it is affecting his marital situation. He confronts Veronica, rapes her, and steals the bust of his wife that she had created. The end result is that Danny leaves with Veronica, while he retreats to his "empty and desolate" moorland cottage to reflect on what he has done. It's not a pleasant story and might well add weight to Alison Oldham's observation that, for Val Baker, "Imagination was what he prized in fiction but his fantasies make unsettling reading".

The dark side of life in Cornwall crops up again in "The Sacrifice" in which the old Celtic ways with Druids and tales of human sacrifice provide a basis for the story. The narrator gets to know Mark and Shelley, a bright young couple who live in a cottage on the moors above St Ives. He meets them in the town: "It's a gay, colourful place, the houses built around a tiny harbour, with blue and white fishing boats bobbing about like corks. In the little pubs by the wharf, painters and their friends gather in the evenings and argue about Picasso and Matisse and Henry Moore".

49

Mark is an archaeologist and often away on explorations, leaving Shelley alone. The narrator begins an affair with her, but soon realises that he's not her only lover: "She was, in fact, a natural nymphomaniac, completely self-possessed and totally unconcerned with anyone's feelings save her own". As for Mark, he is seemingly oblivious to what his wife does, and is obsessed by the Celtic past that he researches. It's a "world of primitive, yet cunning people who lived by different gods, different values". He takes the narrator to an area where there is a large flat stone and says: "Two thousand years ago this place was alive. The priests came up that path, then they formed around the big stone. Fires were lit, men carried in the sacrifice. There was the smell of myrrh and incense. And blood". When asked what the sacrifice was, Mark replies, "A woman".

They throw a party, the theme of which will be everyone dressing up like Ancient Britons, with the culmination being a celebration at the old stone and a mock sacrifice. The guests, some of them hooded like the priests of old, gather around the stone and Shelley lies down on it. Most of the men had been her lovers at one time or another. The moon is suddenly hidden by dark clouds, there is a "wild cry, the like of which none of us had ever heard before", and when it's light enough again to see, Shelley is dead, killed by "the long sacrificial knife" Mark had discovered on one of his archeological digs. But who had murdered her?

Women do seem to have had a largely disturbing influence in Val Baker's stories, and "The Girl in the Photograph" continues this idea as an artist and his wife move to live in an old mill. They are given several old photographs of some of the previous occupiers, and in one of them can be seen a young woman lurking in the background. The artist becomes obsessed with the girl, has clearer copies of the photograph made, and starts to find out more about her. It turns out that her name was Maeve, she was from Ireland, and was the model and the mistress of the old man in the photo. He was Anthony Sampson, a painter who had been quite well-known in his day.

Finding out these basic facts doesn't satisfy the artist, and in the end his need to know more and almost will Maeve into life, despite that she's been dead many years, not only affects his work, but also drives a wedge between him and his wife. In a scene where she taunts him about his feelings for Maeve he assaults her, with the result that she leaves him. In the end, he's living in a dream world, realising that his passion will "consume" him, perhaps to the point of death. He constantly haunts the cliffs where Maeve was known to wander: "Or perhaps, and this I think is more likely, she will be waiting for me out on the wild cliffs, dancing away from me across giant granite steps, out and out towards the mirror of the sea until one day, leaping forward to grasp her hand, I shall be lost with her in some vast eternity".

It's something of a relief to turn to a couple of stories which offer a lighter view of the artistic life of St Ives. "The Potter's Art" is the story of a young potter in St Ives who attracts the attention of an older, wealthy patron. She has a history of taking up various "painters, sculptors, writers, actors, and so forth. But she had never had a real, live potter before". She starts to hang around his workshop, watching him shape his pots and noting that he is physically attractive, as well as being talented. Eventually, she spirits him away to London to establish his work as a "with-it item on the ever-changing panorama of London art life".

He is successful, though not happy about the lady's personal demands on his time and energies. And she is, he has begun to realise, older than she looks. Needing an assistant for his work, "a young girl student by the name of Miranda" is hired. She's pretty and enthusiastic about pottery, and the inevitable happens. They are caught in "an unmistakably compromising position" and the girl is ordered to leave. But the potter exacts his revenge on the older woman in a bizarre way that gives a "twist in the tale" aspect to the story. Some might say that the "twist" brings in the dark element of the other stories. I was reminded of the sort of short pieces that Gerald Kersh used to write when I read "The Potter's Art". Like them, it doesn't waste words and comes to a brisk conclusion.

"Artists in Wonderland" explores a fairly well-worn idea, though in an entertaining way. Dick Drake arrives in St Merry (an obvious St Ives) after packing in his job as a bank clerk and determining to become a painter. The only accommodation he can find in the by-then popular art colony is in an old furniture van. He meets a young woman who works as a model, and she helps him convert the van into comfortable living quarters, and begins to educate him in the ways of the art world. He can't make any money with his paintings, so has to hire himself out as a washer-up at various cafés. He attends a local art school, where the teacher, Alice Sampson, takes him under her wing after "learning that his uncle was the fabulously rich owner of *Drakes Ju-Jubes*", a popular sweet.

Promoted by his teacher, and with the media enticed by the idea of an artist living in a furniture van, Dick soon has an exhibition, despite the fact that his paintings are only half-finished. He's also managed to establish a friendship of sorts with a famous artist who lives in the area, and who appears to be more interested in his collection of vintage cars than in offering Dick any useful advice about painting. Boosted by the media, the presence of a representative from the Arts Council, and the reluctance of anyone, apart from his uncle, to say that Dick's paintings aren't very good, the exhibition seems to be a success. But Dick knows what the true situation is, and when he's offered a well-paid job with his uncle's firm he, and the young woman he'd met earlier, immediately leave St Merry.

Like I said, it's a fairly familiar idea – the gullibility of the art world – but it's handled in an amusing way, and there's no hint of the darkness found in the other stories.

I can't claim that Denys Val Baker was a major writer. He was competent at producing novels and stories that largely skated easily over the surface of the narrative and without delving too deeply into the characters' personalities or motives. Predictability might have been a key factor in their overall effect, even when there was an attempt to surprise. It's mainly their relationship to the lives of certain people, fictional and otherwise, from the St Ives community that interests me. They may not stand comparison wIth Sven Berlin's satirical novel, *The Dark Monarch*, or with Norman Levine's *From a Seaside Town* and his novella, *The Playground*, in their portrait of St Ives, but they can be placed alongside those works as a useful record of fictional accounts of a time and place.

BIBLIOGRAPHICAL NOTE

A Journey with Love. Crest Books, New York, 1956. It had been published in America by Bridgehead Books in 1955, but I've never seen a copy of that edition,

The Face of Love. Sabre Books, 1967. I have not seen this book, but it appears to be a reprint of *A Journey with Love*, though whether or not it uses the full text is not known.

As The River Flows. Milton House Books, Aylesbury, 1974. This is a reprint of *A Journey with Love*, but with the first thirty or so pages omitted, and a short introductory synopsis added. No acknowledgement is made to the earlier editions.

Company of Three. Milton House Books, Aylesbury, 1974.

"A Work of Art" in *A Work of Art*, William Kimber, London, 1984.

"Testament of a Green Eyed Man" in *The House by the Creek*, William Kimber, London, 1981.

"The Sacrifice" in *Martin's Cottage,* William Kimber, London, 1983.

"The Girl in the Photograph" in *The Girl in the Photograph,* William Kimber, London, 1982.

"The Potter's Art" in *The Secret Place & Other Stories from Cornwall,* William Kimber, London, 1977.

"Artists in Wonderland" in *The Girl in the Photograph*, William Kimber, London, 1982.

There are several non-fiction books by Denys Val Baker which are of relevance:

Britain's Art Colony by the Sea, George Ronald, London, 1959. Reprinted in 2000, with an introduction and index added, by Sansom & Co., Bristol.

The Timeless Land: The Creative Spirit in Cornwall, Adams & Dart, Bath, 1973.

A View From Land's End: Writers Against a Cornish Background, William Kimber, London, 1982.

The Spirit of Cornwall, W.H. Allen, London, 1980. A revised edition of *The Timeless Land.*

Other books of interest:

The Cornish Review Anthology 1949-1952, edited by Martin Val Baker, Westcliffe Books, Bristol, 2009.

The Cornish World of Denys Val Baker, by Tim Scott, Ex Libris Press, Bradford-on-Avon, 1994. Scott contributed an article about Val Baker, with bibliography, to the September, 1990, issue of *Book Collector.*

Everyone Was Working: Writers and Artists in Post-War St Ives, by Alison Oldham, Tate St Ives, 2002. A small but invaluable survey of the subject.

From a Seaside Town by Norman Levine, Deneau & Greenberg, Ottowa, 1980

"The Playground" in *Why Do You Live So Far Away?* by Norman Levine, Deneau Publishers, Ottowa, 1984.

The Dark Monarch by Sven Berlin, Finishing Publications, Stevenage, 2009. The original edition, published by Galley Press, London, 1962, was withdrawn after several libel writs were issued against the publisher. The story behind the libel allegations is told in the new edition.

I have only listed the books which directly relate to St Ives and artists and writers. Val Baker wrote numerous other books (novels, autobiographies, local histories, etc.) about Cornwall generally and his activities there. In addition, as mentioned at the beginning of my essay, he published various titles before moving to Cornwall, and edited many magazines and anthologies. A comprehensive bibliography can be found in Tim Scott's biography.

NORMAN LEVINE : FROM A SEASIDE TOWN

The Canadian writer Norman Levine is probably best known in this country for his association with St Ives. In his native country he has a different reputation, one founded on the stories and other material he wrote about it. What he wrote didn't always please his fellow-countrymen, and one book, in particular, *Canada Made Me,* didn't endear him to critics and others anxious to present a positive view of Canada. I think his reputation has recovered in more-recent years, and he's now seen as an important writer when Canadian literature is discussed.

It was his time spent in Cornwall that first interested me, though I wouldn't want to under-estimate the quality of the stories he wrote about growing up in Ottawa, or the family members he met when he re-visited Canada. They are well-written and evocative in their portraits of his mother and father and various other relatives. Levine was always a highly-autobiographical writer, and I've no reason to think that he needed to do much more than register and shape what he saw and experienced. This could be as true of a minor encounter with a waitress or nurse as it was with his sister or an old friend. He may well have lightly-fictionalised what took place, but I would guess that the essential structure of his account had a firm basis in the reality of the situation. He saw the possibilities in what was there, rather than trying to invent events and characters.

If that was true of what he wrote about his experiences in Canada, it was also apparent in the stories he set in St Ives. He may have changed the name of the place, and those of individuals he describes, but the fact remains that it would be almost impossible to read his work and not know where and what he was writing about. Is this a limiting factor? Does it distract from a detached evaluation of the work in a way that purists might say it does? I don't think so. Is Hemingway's *The Sun Also Rises* any less a successful work of art because we know which real-life characters were the models for Hemingway's fictional ones, and we can identify where and when the events described took place?

It's important to note that Norman Levine was mostly a writer of short-stories. He did have a novel, *The Angled Road*, published in 1951 and dealing with his time as a member of the Canadian Air Force based in Britain during the Second World War. And he wrote poetry which was published in the early-1950s in Wrey Gardiner's little magazine, *Poetry Quarterly*, alongside John Heath-Stubbs, Vernon Scannell, and Michael

Hamburger. A couple of poems that I've read – "Crabbing" and "The Fishing Village - quite clearly indicate that he was familiar with Cornwall even then.

It is the short-story form in which he excelled. His bibliography does refer to a second novel, *From a Seaside Town*, but it might be debatable as to whether or not it is a novel, as opposed to a number of interlinking short-stories. I'll have a closer look at it later. The fact that he was mostly producing short stories, a form which has had its ups and downs in terms of attracting attention and readers, and which is not noted for bringing in high fees, points to something that frequently crops up in Levine's writing. He was usually hard-up.

There is a story, "I'll Bring You Back Something Nice", in which the narrator, a supposedly established Canadian writer, meets up with a group of fellow-Canadians he'd been at McGill University with after the war. They've all turned out to be successful, one way or another, having good jobs, marrying wealthy women, and so on. The writer is broke and in London desperately trying to raise some cash. During the course of the afternoon with his one-time student colleagues he follows each to the lavatory in turn and taps them up for a "loan", which, of course, they'll never get back. They only realise that they've all been duped into giving him money after he's left and they talk among themselves. "Our great author", one says sarcastically.

Some might doubt that this story is totally autobiographical. Surely a writer wouldn't want his misadventures like this to be widely known? Perhaps he simply fictionalised a situation in which he'd perceived a certain potential? Perhaps? But knowing Levine's tendency to write directly out of his own experiences, I'm inclined to think he may not have fictionalised very much. In another story, "We All Begin in a Little Magazine", the narrator brings his family to London and stays in a house while the owner and his family are away for three weeks. He discovers that the man is a doctor, and also edits a little literary magazine. The house is full of books, the postman brings piles of review copies and letters every day, and people telephone to enquire about stories and poems they submitted to the magazine months ago. A stranger arrives on the doorstep and says he usually stays whenever he's in London.

The location of the house is given as South London, but it's actually in North London. I know it well. The editor is an old friend of mine and I've stayed there many times over the years. I can testify to the accuracy of the description of it, and to the fact that Levine certainly didn't fictionalise very much, apart from changing the name of the magazine and those of the people who telephoned.

The impulse to make stories out of what he'd observed could sometimes cause difficulties for Levine. In 1961 he published a collection of stories with the title, *One Way Ticket*. The lead story (it's actually a novella of around fifty pages) was called *"The Playground"*, and was quite obviously set in St Ives: "The water in the bay was a thick, deep blue. The sun brilliant. It showed up the fields on top of the cliffs of the far shore; the lower towans with the bald patches on the coarse grass; the long line at the bottom of dazzling sand. And the white lighthouse in the bay, a milk bottle with a camera stuck in its throat. Two French crabbers, anchored beside each other in the deep water, faced the wind".

The story continues with the narrator's vivid descriptions of the town, and also his observations on its limitations. Fishing is declining and increasing numbers of holidaymakers clog up the narrow streets and crowd the pubs. He wants to meet more of the people who actually live there, and gets to know some of what might be called the "artistic community" and goes to "the round of parties in 1959". In a way, though the people concerned do live in the town, they're not native to it, and their way of life is anathema to the real locals. Mothers tell their children: "keep away from them artists". The fact that some of the supposed "artists" are homosexuals doesn't sit easily in a community where "Wesleyan or Methodist" religious values are still strong.

A local man, a garage owner called Starkie, has become involved with the artists and their hangers-on, but beset by debts and other problems he commits suicide. The anger among the locals is noticeable, and one of the genuine artists, a man who was actually born in Cornwall, warns the crowd that Starkie mixed with to stay away from the funeral. Some of the locals are convinced that Starkie was cheated out of his money, others that he had been corrupted by the homosexuals.

I've given a brief outline of the story, and it's much more subtle in its portrayal of place and people than I've implied, in order to highlight that Levine's account, closely based on actual events, angered some people when it appeared in print. He didn't actually name St Ives, and people were obviously given fictional names and their characters loosely described, but it was clear to anyone with even a casual awareness of what happened just who was involved. As far as I know, Levine's story didn't lead to legal action in terms of allegations of libel, and any problems he encountered were related to personal reactions from individuals. They resented the way in which he'd painted a picture of one aspect of a close, small-town society that could cast a bad light on other parts of it which hadn't been caught up in the events concerned.

It needs to be emphasised that people are central to many of Levine's stories, and what they tell him provides the material for what he writes. In "A Writer's Story", the narrator meets an old lady who asks him what he's currently writing. He tells her that he isn't writing anything, and she says, "You mean you don't know any stories? I know lots". She tells them to him, and they're not made-up stories, but people and events from her own life. She introduces him to a friend, a man who says, "I've met lots of writers here", and proceeds to recall visiting D.H. Lawrence and his wife when they lived at Zennor, and meeting Frank Harris. He also recalls seeing Stanley Spencer and watching Augustus John drink "a half bottle of whisky". The way Levine handles these anecdotes, bringing out the character of the person recounting them, and the surroundings where they're told, differentiates him from a journalist looking for local colour, or an academic researching the past. He makes a story out of people telling stories.

In "From a Family Album" the narrator (I use that term, but it's obviously Levine) visits his late wife's ailing mother, and then tells her story. As a girl she'd shown some talent for art, something her parents didn't encourage, and had sent samples of her work to St Martin's. She'd waited for a reply, but nothing arrived. Her life soon followed a standard pattern of work and marriage and family. Many years later, when her mother died, she was clearing out the house and came across a letter of acceptance from St Martin's. Her parents had never shown it to her.

Because Levine was such a skilled storyteller it's possible to simply string together his accounts of human frailties and unusual encounters in an entertaining way. In "I like Chekhov", a small group of teachers from a local school meet in a pub where they all admire the landlord's wife, "one of the attractive women in the town". It's obvious that they, with the exception of Chester, who hasn't been to the pub before, all hope to develop a relationship with her, even though they're married and so is she. When she finds out that Chester is a writer she tells him that she likes Chekhov and invites him into the private accommodation behind the bar. Her husband is away on business. She shows him her small library, and they kiss. When Chester is with the other teachers again it's clear that they're envious of the fact that, in the space of a few minutes, Chester had advanced further than they'd ever done in several years. Their resentment at his success is obvious, but he's not bothered. He's leaving the town the following day.

A story called "Gwen John" isn't really about her, though it does end with a brief account of her life and death: "With the Germans invading, Gwen John left Paris. Got as far as Dieppe. Collapsed in the street. People thought she was a vagrant. Took her to a hospice. Where she died. No-one knows where she is buried. Augustus John was supposed to do a memorial stone. But he never got around to it". Somehow the terse statements match the sad facts of her life generally, and the muted and low-key nature of her art.

I said earlier that Levine's name is usually related to St Ives, and he did live there for quite a few years, and continued to visit the town when he moved away. But I hope I've indicated that the subject-matter of his stories stretched far beyond the art and the artists of Cornwall. He knew Peter Lanyon, Terry Frost, and others, and there is a reference to some-one called Henry in "Soap Opera" who is based on Frost. But the story isn't about him. As Alison Oldham said, it "is remarkable for the way the narrative oscillates between the present, in which the narrator's mother appears to be dying, and different aspects of the past, from his mother's memories of Poland to his own life in St Ives; also for the variations of anger and achievement which recur throughout".

It is the "novel", *From a Seaside Town*", which seems to accent the relationship between Levine and St Ives. The life of a financially-strapped writer is established at the start: "I tried magazines that I never wrote to before. Then waited to see what the postman brought. I found the whole day centred around the postman coming. I'd get up early and wait anxiously until I saw him in the street opposite. Then stand by the window, to the side, so he wouldn't see me. I watched him as he worked the street opposite, before he came here. And hid until I heard the release of the letter slot. I got to know all the postmen's habits. Who was fast. Who dawdled. Who talked".

The local, the everyday life, is an integral part of *From a Seaside Town*, but there are breaks in the routine. Charles Crater, an artist from London, turns up in the town. He's a friend of the narrator, and doesn't really have anything in common with the abstract work that is the hall-mark of the leading artists in Cornwall. His own work leans towards the figurative, even if an often-distorted version of it. He's a character based on Francis Bacon, who Levine was friendly with and sometimes visited in his studio in London: "Against the wall are some canvases, their backs facing the room. In the centre, his easel caked with lumps of paint. And on the floor, in large untidy heaps, are all kinds of picture magazines – from Germany, France, Italy, America, England – with pages torn out of them. Charles constantly searches through picture magazines looking at the photographs".

Other visitors turn up. A Canadian academic looks at something in the window of an Arts and Crafts shop: "a glass container filled with yellow coloured water and some wax. A light was at the bottom. And as the wax was heated it rose slowly in the liquid changing into different shapes. When the wax rose further it cooled and fell back forming other shapes. Then it rose again. He was fascinated by this. Watched it for several minutes. "Somebody could have got a Ph.D with this", he said. It was his highest tribute". Those five words neatly sum up the kind of man he is.

Relatives from Canada come to call. And the narrator goes back to Ottawa to see his mother, and visit his father who is in a nursing home and showing signs of dementia: "And he sat in the chair, not moving, looking out of the plate glass wall. If one of us touched his arm, he looked at us. And if we asked him a question he opened his mouth and got a bit red in the face. Then he would leave us and return to stare at the winter scene outside".

I can't fault the quality of the writing, which seems to me to exemplify Levine's assertion that he's noted for "the cleanness of his prose". He thinks it may be because he had to learn English as a foreign language. "I have a small vocabulary. No long words". It's worth adding that he also once said, "The leaner the language, the more suggestive".

I raised the question earlier about *From a Seaside Town* and its status as a novel, or whether it can be more accurately described as a series of interlocking short stories. In a way, it doesn't matter as long as the whole reads coherently. And it does. But, as a matter of interest, it's worth pointing to how Levine incorporated what had previously been published as stories into the framework of the novel. The incident described in "I'll Bring You Back Something Nice", where the impoverished writer scrounges money from some fellow-Canadians he meets in London, crops up under the title "A Trip to London" as a chapter in the novel. And the story, "Why Do You Live So Far Away?", is also used as a chapter in *From a Seaside Town*. They both do fit easily into the wider pattern of the book. And Levine isn't the only writer who has published short-stories which later appeared as parts of a novel.

I've attempted to give a wider view of Norman Levine as a writer than might be available if he's only seen as someone writing about St Ives. His work on that subject, and the town is in many ways at the centre of his writing, is evocative in that anyone familiar with the place will recognise his short, accurate sketches of its streets and buildings. But the writing stretches out to take in many other things. The subject-matter is not narrow. And when it's dealt with in the kind of precise and perceptive prose that Norman Levine specialised in, the overall effect is impressive.

BIBLIOGRAPHICAL NOTE

From a Seaside Town. Deneau & Greenberg, Ottawa, 1970.

"I'll Bring You Back Something Nice" in *By a Frozen River*. Key Porter Books, Toronto, 2000.

"We All Begin in Little Magazines" in *By a Frozen River.* Key Porter Books, Toronto, 2000.

"The Playground" in *Why Do You Live So Far Away?* Deneau, Ottaway, 1984. Also published as "A View on the Sea" in *The Ability to Forget.* Key Porter Books, Toronto, 2003.

"A Writer's Story" in *By a Frozen River*. Key Porter Books, Toronto, 2000.

"From a Family Album" in *By a Frozen River.* Key Porter Books, Toronto, 2000.

"I Like Chekhov" in By a Frozen River. Key Porter Books, Toronto, 2000.

"Gwen John" in *By a Frozen River*. Key Porter Books, Toronto, 2000.

"Soap Opera" in *By a Frozen River*. Key Porter Books, Toronto, 2000.

"Why Do You Live So Far Away?" in *By a Frozen River.* Key Porter Books, Toronto, 2000.

"Gwen John" and "Soap Opera" were also published in *Something Happened Here.* Viking, London, 1991, "I Like Chekhov", "I'll Bring You Back Something Nice", "We All Begin in Little Magazines", "A Writer's Story", "Why Do You Live So Far Away?", were in *Champagne Barn*. Penguin, Harmandsworth, 1984.

Everyone Was Working: Artists and Writers in Postwar St Ives by Alison Oldham. Tate St Ives, 2002.

St Ives: The Art and the Artists by Chris Stephens. Pavilion Books, London, 2018.

CRYSTAL EASTMAN : ON WOMEN AND REVOLUTION

When recently reading and writing about Greenwich Village in the first decades of the Twentieth Century it became obvious that the male bohemians of those years were, for all their talk of "free love" and "liberation" usually predictable in their actual dealings with women. They expected them to be largely subservient, and it's certainly true that most of the leading roles in whatever they were doing – publishing magazines, organising events, etc. – went to men. The histories of the period have mostly tended to enforce this imbalance by playing down the activities of women who asserted themselves. June Sochen's *The New Woman in Greenwich Village, 1910-1920* (Quadrangle Books, New York, 1972) is one of the few books to attempt to rectify the misapprehension resulting from surveys revolving almost solely around men, or placing women merely in minor roles.

One of the most fascinating of the women activists mentioned in Sochen's book was Crystal Eastman, sister of Max Eastman, and well-known in her own time as a journalist, socialist, and ardent advocate of women's rights. She died relatively young and that, together with the attention focused on her brother, perhaps led to her being forgotten. This new selection of her writings, skilfully edited and introduced by Blanche Wiesen Cook, is therefore welcome.

Crystal Eastman was born in 1881, and demonstrated an interest in social problems, especially those faced by women, at an early age. When she was fifteen she wrote a paper called "Women" in which she said "No woman who allows her husband and children to absorb her whole time and interest is safe against disaster". It was a prophetic statement with regard to her own life because she firmly insisted on following her interests despite a couple of marriages and children. She was aware of the way in which housework, for example, was a form of bondage, and she held the view that the only way for women to achieve real economic independence, in a capitalist society, was for the government to recognise and subsidise housework as skilled labour.

She left college with an MA in sociology, and then took a law degree at New York University. This latter qualification enabled her to make more than a purely theoretical contribution to social reform. She specialised in labour law, and completed in-depth investigations into industrial accidents. These led to her being included on the Employers' Liability Commission where she drafted the New York's first workers' compensation law. Her work in this field was recognised around the

U.S.A. and abroad.

Her experiences researching into labour conditions confirmed her socialist beliefs, and she became increasingly involved with groups which supported the Mexican Revolution, backed major industrial struggles by organisations like the IWW (Industrial Workers of the World), and opposed American entry into the First World War. At the same time she developed her feminist consciousness both as a writer and as an organiser. She had a busy, eventful life which took her to various countries, including Hungary and the United Kingdom, and she involved herself with civil liberties, as well as with socialism and feminism. She also functioned as an editor for the radical magazine, *The Liberator*.

Eastman married an English pacifist, Walter Fuller, during the First World War, and in the early-1920s, lived on and off in England. But her constant urge to work, partly because of the need to earn a living, partly because she was moody and bored when not busy, wore down her health. She moved back to America in 1927, but died within a few weeks of her return. She was just forty-six.

A glance through the contents of *Women and Revolution* will demonstrate the range of Eastman's writing. Mostly produced for magazines and newspapers, the pieces cover such topics as birth control, marriage, pacifism, prostitution, the British suffragette movement, labour conditions, communism in Hungary, the atmosphere on "Red" Clydeside, and the British Labour Party in conference in 1919 when it voted in favour of industrial action to stop intervention in Russia. Her writing was vivid, direct, and totally committed.

There is a need for contemporary feminists to be aware of their forerunners. Crystal Eastman was forgotten primarily because she was a woman, and not because her work was trivial or unimportant. She may also have been overlooked because the people she mixed with – bohemians for the most part – are often treated in a derisory manner by historians. To believe some writers, Greenwich Village in the period prior to 1920 was little more than a hotbed of high jinks, free love, and bad poetry. That a great deal of worthwhile work, both social and literary, was produced is too often ignored.

Some of Eastman's beliefs – her faith in the working-class as a vehicle for change, for example – could now seem naïve, though they may have had seeming relevance at the time. But her overall ideas were generally sensible. And she was in no doubt that, whatever might result from struggles in the economic field, women would still have to fight to gain their own freedom. Her words say clearly how she saw the situation:

"Many feminists are socialists, many are communists....But the true feminist, no matter how far to the left she may be in the revolutionary movement, sees the woman's battle as distinct in its objects and different in its methods from the workers' battle for industrial freedom. She knows, of course, that the vast majority of women as well as men are without property, and are of necessity bread and butter slaves under a system of society which allows the very sources of life to be privately owned by a few, and she counts herself a loyal soldier in the working-class army that is marching to overthrow the system. But as a feminist she also knows that the whole of woman's slavery is not summed up by the profit system, nor her complete emancipation assured by the downfall of capitalism....if we should graduate to communism tomorrow.....man's attitude to his wife would not be changed".

ON WOMEN AND REVOLUTION by Crystal Eastman. Edited by Blanche Wiesen Cook. Oxford University Press. 1978.

EARLY MODERNISTS

Blaise Cendrars was a prolific writer, and is often spoken of as being one of the true innovators in twentieth century literature. But he was not a literary man. A traveller, he roamed across Russia and America before the First World War, working at all kinds of jobs. And he believed in involvement. A Swiss national, he said of his decision to volunteer for the French Foreign Legion in 1914: "As if a poet's place were not amongst men, among his brothers, when things were going badly and everything collapsing, humanity, civilisation and all the rest of it".

The Astonished Man is a record of some of his adventures with the Legion (he lost an arm during an offensive in 1915) and later in various parts of France and South America. It is also a tribute – and Cendrars, like Henry Miller, had a genuine liking for people with all their faults and foibles exposed – to many of the odd characters he met: Gypsies, drug addicts, soldiers, poets. Cendrars seems to have enjoyed being with them all. And he had the capacity to interest his readers in the other writers he mentions, not with the kind of gossip one often finds in literary memoirs, but with anecdotes and descriptions that evoke their writings.

Take Gustave Lerouge, for example, author of over 300 works, many of them published anonymously. Cendrars' interest in him is not that of a highbrow for a popular writer, but a genuine expression of admiration, not only for the man's talents but also for his life-style. It was Lerouge's proud boast that he'd sold the rights to one of his most popular books for a mere pittance. The fact that everyone else was making money out of the book, but that he wasn't involved, was, said Lerouge, a demonstration of how free he was.

That Cendrars was years ahead of his time is obvious from this racy, free-wheeling autobiography. It takes off at tangents about other people's work, returns to chunks of Cendrars' life and treats them almost as if they were episodes in a fictional escapade, and throws in asides about society and literature, usually in a witty and pointed manner.

It is, in fact, not unlike the kind of involved non-fiction which allows the writer to use a form of loose chronicling to deal with his experiences at the level of creativity found in the best fiction. It's a break from the format of the traditional novel, and is what might be called an autobiographical novel.

Not enough is known in this country about Hart Crane's poetry, the main reason being, I suspect, because of the complexity of much of his work. A highly personal and concentrated writer, with little in common with the kind of English and American poets who skate adroitly across the social surface, Cane wrote with an almost-maniacal fervour.

It has, in fact, been documented that he sometimes created his poems while drunk and with the gramophone blaring away. Malcolm Cowley, who knew Crane, went so far as to suggest that the reader has to be in a similarly enthusiastic state to fully appreciate the results. Crane's poems may not have a clear, literal meaning, but their emotional impact – the way they release that hidden intuitive spring – can be considerable.

Besides being a fine poet Crane was, to put it mildly, a personality. A heavy drinker, he was ever prone to get into fights, to break up parties, to end the night in prison, or beaten up in a back-alley. He was homosexual and that added to his problems. It's almost a cliché that poets like this die young, and Crane, with his personal life in chaos and his mind riddled with doubts about his poetry –committed suicide at the age of 32.

As with many others of his ilk – in the world of the arts one can think of Dylan Thomas and Charlie Parker, to name just two – Crane had the kind of charm that made people overlook the drunken escapades and the insults. His friends were numerous and the stories about him enough to fill a book. But he wasn't noted only for his wildness. Some of the best writers of the 1920s admired his work, and he contributed to the great magazines of the day.

He visited Paris and met expatriates like Kay Boyle and Harry Crosby, whose poetry had something in common with Crane's from the point of view of intensity and depth of imagery. And he lived, at various times, in New York and Hollywood. One way or another he came into contact with just about everyone who was anyone in the literary life of the period. John Unterecker's book is notable for the way it places Crane firmly in his milieu, and in doing so, brings it alive.

My own attitude towards any book of this sort is that it should exist as a work in its own right, and help in our appreciation of its subject's work. *Voyager* succeeds on both counts. I did get a little impatient with the accounts of literary squabbles that, in retrospect, can seem almost childish. And some of the minor details in this 800 page book could have been dispensed with. But, taken as a whole, it is an important document and adds to our knowledge of Crane and modern American literature in general.

THE ASTONISHED MAN by Blaise Cendrars . Peter Owen, 1970

VOYAGER: A LIFE OF HART CRANE by John Unterecker. Blond, 1971

HENRY HARLAND IN BOHEMIA

I don't suppose many people read Henry Harland these days. A few academics, perhaps, especially if they're researching the 1890s, and in particular the saga of *The Yellow Book*. The magazine is often held to represent the decadence in full bloom. In fact, with the notable exception of work by Aubrey Beardsley, it often seems quite decorous now, and I'm not convinced that it really appeared to be all that much different when it was first published. It was the notoriety surrounding Oscar Wilde, and the ambiguous nature of some of Beardsley's illustrations, that essentially sounded its death knell. And there had been people waiting in the wings who were keen to find an excuse to attack *The Yellow Book*. To them, it appeared effete and degenerate, and too much infatuated with French literature and art. The suspicious scent of green carnations pervaded the air around it.

Henry Harland was one of the founders of *The Yellow Book*, and its chief editor from 1894 to 1897. It was said that he "did not care greatly for poetry" and what he published in the magazine wasn't always of the highest quality. Katherine Lyon Mix, who wrote a definitive history of *The Yellow Book*, was of the opinion that Harland's finest achievement as an editor was giving space to well-written essays, and that they have survived the years when compared to much of the poetry and fiction that appeared in its pages. Not everyone would necessarily agree with that opinion.

But who was Henry Harland? He was born in 1861 and brought up in America, despite liking to drop hints about coming from St Petersburg, growing up mainly in Rome, and studying in Paris. Under the name of Sidney Luska he wrote several convincing novels about Jewish life in America, despite having no Jewish family links. He does seem to have visited both Rome and Paris in his twenties, though for what purposes is difficult to decipher, but returned to New York. And, according to Mix, in 1884 he married a lady called Aline Merriam, "an American girl of French ancestry". She "was charming, talented, a musician and a writer, and quite in sympathy with Henry's literary ambitions".

The couple moved to Paris in 1887 and then to London in 1889, where Henry effected a transition to a form of literary dandyism that seemed to tie in with the languid mood of the moment. His prose style became more refined and affected, and Mix says his models were French writers like Maupassant, Daudet, and Mérimée : "He was acutely aware of the meaning of style and form, nourishing the vividness of an impression until he could transfer it to well-thought-out phrases". He wrote several novels while he was in London, but it was the short story that showed him at his best.

Harland did set several of his stories in Paris and others in Rome, and it may have been that it was because, in both places, he found people he wanted to relate to. Paris had its bohemians, while Rome had its aristo-cratic expatriates. And in each group he may have perceived a reluc-tance to surrender to bourgeois rules and values. And he could under-stand their distrust of an assertive middle-class, with its own systems of social control and ambitions for power that seemed to challenge the independence of both bohemians and aristocrats. Baudelaire and other bohemians had recognised the threat posed by the bourgeoisie, and the bohemian poet, when he expressed his admiration for the dandies, who were primarily drawn from the aristocracy (Beau Brummell was a no-table exception), was acknowledging their presence in the nineteenth century reaction to mass society, industrialisation, and the rise of a mercantile middle-class.

There is an irony in the fact of Harland's interest in bohemians as sup-posed opponents of middle-class mores. In nineteenth century Paris many of them, and certainly those in the American and British commu-nities of artists, writers, and students, were on the whole from the mid-dle-class and supported in their activities by subsidies from business-based parents and the like. Their bohemianism was largely voluntary and could be terminated at any time should the going get really tough. When they returned to their native land it was often to a comfortable home and, if they hadn't succeeded as painters or poets, to a fairly se-cure awareness that they could always find a reasonable job thanks to family and friends. I think a general impression of these middle-class, part-time bohemians comes through in Harland's stories, as it does in George Du Maurier's *Trilby* (1894) and Robert W. Chambers' *In The Quarter* (1894, though it has been claimed that it was written some years earlier), which had a similar theme to *Trilby*. Both Du Maurier and Chambers had been art students in Paris in their younger days.

Harland's story, "The Bohemian Girl", soon sets the scene with a de-scription of her father often noticed striding along "the Boulevard St Michel" dressed in "velvet jackets, flannel shirts, loosely-knotted ties, and wide-brimmed soft felt hats". He held court to impressionable art students at the Café Bleu and had a studio in Montparnasse. Nina, his daughter, is "a girl or sixteen or seventeen; though tall, with an amply-rounded, mature-seeming figure – if one had judged from her appear-ance, one would have fancied her three or four years older". The narrator goes on to say; "It was a queer life for a girl to live, that happy-go-lucky life of the Latin Quarter, lawless and unpremeditated, with a café for her school-room, and none but men for comrades; but Nina liked it; and her father had a theory in his madness. He was a Bohemian, not in practice only, but in principle; he preached Bohemianism as the most rational manner of existence, maintaining that it developed what was intrinsic and authentic in one's character, saved one from the artificial, and brought one into immediate contact with the realities of the world; and he could see no reason why a human being should be 'cloistered and contracted' because of her sex".

When her father suddenly dies, Nina is compelled to move to distant relatives in England : "From the Café Bleu to a Yorkshire Parsonage". She is completely lost there. As she says in a letter to one of her contacts in Paris: "Are you interested in crops? In the preservation of game? In the diseases of cattle?" She eventually runs away and returns to Paris, where she works as a model, a translator, and gives music lessons. She has male admirers but, following her father's teachings, does not believe in marriage: "If a man and woman love each other, they should be free to determine for themselves the character, extent and duration of their intercourse, as two friends should be".

But some observers felt that "the situation held tragic possibilities. A young and attractive girl, by no means constitutionally insusceptible, and imbued with heterodox ideas of marriage – alone in the Latin Quarter". The inevitable happens and Nina falls in love with a South American who is studying in Paris. When she becomes pregnant he agrees to marry her and leaves, ostensibly to obtain his parents' approval. But once away from Paris he writes to tell her that he is already engaged to marry someone else. Nina has the child, decides to leave the Latin Quarter, and to support herself and her daughter, opens a *pension.* She makes a success of it by being careful about who she allows to live there, and eventually has a regular salon where "on a Friday evening, you would meet half the lions that were at large in the town – authors, painters, actors, actresses, deputies, even an occasional Cabinet Minister. She has become respectable, but "has never accepted the least repentance for what some people would call her 'fault'. Her ideas of right and wrong have undergone very little modification".

It's an engaging tale, tidily told, and if it does have a slight air of disapproval about some aspects of bohemianism, it doesn't push it too hard and the narrator refrains from adopting a moral tone when describing Nina's life.

The lighter side of the Bohemian experience can be found in Harland's stories, "A Reincarnation" and "Mademoiselle Miss". In the former an Englishman arrives in the Latin-Quarter and is surprised to find that, as a popular, published author in his own country, he's unknown in Paris. He is intending to write a novel in which the hero will spend some time in the Latin-Quarter, and so he's in Paris to pick up on some local colour, hopefully from the students he meets. They, realising what a fraud he is, string him along and allow him to make a fool of himself: "He took it for granted that everybody had heard of him, and bridled, as a personal affront, when he met anyone who hadn't. If you fell into chance talk with him, in ignorance of his identity, he could not let three minutes pass without informing you". When he's taken to visit a famous artist he's annoyed that he's not introduced to the man as "a distinguished English author". And he's not interested in the fact that the he's talking to "the most distinguished living painter". It's a briskly-written look at a self-centred mediocrity.

"Mademoiselle Miss" is kinder in intent and concerns a "young and distinctly pretty" Englishwoman who turns up at the hotel where the narrator and his student companions stay. It's not a particularly respectable place, and among the other residents are several young French women whose occupations and activities might best be described as "questionable". The Englishwoman is on her way home after working as a governess in America, is spending a few weeks in Paris, and has an old guide which lists the hotel. It's well out-of-date and the character of the hotel has vastly changed. The students think of themselves as worldly-wise and decide to show the lady the seamy side of Bohemia. She meets up with Aristide Bruant, and even accompanies him at the piano while he performs when his usual pianist is indisposed. And she visits the Rat Mort. She takes it all in her stride, even though she's naïve in many ways, and in the end they all come to respect her and are sad when she leaves. The story is lightly-amusing and not without charm.

There was always a dark side to Bohemia, and Harland was well aware of it. "When I am King" is about a talented pianist-composer who everyone expects will achieve great things. But the narrator meets him many years later playing in a run-down bar in a dockside district of Bordeaux: "Edmund Pair playing a dance for prostitutes and drunken sailors". He hears about the man's story of success in Paris not being repeated in London, the death of his beloved wife, his failure to obtain steady employment as a musician, teacher, or critic. He doesn't betray any self-pity and simply says: "The situation you find me in seems ter-

71

rible to you; to me it's no worse than another. You see, I'm hardened; I've got past caring", And the narrator says; "I stood looking after him till he vanished in the night, with a miserable baffled recognition of my helplessness to help him".

The problem of drugs occurs in "P'tit Bleu", the young woman of that name being "a Latin-Quarter girl" who is alert to the ways of the world and looks on the men who admire her as ready to be exploited. She has little or no regard for anything other than having a good time and raking in any gifts or money offered her. And then she suddenly takes up with an older man, an artist who is also addicted to opium. She looks after him, weans him off the drug, though he frequently relapses and spends whatever they have on opium. But she perseveres and starts him painting again. But then he embarks on one final binge, ends up in hospital, and dies in Dieppe. The narrator does not know about this until later, and is away when P'tit Bleu calls at his Paris address, and never hears from her again: "So she has simply disappeared, and, in the flesh, may have come to.........one would rather not conjecture".

"Funeral March of a Marionette" again touches on the kind of young woman who appears to have been a constant in Parisian bohemia throughout the nineteenth century. Surviving on very little, and with what the respectable would regard as a dubious moral sensibility, she pairs off with various "friends" and others she entertains in her little room on the Left Bank. But the narrator is aware that he often hears her coughing in the night, and is therefore not surprised when one of her companions calls on him to say that she has died, a victim of consumption. It was prevalent in Paris, especially among the impoverished. The narrator looks back on his attempts to help the girl by persuading her to change her way of life, but realises it was all in vain. She didn't want to change, even though she knew how it would end.

The final story I want to consider is the longest. "A Latin Quarter Courtship" ran to 189 pages, so could well be thought of as a short novel, though it's included in Harland's book, *A Latin-Quarter Courtship and Other Stories,* which might give an indication of how he saw it. Stephen Ormizon is a would-be novelist, living in Paris thanks to a generous allowance from his mother. He advertises for someone with a good command of English to make a copy of his novel (this was long before laptops, and even a widespread use of typewriters) and visits the apartment of a D. Personette who replies. There he is greeted by Dr Gluck, "a decidedly pretty, plump little lady, perhaps thirty years of age", who he knows from New York, and who explains that the "D" is Denise, who shares the apartment with her. Gluck is "into animal magnetism, mesmerism, hypnotism, and that sort of thing, a good deal". She describes Denise as "her chum" and her "dearest friend". And they had fallen "desperately in love with each other and vowed never to separate".

Denise turns up and meets Ormizon. Gluck explains who he is and reminiscences fondly about past times with him in New York. Denise pats her hand, "softly stroked it, then kissed it, and murmured 'Chère p'tite Isabel...' 'But' she added, 'you must not think of those times. That was before you knew me. That makes me jealous' ". 'Oh, you sweet thing', exclaimed the doctor, putting her arm around Denise's waist'. 'You have no reason to be jealous. I never knew what real happiness meant until I met you.' "

A little later, Gluck says that she and Denise are "just like husband and wife; aren't we, Denise? And she replies, "Perfectly". Ormizon asks "Which is which?". With our modern sensibilities it's difficult not to imagine that something other than mere friendship is involved in the relationship between Gluck and Denise. But as things develop, Ormizon falls in love with Denise and she with him. He determines to marry her, and decides to break off a commitment he had made at his mother's request to marry her niece. He doesn't love her, nor does he believe that the girl in question loves him. But his mother objects to his marrying a French girl and vows to disinherit him if he does.

It's not necessary to lay out all the plot, which partly involves an American artist, a trip to Meudon, conversations about the comparative merits of French, British, and American authors, and other minor matters. Ormizon does marry Denise with Gluck's blessing, his mother relents and takes him back in the fold, and the couple settle in New York. Ormizon begins to make a mark in the literary world following the success of his first novel. And the story ends: "In addition to their other sources of revenue, they took a boarder. The boarder was a very pretty, plump little lady, not much older than thirty years. And though Ormizon was extremely attentive to her, and apparently very fond of her, Denise never manifested the least symptom of jealousy. Her name was Gluck – Isabel B. Gluck, M.D."

Those with a Freudian frame of mine could have a field day with this story, but I suspect that some readers at the time might have simply shrugged, and said, "That's what comes of living in Paris". Rumours of what went on in the French capital were always likely to lead to assumptions of unconventional behaviour, and the corrupting influence of the bohemian way of life.

Richard Le Gallienne, another writer now little read, knew Henry Harland, and wrote about him affectionately in his memoir, *The Romantic Nineties*: "Harland was one of those Americans in love with Paris who seem more French than the French themselves........He was born to be the life and soul of one of those *cènacles*, which from their café tables in 'the Quarter' promulgate all those world shaking 'new movements' in art which succeed each other with kaleidoscopic rapidity. The most vivacious of talkers, 'art' with him, as with his Parisian prototypes, was a life-and-death matter. Nothing else existed for him. He had no other interests".

Perhaps this intensity came about because of his medical condition. Like his friend, Aubrey Beardsley, he was consumptive, and had been warned by doctors that he had only a few years left to live unless he moved to a warmer and dryer climate. He and his wife left to live in Italy, where he died in 1905. I'm not about to suggest that he was a major writer, and it may be that he is best remembered for his role in editing *The Yellow Book*. One or two of his stories are reprinted in anthologies of 1890s writing, and reprints of some of his books are in the lists of publishers specialising in reclaiming works from the past. I don't know if they are much in demand, though I suspect not. But the short stories I've referred to are not without interest, and if they rarely delve deep into the characters' motives and actions they are well-written and entertaining.

They might also be useful in terms of throwing a little light on aspects of nineteenth-century Parisian bohemia. In *A Latin-Quarter Courtship*, Palmer, an American student who doesn't have a financially-secure background and is always impoverished, explains about Julian's, the art-school he attends and which is the one open to women and foreign students: "But as I was going to tell you, your forty francs a month entitles you to all the privileges of the school. Then the masters, they give their services free-gratis-for-nothing. At Julien's there are Bouguereau, Boulanger, and Lefebvre, the three greatest draughtsmen living. They come to the school three times a week, examine what the boys have done, point out its faults, show you as well as they can how to set it to right. They do this, as I say, for nothing – simply for the love of art; which, I claim, is glorious".

Julian's was a well-known art-school, and the three painters Palmer mentions were all well-established, and were what is usually referred to as "academic" or "traditional" in their approach to art. There are no references to the Impressionists in any of Harland's stories.

BIBLIOGRAPHICAL NOTE

"The Bohemian Girl" in *Grey Roses*, John Lane, London, 1895.

"A Reincarnation" in *Grey Roses*, John Lane, London, 1895.

"Mademoiselle Miss" in *Mademoiselle Miss & Other Stories,* Heinemann, London, 1893.

"When I am King" in *Grey Roses*, John Lane, London, 1895.

"P'tit Bleu" in *Comedies and Errors*, John Lane, London, 1898. This story can also be found in *The Yellow Book*, edited by Fraser Harrison, The Boydell Press, Woodbridge, 1982.

"The Funeral March of a Marionette" in *Mademoiselle Miss & Other Stories,* Heinemann, London, 1893.

"A Latin-Quarter Courtship" in *A Latin-Quarter Courtship and Other Stories,* Cassell, New York, 1889.

The Romantic Nineties by Richard Le Gallienne, Robin Clark, London, 1993. Originally published in 1925.

A Study in Yellow: The Yellow Book and Its *Contributors* by Katherine Lyon Mix, Constable, London, 1960.

Trilby by George Du Maurier. Oxford University Press, Oxford, 1998. Originally published in 1894.

In the Quarter by Robert W. Chambers. Dodo Press, 2007. Originally published in 1894.

JAMES WRIGHT : ABOVE THE RIVER

Do we need a *Complete Poems* from any poet? Not everything a poet writes is necessarily of the same quality, nor is it always interesting. An academic or a would-be biographer might argue that completeness is essential, but I always suspect that poems are like life – they tend to the routine a lot of the time and are consequently forgettable.

These thoughts occurred as I worked my way through James Wright's *Above the River*. There are a handful of his poems that have lingered in my mind over the years, such as "As I Step Over a Puddle at the End of Winter, I think of An Ancient Chinese Governor", "Depressed by a Book of Bad Poetry, I Walk toward an Unused Pasture and Invite the Insects to Join Me", and "In Response to a Rumour that the Oldest Whorehouse in Wheeling, West Virginia, Has Been Condemned". Wright, as you can see, was very good with titles, and the poems themselves are first-rate. They're short, tidily constructed, and point to an ironic appreciation of events. Wright often had a faint air of regret, as if he found the world wanting in many ways, and the best of his poems present that mood in ways that are clear and attractive.

There was, too, an openness about him which led to his writing about anything and everything, though not always with the same degree of success. If, as I suggested earlier, life often becomes routine then attempts to record it in a poem might need to invest the writing with some sort of insight or significance. Wright doesn't manage this at times, and the poems can sound as routine as the incidents they deal with. But it has to be admitted that even his failures can often be interesting, with a striking line or stanza salvaging what would otherwise be a mundane poem. And his handling of technique was often deft. He frequently employed rhyming patterns with great skill, but could also work easily within the framework of free verse. He was, in fact, a real craftsman because the reader is never overwhelmed by the technique. It's there to sustain the language, not dominate it.

I started this review by asking if a *Complete Poems* is necessary, and I have to admit that, in some ways, Wright's book could be a convincing case for completeness. The less-important poems provide a setting for the more-accomplished ones, and the overall impression is of a writer totally committed to poetry rather than just seeing it as something to which he turned on occasions. There is a seriousness here which is both impressive and moving.

It should be noted that the book contains translations, some prose pieces, and a long appreciation by Donald Hall. I'm not sure how many British readers have looked at James Wright's work in depth, but they ought to.

ABOVE THE RIVER: THE COMPLETE POEMS by James Wright. Bloodaxe Books. 1992.

PAUL POTTS : INSTEAD OF A SONNET

Paul Potts is a survivor. Around since the 1940s he has written some fine prose, as anyone who has read *Dante Called You Beatrice* will know. The opening lines of that book set the tone of his writing generally:

"This book is an attempt to tell a woman, while I was standing on her carpet, asking her to marry me, just what kind of a man it was who loved her, and what other love he had, beyond his love of her. Had she but wanted my love she would have had to share it with all of the poor and each of the lonely".

It's fairly intense writing and, as Potts himself says in his introduction to this new edition of *Instead of a Sonnet*, it has a "certain place in contemporary literature". One only wishes that more people were aware of this fact, and that supposedly informed critics and commentators on literature would carry out their function properly and help to keep authors like Potts constantly in circulation.

Paul Potts has also written poems, though he's modestly self-effacing about it. He says that the "poetry of the English language would be no poorer without them and it is unfortunately no richer because of them", which isn't strictly true because some of the poems still merit attention in their own right and not just as souvenirs of an earlier time. They were originally published in scattered magazines and anthologies, and published as a collection in 1944. For this new edition Potts has added ten later poems. The tone hasn't changed over the years, however, and can perhaps be best summed up by these lines from one of the newer poems: "I want to write something holy/Holy about life/Where a kiss is a prayer/And God is worshipped/By the way a woman combs her hair".

The openness, the belief in "simple things", the idea that you pour out the way you feel and it's poetry, are typical of Potts, but it would be unfair to suggest that he does nothing more than pour out his feelings. I would guess that the poems were formed in his mind, and shaped by a sensibility that has a heightened awareness of people and events. They are, in a sense, written before they're set down on paper, so that the actual construction of them on the page is only the final step in a rigorous process. Lesser writers may think they also work that way, but one suspects that they neither feel or construct enough to be able to match Potts.

It's good to see this little book available. The publisher, Charles Graham, mentions that he first met Potts in the French pub in Soho, and my own most recent glimpse of him was in the same place. It seemed apt, bearing in mind the links it has with the lively years of 1940s bohemia. But Potts can't be written off as a mere relic of those days. He's a survivor and, whether writing prose or verse, he's a poet. There are too few of them around – real ones, I mean – for us to ignore him.

INSTEAD OF A SONNET by Paul Potts. Tuba Press. 1978

GARY SNYDER AND THE WOBBLIES

In the "Logging" section of Gary Snyder's *Myths and Texts* there is a reference to the "Everett Massacre November 5 1916". Does it mean much now to anyone other than a dedicated student of Snyder's poetry? Or someone with an interest in American labour history? I would guess that he wrote his poem-sequence in the 1950s when there would have been some people still alive who had memories of the Wobblies and their dynamic, if brief appearance on the American radical scene. I know that the organisation still exists, but its fame largely rests on its activities in the first two or three decades of the twentieth century.

The Industrial Workers of the World (IWW, popularly known as Wobblies) was founded in 1905, its mission being to organise among groups of workers who were often ignored by the predominantly craft unions which dominated labour politics in the United States. So, the IWW went into the mills in Massachusetts where large numbers of immigrant workers were employed, and out to the wheat fields of the mid-West and beyond where itinerant field hands lived rough and followed the harvests. And among the loggers on the West Coast and their often-dangerous work.

I'm not intending to lay down a broad history of the IWW or explain its general policies. It was a union and not a political party, and if it had a theoretical base it was one of syndicalism (or industrial unionism) and a programme of direct action and workers' control. I doubt that many of the grass-roots activists among the Wobblies, or the people they recruited, were too concerned with theory. The usual bread-and-butter issues – shorter hours, higher pay, improved working conditions – were what mattered and strikes were fought on that basis and not to suit theories about revolution.

The Wobblies were seen as dangerous by employers and by local and national authorities, partly because of their success in organising people often seen as difficult to get into unions. But they were also feared because their speeches and pamphlets were frequently inclined to be vigorous in tone, and appeared to sometimes advocate sabotage as a justifiable technique in strike activity. There was never a great deal of evidence to suggest that the IWW actually used sabotage, but people tended to believe that they did. When America entered the First World War in 1917 the government moved to suppress the organisation and put around one hundred leading members on trial in 1918. Most were sentenced to lengthy terms of imprisonment. There were disagreements and splits in the IWW in the early-1920s and many members left to join the newly-established Communist Party.

During its lifetime IWW members suffered a great deal of harassment and violence from the police and local vigilante groups. And it's in this connection that the story behind Snyder's use of the term "Everett Massacre" emerges. The IWW often fought "Free Speech" fights, asserting their right to hold street-corner meetings and other public displays of their message. This resulted in numerous clashes with the police and civic authorities. One of the Wobbly tactics when they encountered resistance to their meetings, and speakers were arrested, was to flood a town with their members so that it would be almost impossible to put everyone in jail.

In November 1916 the town of Everett was experiencing a long strike by shingle weavers. The IWW decided to show support for the strikers by heading to Everett in force. They hired two steamers, one named the Verona, and sailed from Seattle, but when they attempted to land were met by the local sheriff and a large group of armed deputies. A shoot-out started and five Wobblies were killed and many more wounded. The death toll among the Wobblies was probably higher as some of the injured may have fallen into the water and their bodies were never re-covered.

Snyder lists the names of the five known Wobbly dead: Felix Baran, Hugo Gerlot, Gustav Johnson, John Looney, Abraham Rabinowitz. Later in the same poem, he uses what is presumably something said to him by an old logger when he was working among such people: "Thousands of boys shot and beat up/For wanting a good bed, good pay./decent food, in the woods". And he adds two lines of his own: "No one knew what it meant:/ "Soldiers of discontent".

That last phrase was most likely taken from the poem that Charles Ashleigh read at the funeral for the five Wobblies; "Song on his lips he came/Song on his lips he went/This be the token we bear of him/Soldier of Discontent". Ashleigh, an English-born Wobbly, was imprisoned following the big trial of IWW members and was later deported to Britain. His novel, *Rambling Kid*, is about his adventures travelling across America and working with the IWW.

The IWW was a spent force by the time Snyder wrote his poem, though it still had some sort of nostalgic appeal to the Beats. Ginsberg refers to the Wobblies in his poem "America" and in Kerouac's *The Dharma Bums,* Japhy Ryder (Snyder) says: "I was always sympathetic to freedom movements, too, like anarchists in the Northwest, the oldtime he-

roes of Everett Massacre and all". I think the free-wheeling spirit behind the Wobblies, especially those who rode the boxcars as they
moved from place to place in search of work, appealed to those who
saw going "on the road" in romantic terms. And there was also the tradition of Wobbly songs and poems and their newspapers and magazines to provide inspiration for poets and editors.

It was always Snyder's early work that appealed to me. His poems
about going to sea and working in the woods in the Pacific North-West
have stayed in my mind for almost fifty years. "T-2 Tanker Blues",
"Hay for the Horses", "The Sappa Creek", "The Late Snow & Lumber
Strike of the Summer of Fifty-Four", plus the *Myths & Texts* sequence
and the Cold Mountain poems are what I remember. I'm not denigrat-
ing his other concerns with Indian folklore and mythology, Zen Bud-
dhism, and environmental matters. They are all already present in the
works I've mentioned. But it is mostly those early poems that I return
to when I want to read Gary Snyder.

A final note. It intrigues me that not too much attention has been paid
to Snyder's early radical commitments. He had been a member of the
Marine Cooks and Stewards Union, a communist-led organisation
which was hounded by the authorities in the post-war period. His involvement with this union led to him being denied a government job as
a forest lookout in 1954. And he had been a student at Reed College
which had a reputation for its left-liberal tendencies. Some of its staff
were investigated by HUAC and were subsequently dismissed from
their posts.

NOTES

I treasure my copy of Snyder's *A Range of Poems* (Fulcrum Press,
London, 1966). For information about the Wobblies see *Rebel Voices:
An I.W.W. Anthology* edited by Joyce L. Kornbluh (University of
Michigan Press, Ann Arbor, 1968) and *We Shall Be All: A History of
the IWW* by Melvyn Dubofsky (Quadrangle Books, New York, 1969).
Charles Ashleigh's *Rambling Kid* (Faber, London, 1930) is worth read-
ing, but by the time he wrote it he had become a member of the Com-
munist Party and tended to take a critical view of Wobbly aims and
practices. IWW literature was often fairly ephemeral and geared to
strikes and everyday events. For some more-formal writing by Wobblies, see Ralph Chaplin's *Wobbly; The Rough-and-Tumble Story of an
American Radical* (Chicago University Press, Chicago, 1948) and *Bars
& Shadows : The Prison Poems of Ralph Chaplin* (Allen & Unwin,
London, 1922). There is also *Poems* by Arturo Giovannitti (El Corno

Emplumado, Mexico City, 1966). I'm sure that Allen Ginsberg must have known Giovannitti's long-lined, declamatory poems, such as "When the Cock Crows" and "The Walker", when he was young.

SOUTH OF THE BORDER
DOWN MEXICO WAY

People from the United States have crossed the border into Mexico for a variety of reasons. Adventurers, tourists, painters, political exiles, criminals on the run, soldiers chasing Pancho Villa, writers in search of material, and many others. Ambrose Bierce disappeared in Mexico in 1914, and Weldon Kees was rumoured to have gone there instead of jumping off the Golden Gate Bridge in 1955. I'm being selective and whole books have been written about who went into Mexico and why.

The Beats were aware of Mexico, often because it was a source of drugs. William Burroughs moved south of the border in the early-1950s to escape the attentions of narcotics police in the United States. Kerouac and Ginsberg spent some time in Mexico, and Ray and Bonnie Bremser tried to survive there, as she recorded in *For Love of Ray.* There were also writers who went to Mexico as the FBI and the House Un-American Activities Committee turned their spotlights on alleged communists.

The poet George Oppen and his wife, Mary, thought it opportune to head south of the border when their membership of the Communist Party came to light. And the novelist, John Herrmann, was another communist who decided that life in Mexico might be better than being harassed by the authorities in America. He was an interesting character and had been in Paris in the 1920s with Hemingway, Robert McAlmon, and others from the so-called Lost Generation. In the 1930s he became politically committed and joined the Communist Party, and it's more than likely that he had been involved in some sort of espionage activity. It has been suggested that Herrmann knew Burroughs and had visited him on the day that Burroughs shot his wife, though he wasn't present when the incident occurred. What interests me is what Burroughs, known for his right-wing views, might have thought of the communist Herrmann. They would have had something in common by hiding out in Mexico, if not for the same reasons.

We know about the well-known exiles like Burroughs, but there were numerous other Americans in Mexico, scattered around a variety of small towns and villages where rents were cheap and a few American dollars could buy ample food and alcohol. I want to look at a couple of novels based on the American colony at Ajijic on the shore of Lake Chapala. They are *Week with no Friday* by Willard Marsh, and *Where's*

Annie? by Eileen Bassing. Both Marsh and Bassing appear to have been in Ajijic about the same time, in the early-1950s, so presumably would have known many of the same people. They certainly knew some of the same kinds of characters who were living in Ajijic in that period. Like many similar locations with writers and artists in residence it also attracted more than its share of misfits, idlers, drug users, and oddballs, along with the productive, talented people. Of the latter, I have seen references to Alexander Trocchi and ruth weiss having visited Ajijic in the 1950s.

Willard Marsh was born in 1922 in California. He showed some aptitude as a musician (trumpet and trombone) and was skilled enough to pay for his way through college by forming a small band. He served in the armed forces between 1942 and 1945, was at the Iowa Writers' Workshop in 1959/1960, and later held down mostly short-term teaching jobs at various educational establishments, including the University of Southern California. He died in 1970. In between, he spent time in Ajijic, and wrote short-stories, many of which were published in a wide variety of magazines, ranging from *Esquire, Playboy, Transatlantic Review,* and *North American Review* to pulp publications like *Ellery Queen's Mystery Magazine* and *The Magazine of Fantasy and Science-Fiction.* Some of them, those that had appeared in the more-prestigious magazines, were collected in Marsh's book of short stories, *Beachhead in Bohemia.* Several were clearly based on his experiences in Mexico, and others touched on jazz, race relations, and wartime adventures. It's of interest to note that material from the Mexican stories was later reworked into Marsh's novel.

In Marsh's *Week with no Friday,* Warner, a playwright with only minor successes to his name, is living a somewhat desultory daily life in Zopilotl, a village clearly based on Ajijic. His situation might be summed up in an encounter with a friend who invites him home for a coffee. Warner at first declines the invitation, saying he has to "get back on some kind of work schedule". The friend says, "It'll keep till tomorrow, won't it?", and Warner thinks, "The odds were that it would. It had for quite a while now".

Warner isn't earning much from his writing, and Americans can't take jobs in Mexico, so he has to get by in various ways, one of which involves conning tourists into thinking that they've come across some authentic pottery from long ago. He entices a visiting schoolteacher into one of his schemes, but then has an affair with her. Things seem to be going well, but she eventually realises that Warner has used her, and decides to return to the United States. Warner has been living in Mexico on a tourist card which should have been renewed on a regular basis, and when the police catch up with him he has to go on the run. He does make it to Los Angeles, where he soon drifts onto Skid Row and drinks his days away. When he finally pulls himself out of this existence he gets a job as a night clerk in a seedy hotel and takes up with a prostitute who operates out of one of the rooms in the establishment. But he does start to write again, though there's no indication of whether or not his restored-enthusiasm will continue to stimulate him and his written works add up to anything worthwhile.

It isn't a great novel, and perhaps not even a very good one, though it does maintain its interest. Various curious characters crop up, some of them not unlike Warner in their incapacity to settle down to anything sustained. Someone called Beau Blissing is said to have a wife who is a "lady novelist", and this is probably a reference to Robert Bassing, husband of the novelist, Eileen Bassing.

She was born in 1918 and died in 1977. Her novel, *Home Before Dark,* was turned into a film in 1958 which starred Jean Simmons and Rhonda Fleming. Robert Bassing had worked as a producer and screenwriter in Hollywood. It's interesting that the Bassings were in Mexico in the early 1950s, a period when a number of blacklisted screenwriters were there as refugees from the HUAC investigations. I haven't found any evidence that Robert Bassing was in Ajijic for that reason, and it may just be a coincidence that he decided to move to Mexico around the same time. He doesn't appear to have had any difficulty in being credited as co-writer with his wife when they produced the script for the screen version of *Home Before Dark.*

Eileen Bassing's *Where's Annie?* is a better novel than Marsh's from the point of view of plot and personality development. A wider range of characters is introduced into the narrative. Some, such as Willie Chester (based on Willard Marsh) are mentioned only in passing, but others, like Charles, who drifts "around the village wearing an old pair of Marine Corps pants", are given more space. There is Victoria, most likely based on Leonora Baccante, an English-born author of two novels published in the early-1930s. And Harry, a junkie musician who at one time played with various big-bands. He and Charles are friends, largely because Charles has also had involvements with narcotics when he lived in New York. The period is established with references to Bird, Monk, and Tristano. And other names – Stan Getz, Shorty Rogers, Shelly Manne – are scattered around the section about Charles.

Harry is a somewhat cynical and detached individual. He's contemptu-

ous of the "squares" who only "want music as background.....the attention span of the mole-mind of the square is very small". His rant con-
vincingly creates the kind of characters around in the 1950s when the
hipster ethos influenced many musicians and their followers, Victoria
isn't impressed by Harry's outburst, and remarks: "He bangs his spoon
on the tray of his high chair because the world doesn't always listen to
music when he thinks it should". But she's not necessarily totally critical of the hipsters drifting into the village. When Ned, a well-to-do, and
successful artist who has had shows in New York and Mexico City,
expresses his fear of them, she responds: "Oh, they're just lost boys!
Have you no compassion?".

Other people arrive. Margo, a rich lady, who plans to buy property and
turn the village into a proper tourist attraction, and Abel, a black bar-
owner who is killed by Harry in an argument over money. Harry then
kills himself. Victoria, who had witnessed the murder, decides it's time
to leave the village. Charles stays, waiting for a friend to arrive, but
with no plans other than that they'll "blow some pot together". It's a
downbeat ending, with little positive in sight for either of them.

There is, incidentally, an interesting reference in some comments by a
Mexican in the book when, talking about the Americans, he says: "I
have been watching them for years. One sets his bed on fire with his
cigarettes and dies. Another one paralyses himself with peyote and
dies...and he is only twenty-one years old...a poet they say. Many
drink themselves into eternity, taking a slow time about it, destroying
themselves cell by cell". The young poet may be Philip Lamantia's
friend, John Hoffman, who died in Mexico in 1952. Lamantia read
some of Hoffman's poems at the famous Six Gallery event in San
Francisco in 1955. They were both experimenting with peyote in the
early-1950s.

As I said earlier, *Where's Annie?* is a better novel than Willard Marsh's
Week with no Friday. It has more depth and a wider sense of a varied
community. Marsh's book isn't lacking in pace and excitement, but
depends on its central character, Warner, too much. However, both are
valuable for the way in which they provide a picture of Americans in a
bohemian community in Mexico and how they related to each other and
the local people.

NOTES

Willard Marsh's *Week with no Friday* was published by Harper &
Row, New York (hardback, 1965) and Avon Books, New York, (paperback, 1967). *Beachhead in Bohemia* was published by Louisiana

State University Press, Baton Rouge, 1969. Out of curiosity I read one of Marsh's stories, "Everyone's Hometown is Guernica", in the August, 1965, issue of *The Magazine of Fantasy and Science Fiction*. It's a slight account of an artist looking for inspiration, a kitten, and a strange woman who suddenly comes into his life and stimulates him into creativity. But there's a twist in the tale.

Eileen Bassing's *Where's Annie?* appeared in hardback form from Random House, New York, 1963. A paperback edition was published by Dell Books, New York, 1964. A UK hardback edition was published by Longman Green, 1963. Her earlier novel, *Home Before Dark,* came out in 1957 (Random House, hardback) with a paperback edition from Bantam Books in 1958. A UK hardback was published by Longman Green in 1958.

It might be of relevance to note that Willard Motley, a black novelist who spent time in Ajijic, wrote a novel set in Mexico. His *Let Noon be Fair* is a caustic comment on how an influx of Americans has a negative effect on the local community. It was published posthumously, Motley having died in Mexico in 1965. The hardback edition was published by Putnam, New York, 1966, with a paperback edition from Dell in 1966. The UK hardback came from Longman Green, 1966, and the paperback from Pan Books, London, 1969. Motley had been associated with various left-wing groups in the USA and was under surveillance by the FBI while living in Mexico. There is quite a bit about him, and *Let Noon Be Fair,* in *Cold War Exiles in Mexico: U.S. Dissidents and the Culture of Critical Resistance* by Rebecca M. Schreiber (Minnesota University Press, Minneapolis, 2008). It seems that Motley's book was substantially revised and completed by an editor at Putnam's after he died.

One other item of interest may be Georgia Cogswell's *Golden Obsession* (Zebra Books, New York, 1979). She was Willard Marsh's first wife, and her novel, set in Mexico, is a mixture of an adventure story around a search for lost treasure, and a romantic tale almost in the style of a Mills & Boon book, with the attractive young widow winning the love of the handsome visiting American.

THE BEATS : AUTHORSHIPS, LEGACIES

And the Beat goes on. It's now over sixty years since Allen Ginsberg's *Howl* and Jack Kerouac's *On the Road* started it all rolling merrily along. There had been intimations of it before that, but not to the point where it became the object of wide scrutiny by both literary critics and some sections of the general public. I think 1957 may be the year when things began to take on additional speed. As it happened, it was also the year when I finished three years of military service, so returning to civilian life I could observe the growing interest in what the Beats were promoting. Inevitably, a lot of the attention, as expressed in the popular press, focused on the supposed life-styles of the key activists. "Blame these 4 men for the beatnik horror" screamed a headline in *The People* one Sunday in 1960, and beneath it were photos of Burroughs, Ginsberg, Kerouac, and Corso. The accompanying article had much to say about drugs and other matters likely to arouse the prurient or enrage the moralists.

Reception in intellectual circles was generally hostile. "Know-nothing bohemians", sneered Norman Podhoretz in *Partisan Review*, and not many academics seemed sympathetic to Beat writing. Thomas Parkinson was an exception in the USA, and Eric Mottram in England and Edwin Morgan in Scotland were less inclined to dismiss Kerouac and company out-of-hand. On the whole, though, I can't recall much, if any, positive curiosity being evident in academic circles. Bernard Bergonzi said, "I don't think the reader who is concerned with literary values will want to spend much time on them" when reviewing a selection of works by Kerouac, Philip Whalen, Frank O'Hara, and others for *The Guardian*.

Nor was the literary establishment enthusiastic about the arrival of the Beats. Cyril Connolly and Philip Toynbee both wrote dismissive reviews of Lawrence Lipton's *The Holy Barbarians*, though it was admittedly a book that easily lent itself to being ridiculed because of its outlandish claims about Beat aims and achievements. And A.Alvarez was always more than happy to attack Ginsberg and the others for allegedly clinging together for companionship because their work had little credibility otherwise. And that may have been the least of their many sins in his eyes. I've used a few British examples, but there's no reason to think that the situation was essentially any different in the United States.

How things have changed. There is now something of a mini-industry in Beat studies, with journals devoted to examining the poems and novels, degrees to be earned with earnest dissertations, and local and international conferences at which the dedicated gather to exchange information and ideas. I'm not dismissing such endeavours. As a non-academic with a long-standing involvement in writing about specific aspects of the Beat experience, I've hovered around the fringes of this world without wanting to be overwhelmed by it. Still, I can't help thinking that there is a certain amount of amusement (or is it bemusement?) to be had in recalling all those little magazines and small-press publications that we struggled to obtain (and sell, if one was involved in their production) currently being traded at high prices or preserved in special collections.

I have to admit that I now back away from many books about the Beats. They simply can't re-create how exciting it was to wait for the latest issue of *Evergreen Review* or *Big Table* or *The Outsider* to flop through the letterbox, or to get new books from Totem Press, Auerhahn Press, and City Lights, And to receive letters from the poet and novelist Gilbert Sorrentino, the poet and editor Paul Carroll, and the essayist and anthologist Seymour Krim. They were all friendly and informative when I got in touch with them, perhaps because it seemed essential then for people to make contact. And it wasn't for the purpose of furthering academic careers. We just wanted to know what was going on. The Beats weren't the only game in town, and there was a lot of mixing among the players. The whole range of what was referred to as The New American Writing was worth looking into, even if it didn't always in the end appeal. I never could get to grips wIth Charles Olson, John Ashbery, or Michael McClure.

The thoughts expressed above were triggered by reading A.Robert Lee's informative *The Beats: Authorships, Legacies,* which displays an enthusiasm for its subject that is not always found in academic surveys. He seems to genuinely like the work of most of the writers he discusses, and he doesn't restrict himself to a handful of familiar names, or a few well-known books. He usefully roams around the world of the Beats and demonstrates how varied it was. It can't be reduced to a limited area of activity.

Lee's opening chapter, in which he races through "Beat Origins and Circuits, 1940s to 1960s", offers a wide-ranging survey of how the Beats, the major names at least, came together, what their ideas were, and where they met up in print. Little magazines and small presses were of key importance in disseminating work by Beat writers, and they began to flourish in the late-1950s and early-1960s, not only in

New York and San Francisco but also in Chicago, New Orleans, and other locations. Lee does mention some of them, and it would be unfair to take him to task for not referring to others. It would need a separate chapter, perhaps even a separate book, to do justice to them, and even then they probably couldn't all be included with their background stories which, as in the cases of *Big Table* and *The Provincetown Review*, included being taken to court on obscenity charges. The trials and travails of little magazine publishing and distribution involve numerous stories of unsung heroes who wanted to circulate work they thought ought to be read.

Lee also has notes on several anthologies which, he suggests, had important roles to play in drawing attention to the Beats. One of them, *The Beat Generation and the Angry Young Men*, certainly had an influence in terms of giving some people a taste for the Beats, though retrospective views tended to distance them from what were claimed to be dissident voices in Britain. It was hard to see what conventional wrters like Kingsley Amis and John Braine had in common with Kerouac and Carl Solomon. And even in the American section, some of the writers were quick to disown Beat connections.

Chandler Brossard's *Who Walk in Darkness* is sometimes said to be an early Beat novel, but has more to do with 1940s Greenwich Village intellectuals. He was never all that complimentary about the Beats, and wrote an article for *Dude* magazine in 1958 entitled "The Dead Beat Generation". Anatole Broyard was likewise suspicious, and his *New York Times* review of *Visions of Cody* took both Ginsberg and Kerouac to task for inferior writing and more. George Mandel was a talented cartoonist as well as a novelist, and his little book, *BeatVille USA,* neatly satirised the Beats. As for R.V. Cassill, he produced a 1963 article about Greenwich Village for *Cavalier* and spoke of the old bohemian, Maxwell Bodenheim, as writing poetry "worse than Ginsberg's".

I think it's worth stressing that, as Lee points out, most of the Beats, if asked, declined to think of themselves as Beats. They always spoke well of their fellow-poets and novelists, but Ferlinghetti, Snyder, Burroughs were quick to deny the Beat label. Gregory Corso almost laughed it away. The poet Jack Micheline was often linked to the Beats, but identified more with an older bohemian tradition, as exemplified by the likes of Vachel Lindsay and Maxwell Bodenheim. It was one reason why I was drawn to his work. In general, it's only necessary to briefly scan the work of the Beat writers to realise that they differed widely in how they wrote.

1960 was a key year for anthologies, with *The New American Poetry, Beat Coast East, Beatitude Anthology, The Beat Scene,* and *The Beats* all being in the bookshops. I always liked these collections because they didn't only feature Beats even when that word was in their titles, so it was possible to pick up on some interesting writers generally from their contents. Lee says that *Beatitude Anthology* was one of those that "helped point Beat towards canonisation and classroom", but I hope it's stressed in the classroom that a lot of the poems in it were not very noteworthy. I don't think most poems in any context (magazine, anthology, individual collection) are all that wonderful. You need to be dedicated to keep reading them. Poems like "Mexico 5 '59" by Marc, and "Lover" by Jo, both in the *Beatitude Anthology,* might have some sociological interest, and are useful as examples of what minor Beats got up to, but they don't have a great deal else to recommend them.

It may not be strictly related to Beat literature, but then again it perhaps is, when Lee says that "the original 1920s meaning of hipster was one who carried a hip flask of booze". I've come across a few definitions of hip and hipster over the years, though not that one. There used to be a suggestion (stemming from a 1930s Cab Calloway record) that it derived from the practice of lying on one's hip when smoking opium. The most likely explanation, however, emanates from research by David Dalby who found that the Wolof tribe of Senegambia had a word, "'hipi", meaning to "to open one's eyes", so in Wolof "hipi-kat" means "a person who has opened his eyes". A hep cat. A hipster. West Africa was the area where many blacks in America came from as slaves, and where there were close musical parallels to jazz and blues.

Lee proceeds to deal with the leading Beat writers – Ginsberg, Kerouac, Burroughs, Corso, Ferlinghetti, John Clellon Holmes, Michael McClure, Gary Snyder, and Herbert Huncke (a curious inclusion, and perhaps there because of his influence on some of the others rather than his literary talents). His comments on their work are brisk and astute, though he rarely raises questions about its quality. How much of Ginsberg's poetry after the 1950s and into the early-1960s was really good? And wasn't it sometimes true that Burroughs could be repetitive and a little bit of his writing was often preferable to reading it in bulk? Isn't Corso likely to be best-remembered for his fine poem, "Marriage" and a few like "Poets Hitch-hiking on the Highway" and "Birthplace Revisited", rather than those where he adopted a lofty tone and tried to seem significant? And has John Clellon Holmes's jazz novel, *The Horn,* retained the qualities some people initially thought it had? What about Kerouac, whose writing could be variable? He wasn't always a pleasure to read. *Old Angel Midnight* is just hard work.

It might just come down to personal preferences, but it's worth asking the questions. Incidentally, Lee refers to an article called "West Coast Rhythms" by Richard Eberhart that he says appeared in *The New York Review of Books* in 1956. But that publication only started in the 1960s, and the piece in question appeared in the *New York Times Book Review*. Lee gets it right in his notes for the Ginsberg chapter.

There are useful observations on women writers who qualify for an appearance in the Beat category, and it's good to see Diane di Prima receiving attention. It could have been pointed out that memoirs of life among the Beats by Carolyn Cassady, Joyce Johnson, Bonnie Bremser, Hettie Jones, and others often give a truer account of what it was like than most of those we had, whether in fact or fiction, from their male companions. A minor novel like Mimi Albert's *The Second Story Man* also provides a picture of how women were treated by male bohemians. The men were usually concerned to create myths about their personalities and activities, but the women, on the whole, told it as it was. I've never been sure about di Prima's *Memoirs of a Beatnik*, but it was written for Maurice Girodias's Olympia Press, so allowances should be made for its sexual confessions and their truthfulness. It's a personal memory, but I met Carolyn Cassady a few times and corresponded with her. She was a lady with sophisticated tastes, and told me that she didn't particularly care for most Beat writing.

Black Beats are dealt with in the lives and publications of Leroi Jones (Amiri Baraka as he later became), Ted Joans, and Bob Kaufman. I think with Leroi Jones the Beat aspect is best covered in his earlier poems, and his activities, shared with Hettie Jones and Diane di Prima, with the publications, *Yugen* and *The Floating Bear*. Ted Joans was a livewire who I came across in Berlin and Paris, and seemed to crop up everywhere with his energetic poems that quickly demonstrated their influences drawn from jazz and surrealism. Bob Kaufman had a chequered career, marred by various problems, but his best poems retain their power. And his *Abomunist Manifesto* deserves to be remembered as a witty exposition of Beat disaffiliation. Sadly, he became something of a tragic figure.

Mentioning Kaufman makes me think that one aspect of the lives of some of the Beats that isn't often looked at is their early involvement in forms of radical politics. Kaufman had been an activist in the National Maritime Union which, in the 1940s, had a largely communist leadership. Gary Snyder had a background influenced to a degree by IWW

(Industrial Workers of the World) legends, John Clellon Holmes admitted to Marxist-leanings in the 1940s, Carl Solomon had joined the Communist Political Association (the American Communist Party under a different name), Lawrence Ferlinghetti was interested in European anarchist-bohemian traditions, Jack Micheline, who could come across like a proletarian poet in the 1930s style, involved himself in a small radical group for a time, and Stuart Perkoff (based in Venice West, Los Angeles, and not mentioned by Lee) had flirted with communism at one stage. Even the conservative Kerouac had edged around left-wing ideas, as he owned up to in his idiosyncratic way in *Vanity of Dulouz*: "It was great. In those days we were all pro-Lenin, or pro-whatever, Communists". The point I'm making is that when they drifted away from formal politics they moved to bohemia and the Beat and not to middle-class conformity.

I quite admired Lee's book, and I should add that he performs a handy service in attempting to show how the Beat influence carries on through writers who came along later, and in popular music. It does occur to me to wonder what Kerouac would have made of the music that younger Beat enthusiasts enjoy? Lee mentions some little-known figures, such as Martin Matz. His book, *In the Seasons of My Eye: Selected Writings 1953-2001* is of interest not so much for its literary qualities, but for indicating how someone on the fringes of the Beat movement lived and wrote. I do think that characters like Matz would have been around, anyway, Beat or no Beat, and would have just been described as bohemians. There are a few books that I wish Lee had looked into: Kerouac's *Maggie Cassidy*, Holmes's *Get Home Free,* and Lew Welch's *Ring of Bone: Collected Poems 1950-1971* are among them. *Maggie Cassidy* is mentioned, but only in passing. But this is not a complaint and I suppose everyone has fond memories of reading books they would like to see better-acknowledged.

The Beats: Authorships, Legacies is extremely useful from the point of view of not only delivering a swift summation of Beat writing in general, but also for providing a great deal of information about a wide variety of publications relating to the Beats. It has much to offer both for its commentary and its factual details.

THE BEATS : AUTHORSHIPS, LEGACIES

By A. Robert Lee

Edinburgh University Press. 239 pages. £19.99. ISBN 978-1-4744-0397-9

LITTLE MAGAZINES OF THE BEAT ERA

I think the first thing I need to do is offer a definition of what I see as the Beat Era. It's a period in my mind that stretches from roughly 1957 to roughly 1963. This isn't to suggest that the Beat writers, or at least some of them, weren't active before and after those years. But what I'm looking at is the spread of little magazines in that period. It can be argued that 1963 is something if an arbitrary cut-off point and that certain magazines carried on post-1963 and a few continued to maintain what might be called the spirit of the Beats. But Seymour Krim thought that by 1963 the movement had "splintered and broken up". For what it's worth that's my own impression of the Beat literary movement. What many people like to think of as The Sixties, with its emphasis on social protest, rock music, flower power, the hippies, etc., truly got under way around 1963. Underground newspapers and the like began to partially replace little magazines. I think we can see this in the way that a key publication such as *Evergreen Review* began to change. Not only in its format but also in its contents. I'll look a little closer at that later.

It's necessary to go back beyond 1957 to understand why what happened with little magazines late in the 1950s, and into the early Sixties, seems in retrospect quite unusual. There have always been little magazines, of course, printing new and old poets and prose writers. And certain periods, such as the 1920s, gave them a prominence because they published writers who later became famous. If you look at the magazines published in Paris, such as *This Quarter. Transatlantic Review, transition, Broom,* and a few others, their importance becomes evident. And during the 1930s there were more than a few magazines which represented the social and political inclinations of the time. There is a book called *The Red Decade* by Eugene Lyons, originally published in 1941, which, in part, purports to give the lowdown on communist cultural activity in the USA in the 1930s, and mentions magazines like *Anvil, Left, Left Front, Left Review, The Partisan, Blast, Dynamo, Leftward*.....well, I think the titles alone give an indication of where, as the saying goes, they were coming from.

Obviously, I'm dealing primarily with little magazines in the United States. But it may be relevant to mention in passing that the 1940s saw a surprising rise in the number of little magazines published in Britain between 1940 and 1950. There were literally dozens of them, some like *Horizon* and *Penguin New Writing* well-known, others (*Modern Reading, Now, Kingdom Come,* to name a few) less so. What many of them represented was the democratic spirit of the time, and they published a wide variety of writers. What they indicate on the whole is that experimental literature was not of premium concern. Poets and prose writers produced a literature that was often about the day-to-day concerns of people caught up in often extreme wartime situations. It's significant that, as things returned to a kind of normality in the late 1940s most of these magazines closed down. People had other more-pressing concerns about families, jobs, housing. There was less time for reading and writing.

But let me move on to the 1950s and a talk that Saul Bellow's friend, Isaac Rosenfeld, himself a novelist, short-story writer, and critic, gave at the University of Chicago in 1956. It was later reprinted in *The Chicago Review Anthology*, and was entitled "On the Role of the Writer and the Little Magazine". It's a fascinating piece from the point of view of literary history and Rosenfeld has some interesting things to say about the role of the writer in society, the idea and function of an avant-garde, and such matters. But what concerns me here are comments he made about the existence and purpose of little magazines. He was concerned to point out that the rise of the affluent society, and the ways in which writers once seen as avant-garde were now quickly absorbed into the mainstream and available in cheap, attractively-produced paperbacks, had, in his view, destroyed the old idea of an avant-garde. It no longer existed in its original sense. And he pointed to a rise in so-called little magazines published by commercial companies.

One of the best-known was *New World Writing*, a quarterly paperback published between 1952 and 1960. There was another called *Discovery* which lasted for 6 issues in the early-1950s. Both were backed by major publishers. Rosenfeld mentions *Perspectives*, which had funding from a large foundation. It is worth pointing out that early indications of the arrival of some Beat writers could be seen in *New World Writing*, where Kerouac's "Jazz of the Beat Generation" and Kenneth Rexroth's influential essay, "Disengagement: the Art of the Beat Generation" were published. *Discovery*, had contributions from John Clellon Holmes. *New Directions*, founded in 1936, gave space to writers outside the conventional or established institutions. But as Rosenfeld said, none of these, and others, such as *Partisan Review* and *Dissent*, were what he would think of as true little magazines. And there were, of course, the magazines with university backing, such as the *Kenyon Review*, the *Sewanee Review*, and others. Rosenfeld gave his talk to the staff of the *Chicago Review*, a magazine which had a role to play when the Beats started to appear in print. But let me quote him on the subject of little magazines which had secure financial support:

"The little magazines at one time were part of the image of garret poverty and obscurity. Now they survive, but survive with a certain opulence that threatens to crush them. Surely the specific idea of the little magazine, just as the specific idea of the avant-garde, gets lost in such a translation. And that idea was that of a small but vigorous and very vital, active, and conscious group which knew fairly well the sort of thing it stood for even if it had no specific programme and whether or not it had any political allegiance".

Rosenfeld died in 1956 so we can't know what he would have thought of the resurgence of little magazine activity that became evident in the late-1950s. There had been magazines which focused on publishing offbeat material. Cid Corman's *Origin*, started in 1951, might be a good example. And Gilbert Sorrentino's *Neon* kicked off in 1956. There was also the seventh and final issue of *Black Mountain Review* from the famous Black Mountain College in 1957. The Beats and related writers – Kerouac, Ginsberg, Burroughs, Snyder, Whalen, and McClure – all made an appearance.

They were also all in the famous second issue of *Evergreen Review*, the San Francisco issue, which in some ways gave a misleading impression of the Beat movement largely originating on the West Coast. And *Evergreen Review*, though it regularly published Beat writers in its first thirty issues, was not primarily a Beat magazine. It featured a variety of writers from what might be termed the non-establishment literary world. As I remarked earlier, its format and contents altered as the 60s progressed and it picked up on pop music, flower-power, hippies, student protest, pornography, and sensation. The journalist Bruce Cook perhaps summed up the post-1963 issues of *Evergreen Review* when he remarked: "Accretions of bile and hostility seem to have swollen it so that it now almost resembles the ponderous monoliths of American life that are attacked with such monotonous regularity in its pages".

The publication and resultant court case surrounding Ginsberg's *Howl*, published by City Lights Books in San Francisco, and the publication of Kerouac's *On the Road*, more or less launched what can be described as the publicised period of Beat activity. They were in the news and popular misconceptions of what they represented quickly developed. But at the same time there were those who were genuinely interested in the literary aspects of the movement. Irving Rosenthal was, in 1958, editor of the *Chicago Review* and in the Spring and Summer issues for 1958 had used material by, among others, Lawrence Ferlinghetti, Ginsberg, Kerouac, Philip Lamantia, Robert Duncan, Burroughs, and Philip Whalen. It all looks quite innocuous, but in 1958 it came to the attention of a journalist on a Chicago newspaper who questioned whether the university authorities were aware of what was being published in the magazine. The result was that Rosenthal was told that he couldn't use work by Burroughs, Kerouac, and the distinctly non-Beat Edward Dahlberg in his next issue. He and several others linked to the magazine promptly resigned and started an independent publication called *Big Table*, the first issue of which used the banned material from the *Chicago Review* and promptly fell foul of the Chicago postal authorities. The magazine carried on for four more issues (Paul Carroll took over from issue 2), but like so many little magazines was eventually defeated by financial and distribution problems. But it had, in its short lifetime, published not only the usual suspects from the Beats, but also Robert Creeley, Norman Mailer, John Ashbery, and Frank O'Hara. Of particular interest was the fourth issue, devoted to the New American Poets, which offered a variety of poets, including James Wright and Denise Levertov alongside Creeley, Ginsberg, Paul Blackburn, and Harold Norse.

If I can interject a brief personal note, I subscribed to *Big Table, Evergreen Review*, and *The Outsider* and can't forget how exciting and stimulating it was to receive these magazines. I didn't necessarily like everything in them – John Ashbery and Charles Olson were two poets I could never really relate to – but I read everything just to see what was happening in America.

It might be worth mentioning that the *Chicago Review/Big Table* affair was duplicated in Edinburgh in 1959 when Alex Neish imported work by Burroughs. Corso, Kerouac, Ginsberg, and others for an issue of *Jabberwock*, the magazine of the University Renaissance Society. Objections were raised and he resigned as editor and started *Sidewalk* and published Burroughs, Creeley, Michael Rumaker, and more. He was attacked for calling the magazine *Sidewalk* and not *Pavement*, or even *Plainstaines*, and the *Glasgow Evening Times* ran a feature headed "Along the Sidewalk to the Gutter".

I don't think there was ever a genuine Beat literary movement in Britain, as opposed to people playing at being beatniks, but there were editors and poets picking up on what the Beats, New York Poets, Black Mountain Poets, San Francisco poets and others were doing. Mike Horovitz's *New Departures* in its early issues between 1959 and 1962 mixed American and British writers, and the two issues of Tom Raworth's *Outburst* in 1961 and 1963 had a distinctly American focus.

Perhaps the one British poet most likely to be placed under a Beat banner would be Dave Cunliffe, whose magazine *Poetmeat* inclined in that direction. I think a few other publications deserve to be mentioned in the context of making connections with American writers. *Satis,* edited by Matthew Mead and Michael Rutherford from Newcastle, was probably the first magazine in Britain to publish work by Charles Bukowski. And Gael Turnbull's *Migrant* spotlighted Creeley, Ed Dorn, and others.

The black poet, Leroi Jones, as he was known then, started *Yugen* in 1958, with the first issue using some of his associates from the Greenwich Village scene of the time. I doubt that the names of Tom Postell, Ed James, and Ernest Kean will mean much these days, other than to collectors of bohemian ephemera, of which I'm happily one. But once the magazine got into its stride it picked up on the work of most of the leading Beats, as well as New York poets like Frank O'Hara and Gilbert Sorrentino. Jones was married to Hettie Cohen in those days, and though she's doesn't get any credit for it in his autobiography she did contribute to the work of getting out a little magazine. The same can be said for Diane di Prima, an interesting poet in her own right, who was probably the driving force (even if Leroi Jones is shown as co-editor on early issues) behind *The Floating Bear*, a mimeographed newsletter which in its 37 issues packed in a wide range of new and known poets.

In an interview with Di Prima she recalled that 250 copies of the first issue were mimeographed and it was distributed to "painters, poets, dancers....mostly from New York". 250 copies seems to have been an adequate number when venturing into the uncertainties of little magazine publishing, especially if funds are low and distribution has to be done on a personal basis. I recall duplicating just 200 copies of *Move*, a magazine I decided to start in 1964. *The Floating Bear* may have been mimeographed and distributed without the benefits of large distributing agencies, but to look down the index in the 1973 reprint of all the 37 issues is to read a roll-call of the non-establishment poets of the period concerned. They wanted to be in the magazine despite its limited production qualities.

The role of mimeographed or duplicated publications (we used the term duplicated in the UK, I recall) is important. Yes, many magazines were well-produced, especially if like *Evergreen Review* they were backed by a larger organisation, in this case Grove Press. But there were numerous cheaply-produced mimeographed publications. *Beatitude* from San Francisco is a good example, appearing between 1958 and 1960, it had what might be called a loose editorial policy which resulted in a wide variation in the quality of the poems. It would seem that the editorial policy was one of more or less using everything that came in. So, there is a mixture of the well-known names and people who it would be almost impossible to track down. Some simply signed their poems as "Marc" and "Jo". I doubt that, outside a few libraries and private collections, complete sets of *Beatitude* exist. Even an anthology compiled from the magazine, and published by City Lights books in 1960, is out-of-print and expensive to buy on the internet.

The revival of the tradition of the little magazine as the ephemera of bohemia – and in its way the Beat Era might have been the final fling of the old bohemian literary world – meant that people looked back to earlier avant-garde practices and personalities, and in doing so brought some poets and others into circulation again. Walter Lowenfels, friend of Henry Miller in 1930s Paris (he's in Miller's *Black Spring* as Jabberwhorl Cronstadt), and a one-time member of the Communist Party, resurfaced in magazines and edited a couple of anthologies which featured old and new poets, usually those who might have radical leanings. Some elderly Objectivist poets from the 1930s – George Oppen, Charles Reznikoff, Carl Rakosi - were re-discovered and brought back into print.

And a couple of others were involved with little magazines. Jon Edgar Webb (who spent time in prison in the 1930s for armed robbery) and his wife Gypsy Lou Webb launched *The Outsider* from New Orleans with a policy that combined traditional jazz and new poetry. They were old bohemians with a background in the Depression days of the 1930s, and were particularly fond of Charles Bukowski and Kenneth Patchen.. Their story is inspirational in that they sacrificed most things, including home comforts, to get their magazine printed and circulated. I treasure my copies of the five issues (in four, one being a double issue) and they seem like items from a time it's hard to imagine now. The Webb's kind of bohemia just doesn't appear to exist anymore.

There was also Gilbert Neiman, who produced three issues of *Between Worlds* from the Inter-American University in Puerto Rico. Neiman had started his literary career in the 1930s and was a friend of Henry Miller whose *The Air-Conditioned Nightmare* is dedicated to Neiman and his wife. He later had a somewhat chaotic career in teaching because of his heavy drinking, something that Miller noted. But in 1960 he edited *Between Worlds* which appeared on an annual basis for three years. Like Jon Edgar Webb, Neiman was obviously keen to establish a connection between the Beats, and the newer generation of writers generally, and earlier bohemians and avant-garde poets.. He included work by Gregory Corso, Gary Snyder, Whalen, Burroughs, Ed Dorn, and Ferlinghetti, alongside Mina Loy, William Carlos Williams, and Harry Roskolenko.

Roskolenko was a poet and a one-time Trotsykist, and as a merchant seaman was wounded when he got involved in a minor insurrection while his ship was docked in Hamburg. For me, this was always one of the most interesting aspects of the little magazines, that through them I came across poets and prose writers who I knew little or nothing about and so was introduced to not only new names but also many from the past. It was an adventure tracking down their books and, where I could, the magazines they'd been in.

I've attempted to give a broad survey of at least some of the magazines of the Beat Era. There were others I could have included. Tuli Kupferberg's *Birth* started its life in 1958 with an issue devoted to Greenwich Village and Bohemianism, which showed that he knew what was happening as the Beat scene began to expand. And many more, such as *Nomad, Exodus, Foot, Wormwood Review, Intrepid*, and *Kulchur*, a classic little magazine which was representative of much that was exciting and interesting in the arts in its lifetime, which ran from 1960 to 1966. There was also Jay Landesman's *Neurotica*, which, between 1948 and 1951, gave an indication of the way the wind was blowing when it published John Clellon Holmes, Allen Ginsberg, Carl Solomon, Chandler Brossard, and Anatole Broyard. There was also a short story by Larry Rivers, a one-time saxophone player and later well-known as an artist, about junkie jazz musicians. *Neurotica* was a truly idiosyncratic publication. The most-interesting little magazines often were idiosyncratic in that their overall impact reflected the tastes and concerns of their editors. Gael Turnbull's *Migrant* might be a good example with its mixture of essays, letters, poems, and some contributions that were difficult to categorise.

This is the text of a talk given at the Manchester University Symposium on Little Magazines at the John Rylands Library, Manchester, Friday, 6th March, 2020.

THE DAY I MET JACK KEROUAC

I came out of the army in 1957, just in time to get caught up in the excitement that surrounded the advent of the Beat movement. Of course, in those days it wasn't easy to get hold of American publications, and London was the only place you could find a selection that was wide enough to include some of the more-obscure little magazines and poetry pamphlets. This was also true of many British publications. You either got them by mail or in the London bookshops.

So, as often as I could, I'd catch a train from an industrial town 200 miles to the north and spend a day in London. I combined my growing Beat interests with an already-established love of bop and visited the record shops at the same time. Inter-City travel being a bit primitive in the 1950s, the cheapest method was a special-offer ticket that involved travelling out on the overnight service Friday night and returning on the overnight train Saturday night. This gave me a full day in London with an evening free for the cinema or some jazz. It was exhausting but I was younger then and high on bebop and the Beats.

It was on one of those trips that I met Jack Kerouac. I'd been on my usual rounds of Collett's, Dobell's, Zwemmers, and many more, and sometime late in the afternoon I needed to find a public toilet. I was at the south end of Charing Cross Road so I turned into Leicester Square. Down the steps I went and as I reached the bottom I heard a drunken American voice telling the world, or at least that part of it a few feet under Leicester Square, what a great place London was and how the speaker had visited it during the war after travelling down from Liverpool. Weaving slightly in the middle of the floor, and watched by an apprehensive attendant, was a stocky, dark-haired man in a check shirt. He was clutching a bottle and occasionally invited everyone else to have a drink. As I walked past him he saw the records in my hand, and said "What'cha got?" and did a little jig. "Charlie Parker" I replied, and he said, "Oh, yeah, man", and then sang out a fast and funny bebop vocal run which ended with a loud "Ool-ya-koo" that had the attendant even more apprehensive.

I finished and zipped up my trousers and as I moved towards the stairs the man yelled "Go, man" and offered me a drink. I laughed and declined and went back up to the street. It was only later that the dark hair and check shirt struck me as familiar and I realised who I'd spoken to.

Now I know that the precise will want to work out which week it was and whether or not Kerouac could have been in London then. And no doubt I'll be told that the meeting couldn't possibly have taken place. I'm not worried. There was once a young boy saw Shelley plain, and a man might easily have passed Beau Brummell on a Brighton street, so why shouldn't I have met Jack Kerouac one Saturday afternoon in the Gents in Leicester Square?

CIRCLES AND SQUARES : THE LIVES AND ART OF THE HAMPSTEAD MODERNISTS

There are moments when things – people, places, ideas – appear to have come together in a way that, in retrospect, gives them a kind of cohesiveness that might not have been totally evident, if at all, at the time. Hampstead in the 1930s may have been such a location. The activities of a loose group of home-grown modernists, reacting against the art establishment's conventional notions of creativity, coincided with the arrival of avant-garde painters and others in Britain as Nazis and Fascists drove out those not conforming to their limited tastes in art. For a brief period London, and especially Hampstead, became a centre for the forward-looking in painting, sculpture, and architecture.

Two of the key practitioners in the story of the Hampstead Modernists were Ben Nicholson and Barbara Hepworth, a couple who met and became major influences on British art for many years, especially when they moved to Cornwall and were prominent among the painters, sculptors, and others clustered around St Ives. But all that came later.

They were, in the 1930s, leading separate lives, at least initially. Ben Nicholson was the son of a then well-known painter, William Nicholson. William's style was what might be called "traditional" and he had a reputation for landscapes and portraits that had enabled him to live comfortably. He would have preferred his son not to have had ambitions as an artist, but Ben went to the Slade, where he became acquainted with Paul Nash. He travelled around Europe just prior to the outbreak of the First World War, and picked up on some of the ideas, such as Cubism, that were then circulating in France and elsewhere. Caroline Maclean says that when he sent a few of his paintings back to England, his father thought of them as "the work of an untrained eye, both in colour and form". Relations between father and son were never easy, and the situation can't have been helped when Ben brought home his fiancée, Edith Stuart-Wortley, and William charmed her away and married her. Having one's ex-fiancée as your stepmother might not have been the best of circumstances.

Ben met Winifred Roberts, herself a talented artist, and they were married in 1920. As both came from well-to-do backgrounds, they were able to travel extensively on their honeymoon. When they returned to Britain they bought property in Cumberland and started to develop their careers. They exhibited in London, with Winifred's work appealing more to a wider audience than Ben's. Her paintings sold, whereas his –

"irregular geometric shapes....here and there decorated with round spots", according to a hostile review in the *Daily Mail* - failed to attract buyers. But Ben was invited by Ivon Hitchens to join the Seven and Five Society, a group of young painters and sculptors intending to challenge the orthodoxies of the art establishment. Ben was to become quite prominent in the group, easing out people he thought of as "duds" and bringing in fresh blood.

The couple left Cumberland and moved to Dulwich in 1927. They met the ill-fated Christopher Wood, who had studied in Paris and knew Picasso, and it was with Wood that Ben, on a trip to St Ives, "discovered" the work of the primitive painter, Alfred Wallis. Maclean refers to "the friendship and patronage between Ben and Alfred Wallis that lasted many years", though some observers thought that Nicholson had exploited Wallis in various ways by championing his work, raising its prices after paying him very little for it, and benefiting himself.

It would seem that there were some domestic problems, especially since Ben and Winifred now had more than one child to look after, but in 1931 his fortunes started to improve. He was in an exhibition at the Bloomsbury Gallery "with the potter William Staite Murray and a young sculptor called Barbara Hepworth". She was married to another sculptor, Jack Skeaping. Their relationship perhaps wasn't perfect, and Maclean tells the story of how Hepworth arrived at their studio one day to find Skeaping in a compromising situation with "the attractive and sexy-looking" Eileen Friedlander. She was half-undressed and ran out of the back-door and jumped over a fence and into the garden of the monastery next-door. A monk who was reading his breviary calmly ignored her while she got dressed, and then politely showed her the way out. It's a good story, and if not quite true, ought to be.

A relationship between Hepworth and Nicholson developed, with Ben moving between her and Winifred on a regular basis. I have to admit that I found it difficult not to see him as something of an opportunist. When Winifred took their children to Cornwall while he was with Barbara, he pleaded to be allowed to come and stay with her. Likewise when Winifred and the children moved to Paris and Ben again decided that it was the right time to stay with her. As McLean puts it: "Like the move to Cornwall, it had a powerful effect on Ben, who wrote immediately to ask when he might visit". It could be argued that in both cases his desire to see his children had a part in his decision to visit, but somehow I have a feeling that he was the kind of person not likely to pass up an opportunity to further his own interests. It would certainly seem to be true that he was always keen to network and cultivate the right people. He wouldn't be alone in that kind of behaviour, of course.

There was "an explosion of abstraction" in the early-1930s, with Hepworth and Nicholson heavily involved in it. The initial issue of *Axis* edited by Myfanwy Evans, the wife of John Piper, and "the first art journal dedicated to abstract art", appeared in 1935 and lasted through seven further issues until 1937. It played a major role in bringing abstract painting and sculpture to a wider audience than had previously paid attention to it. And it established bridges between British and French painters and sculptors. A slightly later, short-lived publication, *Circle* (a one-shot document-cum-manifesto, and not to be confused with the 1940s Californian magazine of the same name), tried to keep the momentum going, but by 1936 abstraction was facing some opposition from Surrealism.

The famous Surrealist exhibition opened in that year, and drew attention from the press, not only for what was seen as the odd nature of some of the pictures, but also for the odd behaviour of certain of the participants. Salvador Dali paraded in a heavy diving suit and almost died when the helmet wasn't easy to remove. Dylan Thomas offered visitors boiled string in tea cups, asking if they wanted it strong or weak. Sheila Legge "wandered around the Galleries with a dummy leg in one hand and apparently a pork chop in the other". The writer J.B. Priestley wasn't impressed by the antics or the paintings on display and grumpily referred to "moral perversions".

With regard to *Circle*, it's relevant to note that, although Ben Nicholson, Leslie Martin and Naum Gabo got credit as editors, Barbara Hepworth later recalled that she and Martin's wife, Sadie Speight, were also very much involved. They assisted with the research and writing, and "did the layout, we did the corrections, proofing, everything". It might also be of significance to point to the 1936 Abstract & Concrete Exhibition which toured around Oxford, Cambridge, Liverpool and London, and reminded gallery-goers that Surrealism wasn't the only game in town.

With the social and economic situation in Europe continuing to worsen there was an influx of artists, sculptors, and architects into the United Kingdom. The Dutch painter, Piet Mondrian, turned up, as did Naum Gabo and László Moholy-Nagy. And Walter Gropius arrived with his wife, Ise. The spirit of Bauhaus was in the air. There was a profound influence on many British artists and architects. The newcomers didn't always stay too long, some of them seeing Britain as a place of "unsalted vegetables, bony women and an eternally freezing draught". (Walter

Gropius's words). And the looming war situation persuaded people like Gropius and Marcel Breuer to leave for America, where there would be greater safety and a better chance of earning a living. The British weren't always receptive to new ideas in either art or architecture. Maclean's chapter on architectural developments is informative and useful.

Hampstead wasn't just a playground for painters and sculptors, and with the Experimental Theatre and Everyman Cinema on site there were clearly other involvements in the artistic life of the community. Poets and prose writers were also present. W.H. Auden put in an appearance, as did Geoffrey Grigson, with his magazine *New Verse*, and Louis MacNeice was around and chasing after the painter William Coldstream's wife, Nancy. Coldstream didn't have much, if anything, in common with artists like Nicholson, and inclined more to a realist approach to painting. Maclean says "Auden believed that painting, like writing, should be a form of reportage in 1937 and he encouraged Bill to paint things as he saw they were. This became the fundamental tenet of the Euston Road School of which Bill was a founding member in 1937".

A whole catalogue of characters can be encountered in *Circles and Squares*. Virginia Woolf is there, visiting Herbert Read, and reacting against his "vast comfortless studio" where "none of the charm of Bohemia mitigated the hard chairs, the skimpy wine, & the very nice, sensible conversation". Henry Moore appears on the scene, and so do Ceri Richards, Ruthven Todd, Alexander Calder, Graham Sutherland, Roland Penrose, and others too numerous to name. I have to admit that the names, falling fast into the boiling pot of personalities and plots, did bother me at times, and I had to turn back the pages to remind myself who was who when it came to the minor figures. And I couldn't always remember just who had slept with who. I kept thinking of lines from Dorothy Parker's poem, "Bohemia": "Sculptors and singers and those of their kidney/Tell their affairs from Seattle to Sydney./Playwrights and poets and such horses' necks/Start off from anywhere, end up at sex".

Maclean usefully provides an epilogue that briefly tells what happened to individual artists as the Second World War broke up the Hampstead community and, in some cases, drove them away from London altogether. Hepworth and Nicholson moved to St Ives, and it was their presence and influence that was probably as much as anything responsible for the post-war transformation of the small fishing town into a major centre for art that attracted national and international attention. As with any other artistic community it wasn't always sweetness and light, and Sven Berlin took Ben to task for his alleged manipulation of Alfred Wallis's work.

Nicholson eventually moved on, but Hepworth stayed in St Ives. I was never a great admirer of her sculptures until a friend, who is keen on them, took me to the Hepworth Museum in St Ives and I saw them spaced around the garden. They made much more sense to me in that context than in the detached surroundings of an art gallery. As for Nicholson, although I enjoy some of his early, Cubist-influenced canvases, I have never been able to gain anything from his "reliefs", the circles and squares he's most associated with. But then, I have a limited taste for Mondrian's paintings and that kind of geometrical abstraction generally. Surrealism and, in a different way, the realism of William Coldstream and the Euston Road School are much more to my liking.

Circles and Squares is a tidily written and useful book. It would be foolish to suggest that Nicholson and Hepworth have been neglected in recent years, but by putting them in context in terms of their activities in relation to the rest of the Hampstead modernists, Caroline Maclean has provided a valuable service. Her story has additional interest when it reminds us of the importance of the émigré painters, sculptors, and architects who widened the scope of British art in the 1930s. The book has some illustrations, notes, and a Selected Bibliography.

CIRCLES AND SQUARES : THE LIVES AND ART OF THE HAMP-
STEAD MODERNISTS

By Caroline Maclean

Bloomsbury Publishing. 296 pages. £30. ISBN 978-1-4088-8969-5

BILL BUTLER AND THE UNICORN BOOKSHOP

For anyone born after 2000, and some born even earlier, the personalities and literary events of the 1960s and 1970s may be taking on almost-legendary status. The 1965 Albert Hall reading, the rise of "underground" or "alternative" bookshops, characters like Alexander Trocchi and Jeff Nuttall. Did it all seem as important and liberating at the time as it perhaps does in retrospect? From a personal point of view it did lead to lively and interesting encounters with various writers and brought some provocative books to my attention.

Many of those meetings with both people and publications occurred in bookshops, among them Better Books, Indica, Duck Soup, Compendium, and various locations (I recall three) around London where Bernard Stone operated from. There were Grass Roots and Frontline in Manchester, News from Nowhere in Liverpool, and others in Leeds, Sheffield, and elsewhere. It seemed to me, as I moved around doing poetry readings, that just about every city and town had a small bookshop that was trying to break away from the conventional in terms of the books and magazines they stocked. Some of them didn't last very long, and I suspect that most were viewed with suspicion by the local police and civic authorities. They attracted students, bohemians, political and personal misfits, and seemed to hint at drugs, sex, radical politics, and social protest, if not outright revolution.

One of those places where the unusual could be found was the Unicorn Bookshop in Brighton. It was opened in June 1967 by Bill Butler and his partner, Mike Hughes. Butler was an American who had settled in Britain. He had published poetry in *Beatitude*, a mimeographed little magazine in San Francisco. Its seventeen or so issues are collectors' item now because of its Beat connections, though not all of the work in it was Beat, however that term is interpreted. Terry Adams reprints the Butler poem from *Beatitude*, and it's entertaining but conventional. I can recall reviewing a book by Butler in *Ambit* back in the early Seventies. It was called *A Cheyenne Legend* and was published by Bernard Stone's Turret Books. I wasn't too impressed by it, thinking that perhaps the attempts to represent Cheyenne speech relied too much on images and language derived from Western films. But that's another story.

It's not Butler the poet, but Butler the bookseller and publisher, who is the focus of Adams' informative booklet. Besides running the shop, Butler also brought out some publications, among them works by Jack

Kerouac, William Burroughs, J.G.Ballard, W.H. Auden, and Michael Moorcock. Not all of them were "authorised" editions. The Kerouac, for example, came out after Butler had closed the Brighton shop and was living in Wales. It was a bootlegged edition of *Old Angel Midnight*, a work I admit having little time for. It seemed to me something of an indulgence and only ever likely to appeal to Kerouac enthusiasts and academics.

In ordinary circumstances the Unicorn Bookshop might never have attracted interest from outside its Brighton base with a few links to London as well. But it soon became obvious that the police had noticed that it was something a little different from either the standard bookshops or the back-streets businesses that sold what were commonly called "girlie-mags" with varying levels of nudity on display. The police could understand those. I remember a friend of mine who had spent several years as a policeman in Liverpool telling me that when a porn shop was raided the magazines quickly circulated among his colleagues. And if films were seized they soon became standard fare at the stag parties that policeman held.

It was the unusual nature of much of the stock in shops like Unicorn that the average policeman couldn't come to terms with. It all smacked of subversion. And anything like it particularly stood out in the provinces. For someone like Dave Cunliffe in Blackburn or Bill Butler in Brighton to publish and/or sell something that might be sexually challenging in its way, but wasn't recognisable pornography, was to invite attention from the guardians of law and order. It's necessary to understand how narrow-minded much of British society still was in the 1960s and 1970s. But it should also be acknowledged that prosecuting small presses and little bookshops for stocking so-called pornography was also an easy way of stopping them from operating and stocking left-wing newspapers and magazines.

There were several visits to Unicorn by the police, with all kinds of material being seized, including copies of *Evergreen Review* and *Kulchur*, and books by Allen Ginsberg and Herbert Huncke. I'm amused by the reference to *Kulchur* having attracted the attention of the police. A more-serious publication is difficult to imagine, but it was perhaps the unusual spelling that motivated the police to assume that it must be up to no good. The subsequent court case during which Butler was prosecuted under the Obscene Publications Act brought support from various quarters. A lasting example might be the anthology *For Bill Butler*, edited by Eric Mottram and Larry Wallrich, which had contributions from Ginsberg, Ferlinghetti, Lee Harwood, Tom Raworth,

Tuli Kupferberg, and many more. I was more than happy to let the editors use several of my short prose pieces in this publication. It seemed to me that there was something of a mini-campaign of harassment and suppression taking place across the country, and Unicorn wasn't the only establishment raided by the police,

It would be incorrect of me to say that I was in total sympathy with everything that took place in the period covered by Adams. I'm talking about the whole so-called "underground" scene. I wasn't, and a lot of the publications from those years seemed juvenile in their approach to social matters, politics, art, literature, and much else. They were often sexist with regard to how they portrayed women and in that respect sometimes not much different to the pornographic publications they might have looked down on.

It also struck me that there were a lot of con-men around the "scene", all ready to manipulate and rip-off the innocents who believed in the messages about flower power, a summer of love, and other such misleading nonsense. Adams remarks that Butler "had a reputation for the odd bit of 'ducking and diving', covered up by his warmth and charm", and that someone who had been close to him said that he was "often accused of exploiting the talents of his employees and acolytes to further his own ends". But there appears to be others who recall his generosity and the way he helped them to realise their own potential.

It has always struck me that people like Bill Butler, who opened bookshops, published books, started little magazines, and organised events, and rarely made money out of these activities, never have had the recognition due to them. We celebrate poets and novelists, but little would be known of many of them had it not been for the background work supplied by the editors and booksellers. It's good that Terry Adams has taken the trouble to research into Bill Butler's activities. He tells a story of attempts to survive what was, in some ways, a hostile environment. And one in which it was always a struggle to find enough funds to carry on. Along the way Adams pays tribute to numerous other people who worked with Butler in one capacity or another. There are a few surprises, such as the names of three people who, when asked to appear for the defence at one of Butler's trials, seem to have got cold feet and backed away from the situation. I knew one of them, and had met the other two, and it was disturbing to come across them in this context. One might have expected a more-positive response from them.

Terry Adams has produced a useful, informative account of Bill Butler's existence and activities. It should be read by anyone interested in what happened in the 1960s and 1970s. There are few, if any, of the kind of bookshops that Unicorn represented still open. Finding publications like the one I've reviewed can now be difficult. For the record, Beat Scene Press is at 27 Court Leet, Binley Woods, Coventry, CV3 2JQ. They have a list of other relevant publications, and publish *Beat Scene* magazine.

BILL BUTLER AND THE UNICORN BOOKSHOP

By Terry Adams

Beat Scene Press. 49 pages.

SHERLOCK'S SISTERS : STORIES FROM THE GOLDEN AGE
OF THE FEMALE DETECTIVE

Reviewing an earlier anthology edited by Nick Rennison (*More Rivals of Sherlock Holmes,* NRB, June 2019), I pointed to the context in which the stories had originally appeared in print. The late-Victorian and Edwardian periods saw a wide range of magazines and newspapers on sale. They were largely aimed at an audience which didn't want high-brow literature and erudite essays. Entertainment, whether in the form of lively factual articles or popular fiction, was what the editors looked for on the whole. The number of magazines competing for attention on a regular basis meant that they weren't all likely to be successful. Publications came and went. But there was a demand for material and writers could earn a reasonable income if they came up with enough stories to meet deadlines. This did mean that an air of "we don't want it good, we want it Tuesday" was sometimes evident. Not every story – and there must have been thousands of them – was ever likely to warrant being considered a work-of-art, or destined to last beyond the week.

A case in point might be Elizabeth Burgoyne Corbett's "Madame Duchesne's Garden Party", which features a female sleuth named Dora Bell. I think Rennison's own summing up of this story might be useful in explaining why he considered it worthy of inclusion: "The Dora Bell stories are short and uncomplicated, ideally suited to the newspaper readership at which they were aimed. They win no prizes for great originality, but they remain entertaining and easy-to-read". Some of the attraction for readers probably arose from the stories often being built around a particular detective. There were, It seems, several Dora Bell tales, though they don't seem to have ever been published in book form after they'd graced the pages of the *Leeds Mercury* and *The Adelaide Observer*.

I've remarked elsewhere that the lives of the authors often seem as interesting as the stories they wrote, and Corbett (1846-1930) produced novels, one of which uses the basic theme of someone falling asleep and waking up in a different century. Corbett imagined a world where women are in control and lifespan has been extended to around five hundred years. Society is "fairer and less corrupt", but a form of eugenics is practised. It was a subject in the air in the late-Victorian and Edwardian periods and aroused the curiosity of some prominent writers, and not just those who published what might be called fiction for the masses. I have to admit that the title of one of Corbett's crime novels,

"When the Sea Gives Up its Dead" is almost enough to make me start searching for a copy. But would I be disappointed if I read it?

I'd read Clarence Rook's "The Stir Outside the Café Royal" before picking up *Sherlock's Sisters* (it's in *Crime on Her Mind*, edited by Michele B. Slung, Penguin, 1977), and it's another story that is best described as routine. The interest might lie in its brief portrait of the scene around the entrance to the Café Royal. Rook (1862-1915) is remembered, if he is, for his book, *The Hooligan Nights,* which purported to be the authentic story of a young tearaway from Lambeth. Rennison suggests that Rook may not have strayed too far from his study when researching for his book, and that it might have been more than influenced by Arthur Morrison's *Tales of Mean Streets.*

Mentioning Rook indicates that, although the stories have female detectives at their centre, not all of them were written by women. George R. Sims (1847-1922) created Dorcas Dene who solves the riddle of "The Haverstock Hill Murder". Sims – "a journalist, novelist, dramatist and bohemian man-about-town" – was a prolific author, one of his creations being the poem, "Christmas Day in the Workhouse". It's often parodied (the wonderful Billy Bennett did a military-based version, "Christmas Day in the Cookhouse", available on YouTube), but as Rennison makes clear, it was originally designed as "a biting critique of the Victorian poor laws". There were twenty Dorcas Dene stories, according to Rennison, and they were pulled together in two volumes. They are now collectors' items and when I checked the available copies were priced at just over £5,000 for the two.

I first encountered "The Redhill Sisterhood" by Catherine Louisa Pirkis (1839-1910) when Hugh Greene included it in *Further Rivals of Sherlock Holmes* (Penguin, 1976), but it was worth reading again. It features Loveday Brooke, one of the "most interesting and appealing of late Victorian female detectives", who manages to operate successfully in a world largely dominated by men. She doesn't resent them and has an eye for a good-looking chap. The story is intriguing for its period details and starts in London on a "dreary November morning, every gas jet in the Lynch Court office was alight, and a yellow curtain of outside fog draped its narrow windows".

When Brooke is despatched to investigate some shady dealings they are in an area "known to the sanitary authorities for the past ten years as a regular fever nest". Later, there are references to the introduction of electric lighting in more-prosperous locations, and its supposed effectiveness in deterring burglars "If electric lighting were generally in vogue it would save the police a lot of trouble on these dark winter nights". At one point a policeman says of someone, "he has weathered me, after all", presumably meaning that the man has spotted and/or recognised him. I can't recall ever seeing "weathered" used in this way before.

It's also possible to get a picture of Victorian life from a passage in Fergus Hume's "The Fifth Customer and the Copper Key" when the detective, Hagar the Gypsy, enters a room "furnished in the ugly fashion of the early Victorian era........Chairs and sofa were of mahogany and horsehair; a round table, with gilt-edged books lying thereon at regular intervals, occupied the centre of the apartment, and the gilt-framed mirror over the fireplace was swathed in green gauze. Copper-plate prints of the Queen and the Prince Consort decorated the crudely-papered walls, and the well-worn carpet was of a dark green hue sprinkled with bouquets of red flowers".

Hume (1859-1932) was the author of *The Mystery of a Hansom Cab*, said by Rennison to be "the most popular novel of the Victorian era". He published it himself in Australia, when he lived there, and then sold the English rights for £50. When it became a best-seller he didn't profit from it. But he went on to publish over 150 novels and collections of short stories.

I was intrigued by the occurrence of narcotics in a couple of the stories, and Madelyn Mack, the "most flamboyant and eccentric female detective", was created by Hugh Cosgrove Weir (1884-1934) for "The Man with Nine Lives". She chews cola berries as a stimulant when needing to consider the facts of a case. And the victim of a murder she's looking into turns out to have been addicted to "Indian hemp or 'hasheesh' for some time". The murderer finds a particularly clever way of ensuring that the man imbibes a lethal dose of the drug. Amusingly, this story really is one where "the butler did it".

"The Dope Fiends" by Arthur B. Reeve (1880-1936) has Constance Dunlap tracking down a crooked doctor, a shady pharmacist, and a bent policeman engaged in supplying cocaine to, among others, members of the theatrical profession. My thoughts were drawn back to Billy Bennett again. He had an amusing monologue about his mother being so worried that he may become a performer on stage that she gladly accepts his assurance that the powder on the shoulders of his suit is only cocaine and not make-up. But Reeves's heroine has a more-serious purpose in mind and it is to save a young dancer from the grip of the drug. Reeve worked as a journalist, a consultant in crime-prevention, and wrote serials for the early American cinema. I was curious about the date of his story and whether or not it fell strictly within the Victorian/Edwardian category. It seems to have been in a collection of his stories dating from 1916, but may have been published earlier in a magazine. But perhaps I'm niggling?

Another American writer, Anna Katharine Green (1846-1935) highlighted Violet Strange as the focus of some of her short stories. Strange was a rich man's daughter and didn't need to work, but liked to carry out investigations on behalf of a New York private detective agency. She doesn't care to take on murder cases, but gets involved in one involving an elderly lady in a house, described as "of the olden times......it has a fanlight over the front door.........and two old-fashioned strips of parti-coloured glass on either side.......and a knocker between its panels which may bring money some day". The story has a somewhat contrived ending, but Rennison aptly sums it up as "well-written and entertaining".

Green's work included *The Leavenworth Case*, an 1878 novel said to be one of the earliest of all American detective novels. She wrote other novels which featured an investigator called Ebenezer Gryce, "one of the first series characters in detective fiction".

One of the most intriguing and well-written stories in *Sherlock's Sisters* is "The Long Arm" by Mary E.Wilkins (1852-1930). Rennison points out that Wilkins was not a crime writer and the woman at the centre of her story is not a detective in the accepted sense of the word. She is, instead, Sarah Fairbanks, a country schoolteacher twenty-nine years of age, who has been engaged for five years to a young man. But her father opposes the match. When he is murdered suspicion naturally falls on both her and her fiancé. He has an alibi to prove that he was elsewhere at the time of the murder, but she is arrested and charged. She is acquitted, but suspicion lingers, and she determines to discover the real killer. The story-telling does have some originality and flair, and if the ending is a little melodramatic the overall impression is effective.

Wilkins wrote stories based in New England and involving "marginalised characters struggling with the frustrations and constraints of their lives". But Rennison says that although they "won her much praise" at the time of their publication, "today she is probably better known for her stories of ghosts and the supernatural". I have to say I looked in vain for a reference to her in Malcolm Cowley's *New England Writers and Writing* (University Press of New England, 1996), though I was perhaps expecting too much in thinking she might be there. Larzer Ziff does devote a few pages to her New England stories in *The American 1890s: The Life and Times of a Lost Generation* (Chatto & Windus, 1966).

There are other stories that are worthy of mention. "The Episode of the Needle that did not Match" by Grant Allen (1848-1899), has Hilda Wade exposing how ambition can overcome scruples, and professions are sometimes too willing to overlook the faults of the famous. Allen is yet another popular writer who is now almost forgotten. Likewise with Richard Marsh (1857-1915) whose "Eavesdropping at Interlaken" gives us Judith Lee, a young lady with an uncanny gift for lip-reading, even at a distance. It serves her in good stead when she is accused of stealing jewellery in a hotel where she is staying, and she is able to unmask the real thieves. I suppose there has to be a degree of suspending disbelief when reading a story like this – can she really be that gifted? – but it rolls along easily and it's not hard to enjoy its light entertainment .

Sherlock's Sisters is another excellent anthology from Nick Rennison. If one or two of the stories creak a little it's still possible to consider them of some value, even if only for their period charm. And sometimes they offer insights into how words change their meaning or application as the years pass. A young man says he "whipped down the stairs" (meaning dashed down), in the Loveday Brooke story, and it's not something I've heard recently, though I would have said it myself seventy and more years ago. But I'm sure someone will soon tell me that it's still in use. And some readers might want to identify with an old lady in the Baroness Orczy (1865-1947) Lady Molly of Scotland Yard story, "the Woman in the Big Hat", who says, "I hate all this modern smartness and fastness, which are only other words for what I call profligacy". Somehow its relevance doesn't really sound all that old.

SHERLOCK'S SISTERS : STORIES FROM THE GOLDEN AGE OF THE FEMALE DETECTIVE

Edited and introduced by Nick Rennison

No Exit Press. 319 pages. £9.99. ISBN 978-0-85730-398-1

BROADWAY AND THE BLACKLIST

Books about the blacklist during the McCarthy era in the United States usually focus on what happened in Hollywood when hundreds of actors, writers, producers and others were compelled to appear before HUAC (House Un-American Activities Committee) and testify about their alleged membership of the Communist Party. When it came to writers they were often also asked about their union, the Screen Writers Guild (SWG). There are now shelves of books of varying kinds (memoirs, case histories, and more) about the writers, in particular. And dozens of academic essays, and magazine and newspaper articles, plus films.

It always intrigues me that we know very little about the numerous technicians (electricians, carpenters, camera operators, etc.) working in the film industry, who were, perhaps, caught up in anti-communist investigations and allegations of subversion, and so lost their jobs. Is it that they didn't seem as glamorous as actors and directors and producers? Newspapers probably didn't bother to report it if a plumber, who may have been a communist, or even just an active trade unionist, was fired for refusing to testify and name names. And later writers, looking to publish books about the blacklist, have naturally wanted to cover the personalities and events that will arouse a response from the general public. A recognisable name makes for good headlines.

The same might be said of the theatre, where there were investigations, though on nowhere near as big or controversial a scale as in Hollywood. They didn't attract as much publicity. Nor have they been the subject of as much attention in recent years. Which is why K. Kevyne Baar's book is a welcome addition to the library of books about blacklisting due to McCarthyism. However, let me emphasise a point that Baar is keen to highlight. Senator Joseph McCarthy was not in any way connected with HUAC, nor was he ever involved with any of the investigations carried out by that committee. It's just that he was prominent in anti-communist activity, especially with regard to government employees. He made outlandish claims about communist penetration of the civil service and even the armed forces. And so his name is now a catch-all term for purging people seen as subversives.

The significant thing about many of the actors, stage managers, and others, who were summoned by HUAC when it began its investigations into the world of the theatre, is that they had started their professional lives in New York. They moved to Hollywood, and then returned to New York when work in films dried up. But it was often with the Group Theatre and/or the Federal Theatre Project that they had begun to establish reputations for their skills. It needs to be noted, however, that there were not many, if any, well-known actors involved in the theatre hearings. At this late date it's doubtful if many people will recognise names such as Will Geer, John Randolph, and Sam Jaffe, all of them reliable support actors in Hollywood films, unless they happen to have an interest in cinema history. Zero Mostel might be an exception to this rule, having been seen in later films like *The Producers* and *The Front*. The latter was about how blacklisting operated in TV in New York.

There is little doubt about the fact that most of the people concerned probably had been members of the Communist Party, or significantly close to it. The Group Theatre and the Federal Theatre Project (part of Roosevelt's Works Project Administration (WPA) programme to support unemployed theatre workers), inevitably had some communists in their ranks. The 1930s were years of deep economic depression, and communism appeared to be one solution to the problems besetting the United States and other countries. No-one at that time imagined that the play they had been in, the article they had written, the petition they signed, and the demonstration they took part in, were all being carefully logged by the FBI, local police forces, and independent anti-communist organisations. The information would be stored and brought out fifteen or twenty years later to be used as evidence against them when someone refused to reply to the infamous question, "Are you now, or have you ever been, a member of the Communist Party?". Even a favourable review in a communist publication could be counted against an actor or a playwright.

One of the problems facing those called to testify in Hollywood and elsewhere was that they had difficulty in getting support from the organisation (their union) they might have expected to provide advice and assistance. But it does seem that most American unions were not prepared to face up to the rampant anti-communist hysteria in America in the 1950s. They often took matters into their own hands, without pressure from the authorities, and purged their memberships of knowncommunists. The cowardice of unions in failing to support blacklisted members could often lead not just to unemployment, but tragedy. Philip Loeb, fired from a role in a popular radio series, *The Goldbergs,* and "faced with financial hardships which compromised his support of an ailing child killed himself". He had belonged to the American Federation of Television and Radio Artists (AFTRA), but received no help from it. Another actor, J. Edward Bromberg, died of a heart attack probably brought on by the stress he was suffering from. He had been blacklisted and unable to find work.

The Screen Writers Guild (SWG) in Hollywood had backed away from speaking out in support of the Hollywood Ten, the group of writers, directors, and producers who had been sent to prison for refusing to name names and otherwise co-operate with HUAC. It may be true to say that the hearings were a heaven-sent opportunity for anti-communists in the SWG to get their revenge for defeats they suffered in factional fighting in the 1930s. As for the Screen Actors Guild (SAG), its President, Ronald Reagan, happily co-operated with the Federal Bureau of Investigation (FBI) in identifying alleged communists in the union.

It was a different matter when HUAC started to call witnesses from the theatre in 1955 and 1958. The actors' union, Equity, took a firm stance against any form of blacklisting, and even negotiated an agreement with the body representing theatre owners to the effect that no-one would be denied employment because of a refusal to be a "friendly witness" with HUAC. This gave the actors the confidence to refuse to co-operate. It would seem that only one out of the twenty-nine summoned in 1955 freely admitted to one-time membership of the Communist Party and named names of others he said he knew to have also been members. That was George Hall, a minor and not-particularly noteworthy actor. I doubt very much that HUAC gained any great publicity benefit from his testimony.

The 1958 hearings did land a bigger fish when Arthur Miller had to face questions from Committee members. He had a more-prominent profile than earlier witnesses from the world of the theatre (*Death of a Salesman* had been a success), and there was more publicity attached to his appearance. There is a story about Miller being approached by one of the Committee and asked if he could persuade Marilyn Monroe, then Miller's wife, to have her photo taken with the Committee member. The inference appeared to be that Miller might get an easier ride if he agreed. He didn't, and was subsequently questioned about his possible involvement with communists, and his play, *The Crucible*, in which the story of the 17th century witch-hunts in Massachusetts was taken to be an oblique comment on what was happening in America in the 1950s.

A degree of controversy surrounded the investigation of Joe Papp, the founder and producer of the Shakespeare Theatre Workshop which staged free performances of Shakespeare's plays in Central Park. Papp was asked if he had "the opportunity to inject into your plays or into the acting or the entertainment supervision which you have, any propaganda in any way which would influence others to be sympathetic with the Communist philosophy or the beliefs of communism?". Papp replied briefly, saying among other things: "I cannot control the writing of Shakespeare. He wrote plays 500 years ago". After appearing before HUAC he lost his job at CBS, but "opted for arbitration and became the first person to win reinstatement during the blacklist".

Reading about the suggestion that Shakespeare's work might be a useful tool for subversion, I was reminded of an earlier exchange when Hallie Flanagan during her testimony made a reference to Christopher Marlowe, and was immediately asked, "You are quoting from this Marlowe. Is he a communist?". This occurred during the 1938 hearings. Philistinism was never in short supply among HUAC's members.

The hearings into the theatre mostly occurred after those that took place and created such fear and havoc in Hollywood. No-one was sent to prison and though some citations for contempt were handed down, they do not appear to have ever been put into operation. The folk-singer Pete Seeger had been held in contempt at the 1955 investigations, but it was later overturned. If a reference by Baar to the experiences of Charles Dibdin, an actor and television director, are anything to go by, HUAC's activities continued into the 1960s. He had been fired by NBC after his earlier refusal to co-operate with HUAC, but in 1961 he appeared again and testified, which presumably meant that he acknowledged being a member of the Communist Party in earlier years, and also named some names. He then returned to regular work in television.

It is a fact, however, that the blacklist had at least partly broken down by 1960. Baar records that Dalton Trumbo, one of the Hollywood Ten, was openly acknowledged as the screenwriter for films like *Exodus* and *Spartacus*. The signs of a fightback against McCarthyism had been evident from the mid-1950s and McCarthy had shown himself in a bad light as he blustered and argued during the televised "Army hearings" in 1954. He died in 1957 as a result of his alcoholism.

The question arises as to why the actors in New York were better able to withstand attempts to force theatre managers to dismiss alleged communists? The active nature of Equity in terms of negotiating contracts which required employers to guarantee that refusing to co-operate with HUAC was not a reason to fire anyone, obviously had a key role to play. In addition, theatres weren't as reliant on advertising as TV was. Pressure could not be brought to bear by sponsors running scared in the face of opposition to their being seen to be linked to programmes which employed blacklisted writers or directors. Another factor was the nature of the audience for theatre, as compared to that likely to go to the cinema or watch TV. Were theatre-goers more sophisticated and less inclined to see local communists as constituting a serious threat? They were, perhaps, more independent and did not like to be told that they shouldn't go to see a praised play because one of the actors in it had been politically indiscreet twenty years before.

Baar does more than describe the ways in which individuals coped with the problems arising from being called before the Committee. They had to be summoned first, and that involved being served with a subpoena. She has accessed the reports of Dolores Faconti Scotti, a process server for HUAC, and though they are essentially fairly routine documents, in which Scotti describes how she tracked down and served the required summons, they do make for informative reading. The ways in which the individuals concerned reacted varied. Attempting to serve a sub-poena on Madeline Lee, Scotti almost came to blows with the actress in an argument that extended down the street. She also faced some hostility from Sarah Cunningham, but in her report stated that John Randolph, Cunningham's husband, was "pleasant and friendly" when handed his subpoena.

There is information about *Red Channels*, a publication listing the names of actors, musicians, technicians, and others active in TV and radio who were alleged to be (or had been) communists, or who were sympathetic to the ideas of the Communist Party. It was compiled by several ex-FBI agents and used as a kind of guide for management when deciding whether or not it was safe to hire someone. And there was a man called Laurence Johnson, the owner of supermarkets in Syracuse, New York. Johnson "launched a 'Campaign for Americanism' that virtually brought the television industry to its knees". He called for a boycott of any products that were advertised in connection with TV programmes that featured anyone named as a communist.

Broadway and the Blacklist is valuable for the way in which it looks at blacklisting in the theatre and, in certain cases, in radio and television. It is clearly written, has a useful bibliography, helpful notes, and appropriate illustrations.

BROADWAY AND THE BLACKLIST

By K. Kevyne Baar
McFarland & Co. 205 pages. $39.95. ISBN 9-1-4766-7259-5

WILLIAM FAULKNER IN HOLLYWOOD: SCREENWRITING FOR THE STUDIOS

There was an assumption during the hey-day of the Hollywood studio system that if a writer went to work there it automatically led to a decline in his talents. The nature of writing for the screen meant that all kinds of compromises had to be made, and that individuality was much less important than the ability to work as part of a team and accept that one had to function within the conventions that applied in terms of producing a product likely to appeal to a wide audience. There were restrictions placed on what could be dealt with in a film, and how would-be controversial subjects could be approached. Hollywood was an industry of sorts (writers clocked in and clocked out as they would have done in a factory), turning out a variety of goods, some of high quality, some not, and with the profit motive frequently providing the basic reason for production.

Good work could, and often was, created within the system, but it would be foolish to deny that a writer in Hollywood was often employed on what can only be described as hack work. And writing was only one part of making a film. Photography, music, direction, acting, and other factors, were also of key importance. It was probably true to say that, with only a few exceptions, writers were not held in high-esteem by the studios. "Schmucks with Underwoods" was Jack Warner's opinion of the writers he employed. A writer might have had an acknowledged reputation as a novelist or playwright before arriving in Hollywood, but he or she was only ever going to be seen as successful by the standards of most of the film community if they came up with the required scripts for films that won awards and/or made money. There were producers, directors, and others in Hollywood who respected good writing, and tried to support it, but they were few and far between.

Most writers went to Hollywood because the money was good. This may have been especially true in the 1930s, when the Depression had hit America hard and, unless a novel attained best-seller status, it was difficult for authors to earn money from their books. Someone worth referring to is Daniel Fuchs, who had published three critically praised, but commercially unsuccessful novels (*Summer in Williamsburg, Homage to Blenholt, Low Company),* plus stories in the *New Yorker* and elsewhere, and then decided that working in films might provide a better way of supporting his family. I suppose it would be easy to suggest that he is an example of a writer who failed to come up with any writing of consequence after moving to the film capital, but it would be an unfair judgement. A later short novel, and some stories, demonstrate that he hadn't completely turned his back on anything other than screenwriting. But he seems to have adapted well to the studio system and stayed on the West Coast for the rest of his life. He was teamed with William Faulkner on at least one occasion.

Faulkner himself never pretended that he was in Hollywood for anything but the money. Although a published novelist and short-story writer, he had, at that point in the 1930s, not achieved any sort of popular success. When the opportunity arose to earn money as a screenwriter he appears to have seen it as a way to look after his family and buy time to work on his novels. It's obvious that he would have preferred to have been at home rather than in Hollywood. And it's debatable how seriously he took the work he was hred to carry out in the studios. Stefan Solomon sets out to show how his contributions to various films were valued, and that the practice of working on screenplays had an effect on Faulkner's writing in his novels. Because of the nature of writing for films it's often difficult to determine just where he contributed to a script. He received on-screen credits for six films, and is said to have been involved with around fifty in total. It's worth quoting what Faulkner himself once said: "I'm a motion-picture doctor. When they find a section of a script they don't like I rewrite it and continue to rewrite it until they are satisfied. I reworked sections in this picture. I don't write scripts. I don't know enough about it".

Opinions about how much Faulkner contributed to even the screenplays where he received a credit are divided, as are those about how he viewed his role as a Hollywood writer. When Howard Hawks directed *Land of the Pharaohs* in 1955, the screenplay was credited to Faulkner, Harry Kurnitz, and a relative newcomer, Harold Jack Bloom. Solomon notes that Faulkner happily acknowledged that Kurnitz did much of the writing for the film. And there are some instructive reminiscences by Bloom in Max Wilk's *Schmucks with Underwoods: Conversations with Hollywood's Classic Screenwriters* (Applause Theatre and Cinema Books, New York, 2004) which throw light on Faulkner's general behaviour while on location in Italy. Bloom's opinion was that he viewed it as a holiday with pay and made the most of little luxuries (wine, meals in expensive restaurants, etc.) that could be added to the studio expense account. He also thought that Faulkner was there because Howard Hawks, an old friend, wanted him to be, and was conscious of having his name on the screen credits as a matter of prestige. Faulkner's reputation as a novelist was beginning to flower by the mid-1950s. It perhaps needs to be said that, whoever contributed what to *Land of the Pharaohs,* didn't make a very good job of it. The writing was routine at best, and the film notable only for its spectacle.

As for Faulkner's attitude towards film-making in general, it appears to be true that he didn't hold it in high regard. He must have been competent enough with what he did, otherwise he wouldn't have been kept on the studio payrolls for any length of time. But it was just a job and a way of earning money, and I think other writers, more attuned to the idea of screenwriting as a profession with its own particular skills, recognised that Faulkner didn't have their sense of commitment to the practice. Nunnally Johnson, a well-regarded writer and producer, said: "Faulkner worked on a script for me once but I never thought for a moment that he had the slightest interest in either that script or anything else in Hollywood". And Harold Jack Bloom, who as noted earlier, had known and talked with Faulkner, was of the opinion that: "He had no respect at all for films. He didn't consider anything about the movies as an art form. He felt that doing anything in films was getting money for nothing, and he certainly wanted the money".

On the other hand, a talented director like Jean Renoir recalled that Faulkner's admittedly small contributions to the screenplay for *The Southerner* were of great value. And Howard Hawks claimed that Faulkner "contributed enormously" to the making of *Land of the Pharaohs*. It's amusing to read what Faulkner said of the film: "It's the same movie Howard has been making for 35 years. It's *Red River* all over again. The Pharaoh is the cattle baron, his jewels are the cattle, and the Nile is the Red River. But the thing about Howard is, he knows it's the same movie, and he knows how to make it".

The relationship with Howard Hawks is an interesting aspect of Faulkner's time in Hollywood, and five of the six films that earned him on-screen credits were directed by Hawks: *Today We Live, 1933; The Road to Glory, 1936; To Have and Have Not, 1944; The Big Sleep, 1946; Land of the Pharaohs, 1955.* The sixth, *Slave Ship,* was directed by Tay Garnett in 1938. It has to be accepted that Faulkner didn't have the only credit for any of these films, and various writers shared recognition with him. For *Today We Live,* for example, he was credited for dialogue and the film having been based on his short-story, "Turnabout". *Slave Ship* acknowledged that he provided the story but others the screenplay. He was credited with the screenplay of *The Road to Glory,* though with another writer, Joel Sayre. Jules Furthman accompanied him in the credits for *To Have and Have Not* and *The Big Sleep,* with Leigh Brackett added to the latter's credits. And we know about *Land of the Pharaohs* and its trio of writers.

Obviously, with several people involved and credited, and probably others who tinkered with the screenplay as it was developed (standard practice in Hollywood; Faulkner was one of six writers employed on a film called *Country Lawyer,* and at least one other was later called in), it's often difficult to ascertain who wrote what. But Solomon's diligent research work has unearthed some documents that can be linked to Faulkner. And the discovery of the "treatment" for *Sutter's Gold* (based on a novel by Blaise Cendrars) by another academic enables Solomon to discuss Faulkner's writing for Hollywood in relation to two novels – *Absalom, Absalom!* and *Pylon* – to discover if there were any influences in either direction. His comments may hold more relevance for students of Faulkner's literary works than those of film history, but they are generally informative. It's fascinating to note how he incorporated "non-human sound" when writing for films as support for dialogue. Faulkner may have been prone to say that the only aspects of cinema that interested him were newsreels and Mickey Mouse, but he does seem to have well-aware of the potential that the introduction of sound offered once it was introduced into films.

If Faulkner had only six on-screen credits, but is reputed to have worked on at least fifty films, it's possible that some of what he did made a difference to what are now considered lasting examples of the range of films Hollywood could turn out. We're told that he contributed, in one way or another, to *Gunga Din, Mildred Pierce, Drums Along the Mohawk,* and *Stallion Road*, to name just a few of them. *Stallion Road* was based on a novel by Stephen Longstreet, who was given sole credit for the screenplay. But Faulkner had done the initial adaptation of the novel, and Longstreet later said it was "a magnificent thing, wild, wonderful, mad. Utterly impossible to be made into the trite movie of the period. Bill had kept little but the names and some of the situations of my novel and had gone off on a Faulknerian tour of his own despairs, passions and story-telling".

There were also films that Faulkner worked on but which were never made. *The Life and Death of a Bomber*, a projected wartime morale-booster, was one, and a planned film about General De Gaulle another. And, though *The Left Hand of God* did eventually appear, with Humphrey Bogart as its male lead, its initial stages, on which Faulkner was employed, were interrupted because of objections by the Hollywood censor, the Hays Office, anticipating potential negative comments by the Roman Catholic Church. The story involved someone disguising himself as a priest in order to escape from the Japanese, and it was felt that it would be unacceptable for him to be seen in the film as being involved in any sort of ceremony that he wasn't qualified to conduct. The screenplay for the released version of the film was written by Alfred Hayes, a talented novelist whose *My Face for the World to See* and *In Love* are rightly considered minor classics.

Having spent so much time at the cinema when I was young, and continuing my interest in films since the 1940s, I was constantly entertained and intrigued by what Solomon had to say. His passing references to other writers that Faulkner teamed up with, if sometimes only for a short time, caught my attention. He revised a screenplay for *God is My Co-Pilot* which had originally been written by Steve Fisher, though in the end two other writers, Abel Finkel and Peter Milne, were credited when the film was released. Fisher had a long career in Hollywood, but was also a prolific writer of pulp novels, a couple of which – *I Wake Up Screaming* and *No House Limit* – are still worth reading. I pointed to Daniel Fuchs' presence in Hollywood earlier in this review (he co-operated with Faulkner on *Background to Danger*, based on an Eric Ambler novel, with W.R. Burnett, a popular crime novelist, getting credit).

There were a couple of occasions when Faulkner might have come into contact with the Hollywood Left of the 1940s, though he clearly had no political affiliations himself in that direction. He had been one of the group of writers, including Frank Gruber, Thomas Job, Robert Rossen, and A.I.Bezzerides, working on a screenplay for *Northern Pursuit*. It was expected that Gruber and Rossen would receive acknowledgment for it, but Rossen handed his credit to a fellow-communist, Alvah Bessie, who needed on-screen recognition to secure his continued employment in Hollywood. Solomon says that "Faulkner and Job seemed particularly incensed by the closing of party ranks here, and Gruber would later recall it as a 'Communist conspiracy' ". The Party link cropped up again when Faulkner's novel, *Intruder in the Dust*, was turned into a film in 1949. The screenplay was written by Ben Maddow, who had a radical past and was blacklisted, but found a way back into films when he agreed to name names later in the 1950s. It's not known if Faulkner had any input in the making of the film, or if he had ever met Maddow.

I realise that I'm indulging myself by referring to other writers and their publications, but the fact of work in Hollywood being a collaborative effort does incline me to wonder how far Faulkner was aware of his fellow-writers' achievements? Bezzerides had published a couple of novels (*Thieves' Market* and *The Long Haul,* both reprinted in recent years) and Frank Gruber was well-known for his crime novels. And Harry Kurnitz, who I mentioned earlier in connection with *Land of the Pharaohs*, wrote plays, and several entertaining novels, one of which, *Invasion of Privacy*, mocked some of the pretensions associated with the film industry. Solomon merely refers to him as a "young writer" but he was well into his forties when he knew Faulkner and was already an established-screenwriter with credits dating back to 1938.

William Faulkner in Hollywood has much to recommend it to both students of the novelist's work and those fascinated by the broad history of how screenwriters fared within the Hollywood studios system. Stefan Solomon is informative about how screenplays were produced and the problems that writers faced when attempting to outline something worthwhile in the face of demands to direct their work solely towards commercial success. He writes clearly and objectively and although his evaluations of the plots and characters of Faulkner's novels might be aimed more at a literary rather than film readership they are never less than direct and instructive. The book operates on more than one level. It is well-researched, has ample notes, and a useful bibliography. I think it should be pointed out that there is little biographical information about Faulkner in it, and anyone wanting details about his private life, his battles with the bottle, and similar matters, will need to look elsewhere. This is not a drawback to enjoyment of Solomon's book. His focus is on the work that Faulkner did in California, and not what personal adventures, or misadventures, took place there.

WILLIAM FAULKNER IN HOLLYWOOD: SCREENWRITING FOR THE STUDIOS

By Stefan Solomon

The University of Georgia Press. 301 pages. £27.50. ISBN 978-0-8203-5789-8

JOHN DOS PASSOS, JOHN HOWARD LAWSON
& *MOST LIKELY TO SUCCEED*

John Dos Passos' novel, *Most Likely to Succeed*, was published in 1954 in America and 1955 in Britain. He had, in his younger days, been inclined towards the Left, but by the 1950s was what can only be described as a conservative in his political thinking. The process of moving to the Right had taken place over a number of years, but prominent among the factors shaping his opinions were his experiences in Spain during the period when the Civil War was raging there. They occasioned a notable falling-out with Ernest Hemingway, among other things.

Dos Passos had a friend, a Spanish academic called José Robles, who had been teaching in the USA, but was visiting Spain when the Civil War started and decided to stay and help the Republican authorities. He acted as a translator for a senior Russian agent who was involved with the International Brigades, which were always under communist control, and who was also participating in the communist-dominated reorganisation of the Republican army. At some point the Russian came under suspicion because of his doubts about the purges that were being carried out against non-communist republicans like the anarchists and members of POUM (Workers Party of Marxist Unity), who were accused of being Trotskyists. Robles, as his translator, was arrested by the secret police, probably because it was considered he knew too much, accused of being a fascist spy, and shot, seemingly without any kind of trial. There were other reasons given for getting rid of Robles. He had a brother who supported Franco and was said to have helped him in various ways. And he had talked too openly in cafés about Republican military objectives.

Dos Passos was concerned that Robles appeared to have vanished without trace, and became increasingly curious when he received only vague replies to enquiries about his whereabouts. When he raised the matter with Hemingway, who mixed with officials in the Spanish government, he was told that certain things were necessary in wartime and he should stop asking questions. One man's fate was insignificant in the grand scheme of things. I have given only a brief summary of the mystery surrounding the death of Robles, and a more detailed account can be found in the book by Stephen Koch listed in the Bibliographical Note appended to this essay. It's worth noting that Dos Passos was also aware of the arrest, torture, and killing of Andrés Nin, head of the

POUM, by the communist-dominated security services.

Some years later, Dos Passos wrote an anti-communist novel, *Adventures of a Young Man*, in which an idealistic young man is radicalised in the 1930s, and joins the Communist Party. He gets involved in strikes and other activities, but begins to realise that the interests of the Party take precedence over those of the people it claims to be supporting. When he expresses his doubts openly he is expelled from the Party. He decides to go to Spain to enlist in the fight against fascism by joining the International Brigades. But, as a non-communist, and in fact someone who was thrown out of the Party, he's viewed with suspicion. And the suspicion grows when he's seen talking to an anarcho-syndicalist he knows. He is brought before a disciplinary hearing and accused of being a Trotskyist, a counter-revolutionary, and a fascist spy. He is sent to the front-lines and given what is a task almost certain to result in his death. It's a way of disposing of him without having to fulfil the formalities of a court-martial or other legal requirements.

When Hemingway and Dos Passos were watching the war in Spain wind it ways towards its disastrous end, in Hollywood John Howard Lawson was writing the screenplay for a film called *Blockade* which had its basis in the war. Lawson was a member of the Communist Party and a leading light in the Screen Writers' Guild, the union representing their interests, and often noted for its factional fights and its struggles with management. It would all come to a head in the post-1945 period when the House Un-American Activities Committee (HUAC) hearings focused heavily on the activities of writers who were alleged Party members. Sometimes, it wasn't even necessary to be a Party member to be thought of as subversive. "Are you a member of the Screen Writers' Guild?" was a question asked alongside "Are you now or have you ever been a member of the Communist Party?".

Lawson had known Dos Passos in New York in the 1920s when both were involved with the New Playwrights' Theatre (The Craftsman's Theatre in *Most Likely to Succeed*), which was, according to Stephen Koch, "a modernist enterprise organised by John Howard Lawson, and its star author was Lawson's fellow ambulance-driver John Dos Passos". The reference to being ambulance drivers brings out the fact that both, like Hemingway, Malcolm Cowley, e.e. cummings and other young Americans, had been volunteers in the Red Cross during the First World War. The theatre they started was devoted to "radical" and "expressionist" plays, and if Koch is to believed, was "unobtrusively supervised" by V.J. Jerome and Alexander Trachtenberg, two of the American Communist Party's cultural commissars. Koch also asserts that its "true purpose" was to "help Stalinise the New York vanguard, while assisting its founders, above all John Howard Lawson and Lawson's political sidekick, Frances Faragoh, make their move to Hollywood". A couple of Dos Passos' plays, and several by Lawson, did achieve some critical attention, if not popular success, and by the late-1920s Lawson and Faragoh were in the thriving film capital.

Faragoh doesn't seem to have ever had any major successes as an actor, but Lawson did build up a reasonably impressive list of films he had worked on. Like anyone functioning in Hollywood, he was often faced with trying to make something worthwhile out of indifferent material. But when he wrote the screenplay for *Blockade*, he may have thought that he was being given an opportunity to deal with a subject, the Spanish Civil War, that was close to his heart. The reality of the situation soon told him otherwise. Censorship and commercial interests determined that, though an informed viewer might easily guess that the action was taking place in Spain, the film made no reference to that fact. Groups with a special interest, the Catholic Church for example, objected to what they thought was communist propaganda in anything that appeared to be favourable about the Loyalists or unfavourable about the Nationalists. For their part, the studios were wary of promoting anything that might affect distribution of the film in America and Europe.

A couple of films made during the Second World War gave Lawson greater opportunities to openly express his anti-fascist feelings. *Sahara* starred Humphrey Bogart as an American army sergeant leading a disparate group of characters to safety in North Africa. Lawson managed to work sentiments about racial prejudice into the script in a way that suited the wartime calls for co-operation between all races, colours, and creeds in the struggle to defeat fascism.

The other film was *Action in the North Atlantic*, and I have to admit to a personal fondness for it. The story of a group of American merchant seamen taking supplies to Soviet Russia very much caught the mood of the moment when Russia was an ally and singing its praises was looked on positively. Did Lawson work propaganda into his screenplay, as would later be alleged? There are a few scenes which probably could arouse the suspicions of red-baiters. In one, a group sits around a table in the National Maritime Union (a communist-controlled union) hiring hall, and a young sailor expresses his reluctance to go to sea again after the ship he was on had been sunk. An older sailor remonstrates with him and points out how fascism threatens everyone. This man later in the film, when asked what "tovarisch" means, says, "It means comrade, and that's good". And there is a scene where crew members apprehensively watch a plane approaching until someone shouts, "It's one of ours", and the camera pans upwards to indicate Russian markings on its wings.

None of Lawson's writing for films appears to show him inserting outright communist propaganda into his scripts, but he was accused of doing just that when summoned to appear before the House Un-American Committee (HUAC) in 1947. A combination of suggestions about his work, and references to his activities in the Screen Writers Guild (SWG, but called the Filmwriters' Association in *Most Likely to Succeed)* pinpointed him as a leading communist in Hollywood. When he blustered and argued with the Committee, and refused to co-operate, he was, as one of the famous Hollywood Ten, sentenced to a term in prison. After that, he did little direct work in films, though he wrote and taught about them.

It's obvious that, as Dos Passos moved to the right, and Lawson further to the left, their previous friendship had broken down. When Dos Passos's novel, *Most Likely to Succeed,* appeared in 1954 it would have been clear to informed readers that the central character, Jed Morris, had, in some respects, more than a passing resemblance to John Howard Lawson. Both the fictional and the real-life character had started their careers in off-Broadway left-wing theatre circles in New York, had a limited amount of success as playwrights, and moved to Hollywood. There may be something of Morris's womanising in Lawson's activities. He was married but had relationships with other women, including, it has been suggested, a long affair with the novelist, Dawn Powell. We are, of course, dealing with a novel, so it's not necessarily a reliable guide to the character and actions of an actual person, especially when it comes to sex, where it might not always be obvious what someone thinks and does.

Is it different with politics? Dos Passos had known Lawson sufficiently well over the years to be able to assess his capabilities for political thinking. The testimonies of others who knew him do indicate that Lawson had the capacity to absorb Marxist theory and use it for the analysis of film techniques and achievements. But it has also been asserted that, when it came to dealing with people, Lawson could be dogmatic and that he had a tendency to accept the Party line and, where necessary, impose it on others. His position during the debate surrounding Albert Maltz's alleged deviation from Party policy regarding the role of the writer might be interesting to consider.

Maltz, a novelist and fellow-screenwriter, had written an article saying that writers ought not to be expected to follow a Party line when it came to what their subject-matter was and how they wrote about it. They should be free to make their own decisions regarding such matters. He was attacked by several other writers, including Alvah Bessie, Dalton Trumbo, and John Howard Lawson, all of them essentially insisting that art is a weapon to be used in the class war. Gerald Horne says that: "Lawson was not on the side of Maltz. In fact, according to some, he was leading the charge against him, burnishing his reputation as the Party's ideological enforcer". There are some relevant observations on Lawson's grasp of Marxism, and his application of it in relation to works of art, in Nancy Lynn Schwartz's *The Hollywood Writers' Wars*, and the consensus seems to be that he could be very authoritarian when deviations from Party policies came to light.

Jed Morris, the Lawson-like character in *Most Likely to Succeed*, is dogmatic, but largely because he doesn't really understand Marxist theory too well and simply parrots the Party line when a problem arises. He's impressed when he meets Party bureaucrats like V.F. Calvert (based on V.J. Jerome, a communist ideologue who sometimes visited Hollywood to lay down the law regarding what writers there should be doing to further the cause). But he's similarly impressed by some of the studio executives he meets, in particular by Milt Michelson, a dynamic young producer who dies unexpectedly from a heart attack, and who is probably modelled on Irving Thalberg. Scott Fitzgerald also took him as the inspiration for Monroe Stahr in *The Last Tycoon*. Jed is as swayed by their seeming enthusiasm for creating film as art as he is by communist enthusiasm for a supposed better society. In both cases their actual aims are much more prosaic. Money and power.

I propose that Dos Passos was doing more than settling old scores when he created Jed Morris and charted his collapse into mediocrity in the money-markets of Hollywood. As well as exposing the influence and machinations of the Communist Party among the Hollywood community, and in particular its writers, I think he was also emphasising a point often made by communists and conservatives alike. Moving to Hollywood was likely to lead to a diminution in one's talents as a creative writer. Too many other people – directors, producers, actors, writers – could interfere with one's screenplays. And the basic material was often not likely to make any great demands on one's creative imagination. There might be an irony in the notion of the Communist Party adopting a lofty position with regard to a writer's work being almost sacrosanct and not open for interference from outside sources. The Party had more than once attempted to shape the direction of novels written by screenwriters, as witness the arguments surrounding Budd Schulberg's *What Makes Sammy Run?* and Nathanael West's *The Day of the Locusts*. In Schulberg's case he resigned from the Party rather than agree to demands that he make certain changes to the text.

The HUAC investigations and subsequent blacklisting of many writers are not part of *Most Likely to Succeed*. The novel comes to a conclusion when Jed is warned by his Party contacts that Marlowe, the woman he had met on board ship at the start of the novel, and who has turned up in Hollywood years later and become his mistress, is probably an informant for the FBI. So, it's more than likely that they'll have details of his involvements besides the more-obvious ones like making speeches and signing petitions. The HUAC hearings brought out the fact that the activities of left-wing writers had all been carefully noted and filed for future use, even during the war years when everyone considered it safe to support Russia. Given the details of Marlowe's associations with the FBI and right-wing politicians, Jed collapses and asks his friends to call a doctor.

We know that Lawson's career in Hollywood came to an end in 1947 when he was convicted and imprisoned after his confrontation with HUAC. So Dos Passos' novel isn't meant to parallel Lawson's life, even if there are sufficient signs to point the reader in the direction of understanding where the inspiration for its central character came from. And some of the minor characters can also be linked to actual people who knew Lawson. Eli Soltair, a failed playwright and a man who leaned more towards the free-wheeling American radicalism exemplified by the IWW, was based on the curiously-named Em Jo Basshe. He had been present in the 1920s when Lawson and Dos Passos were active in New York, and had been one of the founder members of the New Playwrights' Theatre. He had two or three plays produced, but without any great response, and died in 1939. His fictional counterpart at one point turns up in Hollywood, but Jed has moved on from what he represents: "Greenwich Village, artists, what a dead end. He was through with drunks and Bohemians and addle-headed liberals".

I don't think that anyone could claim major status as a novel for *Most Likely to Succeed*. But it is of interest as an admittedly satirical account of left-wing writers supposedly plotting revolution while making good money in the Hollywood dream factory. It's easy to see why they were sometimes referred to as the "swimming pool Soviet". I don't want to detract from John Howard Lawson's principled stand against HUAC, even if it was a blunder in its application. He went to prison, and lost his position in the film industry by defying the Committee. Dos Passos possibly portrayed him unfairly in some ways by making his fictional counterpart less-intelligent, and more-opportunistic than Lawson probably was. But he was writing a novel and not a factual account, so was at liberty to shape people and places to suit his overall intentions. And by the early-1950s he was firmly of the opinion that those writers who had surrendered their individuality to either the notion of a communist utopia or the lure of Hollywood fantasy were lacking in both intelligence and integrity.

It does occur to me to wonder if Dos Passos wasn't also influenced when writing *Most Likely to Succeed* by the stories of other playwrights who had moved from New York to Hollywood. George Sklar had a success in both New York and London with *Stevedore* which starred Paul Robeson. He went to Hollywood, but was never in great demand as a screenwriter. He was involved with now-forgotten films like *City Without Men* and *Next Comes Courage*, and contributed additional dialogue to the screenplay of *The Bandit of Sherwood Forest*, though without receiving screen credit for it. He was blacklisted in 1951 after being named by Martin Berkeley who with Budd Schulberg had also worked on *City Without Men*. Both co-operated wIth HUAC when summoned to testify.

And there is the case of Clifford Odets, probably the most-acclaimed left-wing playwright in New York in the 1930s. Like Lawson and Sklar he took his talents to Hollywood, but when HUAC arrived in the early-1950s he co-operated and survived to carry on working in films. It has sometimes been the case to dismiss Odets' work in films, but his screenplays for *None But the Lonely Heart* and *Deadline at Dawn* are worth paying attention to, and the later *Sweet Smell of Success* is excellent.

Something else that Dos Passos brings out in his novel is that the Party was regularly looking for funds to support its various activities. It has been suggested that it was, in fact, the prime source of its interest in the screenwriters. As comparatively well-paid writers, they could afford to give generously to any cause the Party propagated. If they were actual Party members they were expected to contribute a regular portion of their earnings to the Party.

BIBLIOGRAPHICAL NOTE

Most Likely to Succeed by John Dos Passos. Robert Hale, London, 1955.

Adventures of a Young Man by John Dos Passos. Constable, London, 1939.

The Best Times: An Informal Memoir by John Dos Passos. Deutsch, London, 1968.

The Fourteenth Chronicle: Letters and Diaries of John Dos Passos edited by Townsend Ludington. Deutsch, London, 1974.

The Life of John Dos Passos: Twentieth Century Odyssey by Townsend Ludington. Dutton, New York, 1980.

Dos Passos: The Critical Heritage edited by Barry Maine. Routledge, London, 1988.

The Breaking Point: Hemingway, Dos Passos, and the Murder of José Robles by Stephen Koch. Counterpoint, New York, 2005.

Double Lives: Stalin, Willi Munzenberg, and the Seduction of the Intellectuals by Stephen Koch. HarperCollins, London, 1995.

Hotel Florida: Truth, Love and Death in the Spanish Civil War by Amanda Vail. Bloomsbury, London, 2014.

The Final Victim of the Blacklist: John Howard Lawson, Dean of the Hollywood Ten by Gerald Horne. University of California Press, Berkeley, 2006.

The Hollywood Writers Wars by Nancy Lynn Schwartz. Knopf, New York, 1982.

Tender Comrades: A Backstory of the Hollywood Blacklist by Patrick McGilligan and Paul Buhle. St Martin's Press, New York, 1997.

Communism in Hollywood: The Moral Paradoxes of Testimony, Silence, and Betrayal by Alan Casty. Scarecrow Press, Lanham, 2009.

Red Star Over Hollywood: The Film Colony's Long Romance with the Left by Ronald Radosh and Allis Radosh. Encounter Books, San Francisco, 2005.

JOHN NASH : ARTIST AND COUNTRYMAN

John Nash was for many years overshadowed by his brother, Paul. Perhaps he still is in most people's eyes? Paul Nash's reputation as a war artist has been reinforced over the years with various exhibitions and books about both the First and Second World Wars. There are classic images that seem to capture the essence of the grim trench war of 1916, or the spectacle of aeroplanes leaving vapour trails in the sky as they weave around each other during the dog-fights of 1940. Paul Nash also has some kudos attached to his name because of his involvements with British Surrealism in the 1930s. Authors often like to write books about movements in art, and being linked to one or other of them tends to ensure that a painter will have a place in such surveys. There is, too, the fact that Paul Nash "was more worldly, more ambitious, and much more alert to art politics than his brother".

I can't imagine John Nash ever getting too involved with groups and movements, though he certainly had friends in the world of the arts. And, when it came to portraying war on canvas he did spend months as a war artist towards the end of the Great War. But before that he had served on the front line and taken part in some of the fierce fighting of the time. When it came to representing the situation in France his "Over the Top" is probably a realistic portrayal of how it was. The soldiers, having clambered out of their trench are trudging toward enemy lines, their heads bowed, and their rifles carried loosely at their side and not aggressively. They give the appearance of exhaustion and resignation as they walk wearily into what is certain to be sustained enemy shelling and machine-gun fire.

Once out of the army it became obvious that there was more to JN (I'm going to follow Andrew Lambirth and refer to JN rather keep spelling out his full name) than as a minor war artist. Born in 1893, he showed some early skills at drawing, but unlike his older brother (born 1889) he had little or no formal training as an artist, and was more or less self-taught. He was said to have later expressed regret about not attending art school, but Lambirth is of the opinion that Nash never really felt inadequate for not having that experience: "What could it have taught him that he didn't learn for himself or absorb from friends and contemporaries?".

Nature was JN's chief inspiration, though he clearly picked up ideas from other painters. And there is "a convincing argument for the influence of Cezanne in the 1920s". But it is his landscapes that are probably what he is best-known for, and they engaged "with a simplification of landscape forms which nevertheless enhanced their significance". What he was after was producing a painting that was simply good to look at, and not meant to "educate" the viewer. In Lambirth's words: "The artist's job is to entertain and give pleasure, not to instruct". In an age where the political seemingly has to run through everything, the continuing popularity of JN's work among non-specialists lies in the fact that people just like to look at it. The same can surely also be said about the art of Eric Ravilious, a friend of JN's who tragically died young. Both artists took the real world, whether rural or urban, as their model, and then invested it with their own idiosyncratic colourings and designs.

JN had some success prior to the First World War, particularly as a water-colourist, and joined the New English Art Club, which had been established as a counter-force to what was seen as the establishment dominating the Royal Academy and other institutions. Among his contemporaries were young moderns like William Roberts, Robert Bevan, Charles Ginner, Spencer Gore, Harold Gilman, and Wyndham Lewis. Influences from abroad, primarily France, were affecting all these artists. Lambirth points out, however, that both JN and Paul Nash were producing work that "struck an instantly modern note without an apparent debt to all these influences, as if they had produced a home-grown version of Post-Impressionism without any of the usual awkward traces of hybrid origin". It was a lively period when groups formed, fell apart, and formed again under different names: the Fitzroy Street Group, the Camden Town Group, the Cumberland Market Group. Whenever I visit Judd Books in Marchmont Street I think of the area in 1913 and both JN and his brother living there.

An idea of JN's character can be gained from Lambirth's comments about him dressing "unobtrusively, more like a plantsman or country-man than as a painter". In this, he was akin to Robert Bevan, who Lambirth describes as "more like a countryman familiar with dogs and horses than a bohemian artist". It's an interesting area to explore, this need to portray oneself as just an ordinary person and not a pretentious poet or painter. It doesn't only extend to outward appearance, but can be heard in conversation, as when JN stated that he preferred gardening and fishing to painting. It may not be as pronounced now as it used to be, colourful and casual dress being more in evidence in society generally, but I suspect that a kind of bluff, down-to-earth Englishness still persuades many people that a person is basically sound. But beneath the conventional façade, JN did live a bohemian life in some ways, often short of money and with a reputation as a philanderer.

When JN finished his wartime service, as an infantryman and later a war artist, he soon settled into the life of a fulltime artist. There doesn't seem to have been any major changes in what he aimed for, and a watercolour called "The Cornfield" ("The whole composition is superbly managed and patterned with the glorious tensity that comes over farmland with ripeness and repletion at harvest time", in Lambirth's words) establishes the pattern of what he mostly did throughout his lifetime. Aside from the very early lessons he may have drawn from French Post-Impressionists, or his English contemporaries, it's probably true to say that JN never essentially altered his basic style. Lambirth refers to "The Cornfield" as "an image of pastoral idyll, and thus very dear to an Englishman's heart". I'm not sure I can accept the generalisation that all Englishmen share a liking for a "pastoral idyll" and it tends to make me feel that people in the home counties don't see the rest of the country, especially in the industrial North and Midlands, as really England.

Let me say at this point that I've no complaint to make about JN or any other artist establishing and maintaining a style throughout a lifetime. As long as they continue to sustain a high level of technical competence, and an imaginative interpretation of subject-matter, it doesn't seem essential that they should "make it new". This is true of representational art, though I have my doubts if it is applied to abstraction, where there are fewer places to go. After the Abstract Expressionists, and the St Ives artists in Britain, it always struck me that a lot of abstract art had reached a dead-end.

JN was included in the English section of the Venice Biennial in the 1920s, worked briefly as an art critic for the *London Mercury*, and contributed humorous drawings to various publications. It's significant that he no longer felt a need to align himself with any group or movement, and he went on the attack against them, writing that: "There is a distemper prevalent amongst artists of today. I refer to the mania for group forming". He pointed out that groups always had a spirit of dissension which led to "disgruntled diaspora" and characterised what he thought was "an inherent distrust of each other which all artists seem to possess". He might have added that ambition and ego are usually not in short supply among artists and writers. JN was not often thought of as being saddled with either affliction, though later in life Vera Coker, wife of Peter Coker, a painter who became friendly with JN, described him as "very self-centred, with quite a high opinion of himself".

Earning a living as an artist often requires turning to various activities in order to make money. Artists teach (JN's students often remembered him as usually positive and helpful in his comments on their work), they provide illustrations for commercial enterprises, and they experiment with different techniques. JN became highly proficient with wood-engravings and produced many of them as book and magazine illustrations. Lambirth remarks that critics have pointed out that "only twice had England led the world in the arts- first with watercolours and secondly with wood engravings". And he quotes another commentator saying that wood engraving "requires greater integrity in craftsmanship than any other means of reproduction". It's possible to see what is meant when one looks at the 1922 "A Gloucestershire Cottage", a wood-engraving "with its lucid design and sumptuous textures, the bushes and plants contrasting lyrically with the façade of the cottage". I must admit that my own favourite from the selection of wood-engravings in the book is the 1924 "Common Objects", with its collection of a cat, a kettle, a cushion, an umbrella, a book, and more, all of it wonderfully striking.

JN's chief interest was always in landscapes, and he was constantly looking for new places to focus on with pen, pencil, and brush. In this he was assisted by his wife, Christine, who was far more practical about everyday matters than he was. But I ought not to ignore JN's skill as a botanical illustrator, and he produced numerous illustrations for books and magazines: "JN became expert at depicting the decorative structure of plants and flowers. Although always text-book accurate, he was also able to draw plants as if they were really alive and capable of wilting or flourishing". The accompanying illustrations to Lambirth's comments certainly appear (to my admittedly town-bred eye) to bear out the accuracy of his assertions.

With his landscapes there is no doubt that JN was not a mere copyist, and the overall lay-out of a painting determined what was left in or left out. Once, when he asked a student why he had shown some daffodils in a painting, the student replied, "Because they were there". The person observing this incident thought that JN would have left them out: "He simplified a subject". When I look at something like the fine 1953 oil painting, "Frozen Pond" or the equally impressive 1950 "A Barn Wormingford", and the ravishing 1959 "Wild Garden, Winter", and "A Pond Near Cambridge", I'm minded to reflect on what may or may not have been edited out of the pictures as JN established their pictorial structures. It was certainly rare for figures to appear in his landscapes, for example, even if they had been there as he sketched what he could see. Or wanted to see?

140

He did move way from gardens and ponds and farms, and painted some non-rural scenes, though not of the streets of the cities. I don't think that he would have wanted to paint pictures of shop-fronts and bustling shoppers. He did like to look around dock-areas in Bristol, Great Yarmouth, and Ipswich, and some of the watercolour scenes he captured in those places do sometimes remind me of Eric Ravilious. The clarity of the lines is impressive.

John Nash died in 1977. There had been a retrospective exhibition of his work at the Royal Academy in 1967, and a major museum show in 1971 which opened in Chelmsford and later moved to Worthing. But, as Lambirth points out, there hasn't been another big exhibition since then. It isn't because his work has declined in popularity with a wide public. When people see it they like it. And it makes me wonder if that isn't part of the problem? Its popularity may damn it in the eyes of curators and critics raised on academic theory and abstract art. JN himself had little time for theory and I suspect the same might be said of Andrew Lambirth, whose writing is always clear and directly related to the subject. Some years ago I bought *The Spectator* regularly just so I could read the review pages and especially Lambirth's column. I have his volume of selected writings from *The Spectator*, and this splendid book about John Nash will make an excellent companion to it.

JOHN NASH : ARTIST AND COUNTRYMAN
By Andrew Lambirth
Unicorn Press. 352 pages. £40. ISBN 978-1-916495-70-8

THE POSTER : 200 YEARS OF ART AND HISTORY

On my wall, near where I'm writing this review, is a large calendar. As with so many of its kind these days the monthly illustrations are set around a specific theme, in this case Art Nouveau Posters. They're colourful and attractive, and conjure up the period when they were first displayed to draw attention to a particular product (cigarette papers, corsets), or a personality (Loïe Fuller, Germaine Gallois) from the Parisian theatre world. There is also one, by the American designer Edward Penfield, for the cover of a Poster Calendar for 1897.

The fact that a calendar featuring posters had commercial potential by that date is indicative of how popular posters were. In Paris they had already become collectors' items. Shops were established to sell them, exhibitions were held to display their variety and invention. And there were stories of people prowling the streets at night to strip posters from walls almost as soon as they were put up. Posters perhaps hadn't achieved status as an art form, even if some practitioners of the fine arts were involved in preparing them for advertising purposes. Toulouse-Lautrec is an obvious candidate with so many splendid examples, including his classic poster-portrait of Aristide Bruant. The cultural establishment remained aloof about them. They were often looked on as "the poor man's art" due to their being viewed outside galleries by people who had little or no money to purchase a painting. It didn't cost anything to stand and stare at them in the streets. And if a poster or two could be obtained for little or no expense, they could be used for decoration in the home. I have a couple on my walls.

The original point of posters was to provide information. In their simplest form they notified the public of forthcoming events and new rules and regulations. They might be better described as notices. Some were meant to promote a product. There is an illustration of a lithograph from 1842 which showed the uses and effects of Martin's Beer. It's an early example of poster advertising and is noticeably limited in terms of colour. It was only later that techniques developed sufficiently for lithographs to be produced in a variety of colours. A scene of people clustered around an advertising column in Berlin in 1855 appears to suggest that most of the items displayed employed words rather than pictures to impart their messages, whatever they were.

As lithographic techniques advanced and the quality of production, particularly in the application of colour, improved, so did the uses of posters. The Paris of the 1890s became noted for them. The term Art Nouveau was associated with the style, and Alphonse Mucha with its typical idealised female figures – "the personification of lithography" - and the "elaborate decorative circular" designs that marked so many of his paintings. Those designs, which sometimes seemed to be like a halo, may have been lampooned by Alexandre Steinlen in his memorable 1896 poster for the Cabaret Chat Noir. Steinlen favoured cats and his charming 1894 poster advertising sterilised milk showed a little girl sipping it from a bowl while three cats cluster around and look appealingly at her. Steinlen wasn't touched by the Art Nouveau fashion as much as some other artists, and his 1900 poster advertising the socialist magazine, *Le Petit Sou,* while eye-catching has little decoration about it. It's a harsh, near-realistic scene of social protest.

That term "eye catching" is precisely what posters, at least those primarily designed for public display, were meant to be. According to Leonetto Cappiello, "a poster should be a dab of colour on a wall that captivates passers-by already from a distance". His 1912 "I smoke only Le Nil", which has a rampaging elephant seemingly trumpeting "its preference for a certain cigarette paper" immediately fulfils that requirement. A later poster practitioner, A.M. Cassandre, active in the 1920s and 1930s, and regarded "as the most important poster artist of the 20th century, stated that "Unlike a painting, a poster tends towards a collective, applied art, and strives to eradicate individual peculiarities, along with the traits of the artist, in particular his handwriting. A poster is a mass-produced product designed to fulfil material needs and commercial functions". What appears to be a disclaimer in both Capiello's and Cassandre's statements about their status, or otherwise, as artists, might be viewed as contrasting with earlier poster painters like Mucha, Toulouse-Lautrec, and the great Jules Chéret, who would certainly have thought of themselves as fulfilling the role of an artist. And what of Bonnard, who did some poster work? How much did he distinguish it from his gallery paintings? Did he think of himself as less than an artist when designing a poster?

Not all posters were destined to be of use as advertisements for commercial products. The First World War employed them for recruitment purposes, as with the famous James Montgomery Flagg one of a forceful Uncle Sam pointing a finger and a large I WANT YOU FOR U.S. ARMY emphasising that it was part of a patriotic drive in 1917. America had joined the Allies confronting Germany and its supporters. The major combatants all used posters for propaganda, with, it seems, the British and French often focusing on the alleged brutality of the Germans.

Propaganda became a major theme in poster production. The Nazis used it to demonise both Bolsheviks and Jews in the 1930s, with startling images of grotesque Red Army men looming over terrified German women, and warped-looking Jews leering at viewers. The inference seemed to be that Bolsheviks were often Jews and Jews often Bolsheviks. There was a similar use of stereotypical figures on some Republican posters from the Spanish Civil War. The workers, and the fighters from the International Brigades, were shown as sturdy and heroic, Franco's forces as much less so.

That was one side of the poster art of the 1930s, and another was the promotion of travel. Trains, planes, ships, and cars were favourite motifs, all implying speed and the pleasures of relaxing in far-flung places. A 1935 poster by Cassandre placed the liner *Normandie* in the centre of the layout, with its bow appearing to loom over the viewer. Information relating to the owners of the ship and the route it takes is located below the bow so that the eye travels down to it. A relatively simple but effective advertisement. Roger Perot's 1933 poster for Delaheye has a fast-moving car hurtling towards us, and Cassandre's *Nord Express* focuses on the forward movement of a sleek train.

There are not many posters advocating air travel, probably because it was a luxury in the 1930s and largely limited to the well-off. Nor is there a lot about the encouragement from posters to travel by train within one's own country. But it's unfair to pinpoint limitations, because no one book can take in all aspects of posters. Still, the interested reader might like to look elsewhere for some of the posters for various rail companies operating services in the 1930s to English resorts in Cornwall and along the South Coast. I recall an exhibition of them at the Dulwich Gallery in London some years ago. They were sometimes by painters practising in the fine arts, and who found it useful to earn a little money from commercial work. It's of value to contemplate the relationship of posters to fine art works. A painting like Stanhope Forbes's *On Paul Hill*, which hangs in the Penlee Gallery in Penzance, might not look any different if it was used as a rail poster advocating a visit to the location concerned. Would the addition of a few words impose a different meaning on the painting and distract from its consideration as a work of art?

One of the things that struck me as I looked at the dozens of illustrations was that sometimes simplicity worked best. This is not to imply that the colourful, more detailed posters were less than interesting. I'm a great admirer of Mucha and others like him. But it is occasionally evident that a good effect has been achieved with a minimum of fuss.

Charles Rennie Mackintosh's 1895 poster for the Glasgow Institute of Fine Arts might be seen as within the Art Nouveau framework, but its lines are relatively straightforward, its colours simplified, and the overall design tidy. Charles Loupot reduces the layout of the 1929 Le Cafè Martin advertisement to a single cup of coffee against a creamy background with the café title and address beneath it. Herbert Leupin's 1953 Coca-Cola layout is based on the spidery outlines of a chair, music stand, and trumpet, with a realistic-looking bottle and the slogan, "Pause: Drink Coca-Cola". It works well, and seems very much of its period, with the musical link, and especially the trumpet, possibly pointing towards the cool sounds of jazz that were popular at the time. David Stone Martin, who did the art work for numerous jazz albums of the 1950s, sometimes used the bare-outline style of illustration, though his work was varied and he would easily move into other areas to suit the nature of the music or performer concerned.

Art Deco dominated a lot of 1920s poster design, and we're told, "was much more widespread and commercially successful than avant-garde graphic design". Although it's sometimes difficult to determine where Art Deco separates itself from avant-garde work, it may be that commercial outlets, as opposed to artistic ones, preferred a less aggressive format for advertising their products. But it's not easy to know just where to draw a line, if one needs to be drawn, between different groups or movements. They easily spill over into each other, and it seems obvious to me that individual artists would call on various styles to produce a successful poster.

Advertising has never been slow to take inspiration from whatever source it finds useful. The reverse might well be true, with artists using aspects of commercial art to finalise fine art productions. Look at Andy Warhol's work, for example, where everyday products are displayed in a manner not much different from how they appear in a supermarket. Or there is Roy Lichtenstein, famous for items like "Crying Girl", an announcement for an exhibition at the Leo Castelli Gallery in 1963 when Pop Art was riding high on the cultural scene, and the inspiration came from comic books and magazines.

I'm inclined at this point to raise the question of what might be called direct appropriation of a work for advertising purposes. A classic example might be "Bubbles", a painting by Sir John Everett Millais which, when exhibited at the Royal Academy in 1886 had the title, "A Child's World", and pictured a small boy blowing bubbles. It eventually came into the possession of someone connected to the Pear's Soap Company who had the bright notion of using the painting to advertise

145

its product. A similar idea was used when George Dunlap Leslie's "This is the way we wash the clothes", another Royal Academy painting, was slightly adjusted to advertise Sunlight Soap. Millais' reputation suffered because of the way his work was tied in with the world of commerce. But, again, did the placing of a few words on each canvas immediately invalidate the paintings as works of art?

There was something of a return to Art Nouveau on the West Coast of the USA in the 1960s and this, with the sort of Psychedelic Art that could be found wherever the so-called "underground" was in evidence, seemed to be symptomatic of the era of hippies, drugs, rock music, and general hedonism. But if the "Summer of Love" was supposed to sum up the atmosphere of the period it wasn't always that way. The 1960s were years of protest, and posters were produced to represent it. The events of May 1968 in Paris saw the streets sprouting them in a chaotic way, with often seemingly simple messages such as "Be young and shut up", and a large shadow of De Gaulle holding a hand over a young man's mouth. Opinions might vary as to how much of a challenge to authority 1968 in Paris really was, but there's no denying the seriousness of the situation in Vietnam. An offset print of a photo of the bodies of men, women, and children slaughtered by American soldiers bore the words: "Question: "And babies? Answer: And babies". It made a shocking 1970 poster which can still disturb the viewer. And 1968 saw Russian tanks rumbling into Prague, and quickly-formulated posters protesting against the invasion appeared in the streets.

Posters behind the Iron Curtain were, on the whole, not likely to challenge the role of the Communist Party. Examples of Russian posters from the time of the Revolution and the establishment of the Soviet state, demonstrated that they could be used to good advantage to attack the enemy, and to urge workers to throw their weight behind drives to increase productivity. What I do find particularly interesting about posters from Iron Curtain countries are those that came from Poland. They are well-represented, and their inventiveness is striking. They were not political, nor necessarily designed for propaganda purposes. A Poster School had been established in Warsaw in the 1950s and "a lively, narrative poster scene developed, in which the personal style of individual poster artists played a decisive role". It's pointed out that posters were often produced for sale, rather than for practical use in advertising.

The digital revolution affected the design and production of posters: "Designers were fascinated by the possibilities of digital image editing at an early stage". April Greiman seized on the opportunities to create posters for institutes and conferences that could feature "more extensive amounts of texts, and sometimes entire conference programmes and timetables". There are both advantages and disadvantages with digitalisation: "Compositions are becoming more detailed; there has been an increase in collage-like designs, and there is a mix of different techniques such as illustrations, photographs, cartoons, and handwriting........Image ideas travel round the world at the speed of light, and so national styles are increasingly losing their identity.......designers are no longer able to maintain control over their designs.......Large marketing companies and agencies have long since taken over the marketing of consumer goods or even political parties.......Individual design has been pushed back into the cultural sector, if it has not withdrawn completely into exhibitions or competitions".

It's relevant to note that later examples of posters sometimes do not have an individual artist's name attached to them but rather the name of an agency. If a name does occur, it's that of an "art director" who presumably presides over a team of designers busy at their computers. It seems a long way from Mucha and Toulouse-Lautrec and dozens of others who across the years laboured to finish posters that could combine a commercial message with some artistic invention. Is what those working in the digital world do any different? A poster from the Wieden & Kennedy Agency advertising New York City basketball seems to me to have genuine imaginative qualities. I suspect there are still plenty of people who will question whether art produced for commercial purposes can ever be compared to that which is defined as fine art. But it could be that, as much fine art has moved into abstraction, conceptual art, and related fields, the general public has drifted away from the galleries and, if they need art in their lives, might prefer to find it in in the posters they see in the streets and shops, and the advertisements on TV and at the cinema.

There is so much to absorb in *The Poster*, and I'm conscious of having only referred to a small selection of the work emanating from the story of the historical development of posters, and the techniques that made them possible. I should add that there are some useful explanations of those techniques. And I was constantly coming across stand-out items like Saul Bass's poster design for the film, *The Man with the Golden Arm,* an image that has stayed in my mind since I first saw it in the 1950s. Superbly illustrated, and with accompanying texts that are notable for their clarity, *The Poster* is a wonderful guide to an art form that has its own intentions and achievements.

Published in conjunction with the exhibition The Poster: 200 Years of

Art and History, held at the Museum für Kunst und Gewerbe, Hamburg, 28th February to 20th September, 2020.

THE POSTER : 200 YEARS OF ART AND HISTORY
Edited by Jürgen Döring and Tulga Beyerle
Prestel. 383 pages. £45. ISBN 978-3-7913-5985-4

MODIGLIANI

Olaf Mextorf's introduction to this book quickly establishes a picture of a man who, whatever else he did, became a model for the notion of the doomed artist: "He was handsome, reckless and dangerously ill". He drank and drugged to excess, "women found him irresistible", and he was talented. He might well have gone down as one more bohemian character who cut a path through artistic Paris in the early years of the twentieth century and was then largely forgotten, but for one thing. The "talent" which, in the form of his paintings, assured him of immortality. He wasn't just a proficient artist with an assured touch when it came to applying colour to canvas. Modigliani created something new and original and left behind paintings which are recognisable as only his.

Born in 1886 in Italy, Modigliani was rarely free from illness as a child, a factor which, when added to the tuberculosis he later suffered from, probably shaped his desire to live life to the full while he could. He was known to admire the writings of Verlaine and Rimbaud, and even when an art student frequented brothels and regularly used alcohol and cannabis. He identified with the role of the artist "on the edge of society". It was inevitable that he would soon move to Paris, which he did in 1906. The city was then the centre of the art world and teeming with painters and sculptors from many countries. And it was the focus for new ideas. Impressionism had changed attitudes in many ways, and other movements soon followed – post-impressionism, symbolism, fauvism, cubism.

Modigliani became friendly with the German artist, Ludwig Meidner, and with Maurice Utrillo who shared his liking for a lifestyle often revolving around drink. But he was painting, and in 1907 exhibited at the Paris Salon d'Automne, and in 1908 at the Salon des Indépendants, both of which highlighted the works of the current avant-garde. I think it's true to say that Modigliani was still formulating his own style at this time. His 1907 painting, "Jewish Woman", puts me in mind of works by Picasso from his Blue period. Mextorf says that he "mixed with Jewish artists in Paris, where he may have met the young woman who posed as a model for him".

Montmartre, where Modigliani initially lived when he arrived in Paris, was being replaced by Montparnasse as the area where artists and writers congregated, and he moved there in 1909. He had met the painter Chaim Soutine, who became one of his drinking companions, and the sculptor Brancusi. I think we now tend to primarily look at Modigliani the painter, but he did produce many sculptures, some of them showing how he was influenced by non-European cultures. It's said that he had been friendly with Italian construction workers in Paris, and that they loaned him tools for sculpting and provided the materials from which he chiselled his heads.

An early item that particularly caught my attention is a drawing from 1911 of the Russian poet, Anna Akhmatova. Its simplicity is striking, being little more than a "few thinly spaced lines" and a small head. Mextorf suggests that there is some affinity in this work with that of the "British illustrator and graphic artist, Aubrey Beardsley". The deftness with which Modigliani creates a personality with seemingly little effort certainly does have some resemblance to Beardsley's work.

Modigliani lived in poverty in Paris, and it was during this period that he met the British painter, Nina Hamnett, whose portrait he painted in 1914. It shows an attractive woman and is certainly a world away from photographs of the Hamnett who is mostly remembered as an alcoholic habitué of the Soho watering holes of the 1930s and 1940s. Hamnett, in turn, introduced him to the writer Beatrice Hastings, with who Modigliani had a "tempestuous affair". Her early impression of him hadn't been favourable, but she soon declared herself "completely crazy about the pale, brutal bastard". His portrait of Hastings is curious and has a "secretive, somewhat melancholic aura.......In parts of the canvas, an almost brittle application of colour makes the picture appear like a slowly fading memory". Was Hastings fading from Modigliani's life when he painted her picture?

Modigliani may now be noted for his paintings of nudes, but when they were first exhibited in Paris they attracted the attention of the police and had to be withdrawn from public display. A lot of the fuss seems to have centred around the pubic hair that all the models clearly have. It was a convention that nudes usually had that part of their bodies either hidden or clean-shaven. Did Modigliani deliberately seek to cause a scandal by showing the pubic hair? He certainly liked to shock the bourgeoisie with his behaviour, and it may be that he would have been aware that the sight of the tufts would invite a reaction.

It might be worth adding at this point that it was often assumed that Modigliani usually had "more than just an artistic interest in his models". And it does seem true that what he captured on canvas wasn't only a matter of form in terms of curves and colour. There does appear to be a suggestion of sexuality in the way the models are posed. Look at the 1918 "Young Woman in a Shirt", of which Mextorf says: "The painting's transience corresponds to the fragile moment of intimacy that Modigliani is aiming to express. It is uncertain which role the painter himself played in this context". He also discusses the 1917 "Reclining Nude", and says that Modigliani's approach to the subject can be seen as "reducing nudity to sex". Are his models "objects of degraded male fantasies?". He adds: "opinions oscillate between transcendence and a suspicion of pornography".

It's Modigliani's portraits that seem to me to me to hold more interest, skilled and provocative as the nudes may be. As a prominent member of the Montparnasse artistic community he frequently painted his friends and associates. Early portraits such as those of Paul Alexandre (an enthusiastic patron and collector of Modigliani's work) and Baroness Marguerite de Hasse de Villers (a socialite with an occasionally difficult character) are both accomplished, though the Baroness rejected her portrait. His portrait of the Mexican artist, Diego Rivera, "deviates from his otherwise typical stylisation", and a portrait of Picasso is described as "curious" and "characterised by a sketchy and fleeting application of colour".

The Polish art dealer Léopold Zborovski had been introduced to Modigliani by the artist Moise Kisling, and he and his wife helped to look after him in his final years. Modigliani painted portraits of both Leo and Anna Zborovski. With Leo, he captured a man with a quizzical expression on his face. Is he weighing up the artist or the world in general? When it came to Anna, known as a woman who was "cultivated, self-controlled and reserved," he saw her as "at peace with herself and unapproachably beautiful". Mextorf says that, although she disapproved of Modigliani's lifestyle, she "repeatedly posed as a model for him". She was presumably someone in whom his interest didn't get to extend beyond the artistic.

Others painted by Modigliani included Soutine and the portrait has "restless brushwork that appears to echo Soutine's personality, described as unrefined". When he produced a portrait of the Russian sculptor Jacques Lipschitz and his wife Berthe, he charged "only ten francs and some alcohol". With the poet, critic and painter Max Jacob – "Jewish, a homosexual and a drug addict" - he saw someone whose "true feelings.....seem to be hidden from view by an inner barrier". There was also an expressive drawing of the Swiss poet and novelist Blaise Cendrars, author of, among other things, the wonderful long poem, "Easter in New York". Cendrars had joined the French Foreign Legion in 1914 and had lost an arm in 1915. Like his drawing of Anna Akhmatova, Modigliani's few lines pack in a great deal in terms of cap-

151

turing something of Cendrars' presence in the world.

Modigliani's final years are probably those that many people may know about, the nature of his death and its consequences having been chronicled in various novels, films, biographies, and articles. He had never been without a female companion in his life, and in 1917 met Jeanne Hébuterne, a nineteen year old art student, "a beautiful young woman with blue eyes and thick, reddish brown hair". There was an immediate attraction between them and it was not long before she had moved in with the thirty-two year old artist. He was achieving some success, but was still "entirely destitute". To complicate matters even further her parents – staunch middle-class Catholics – disapproved of her relationship with the older Jewish bohemian painter.

There are two portraits of Jeanne in the book. One, a head-and-shoulders, brings out something of her fragile beauty, while the other, painted in 1919, shows her when she was carrying their second child. Life with Modigliani had never been easy for Jeanne. She was sometimes described as "quiet, weak and willing to make sacrifices", presumably to hold on to his affections. He had continued to indulge in drink and drugs and to associate with other women. There must have been some inner depth in her character which enabled her to tolerate the unfaithfulness, poverty, and even the verbal and physical abuse Modigliani directed against her.

Things came to a head in January 1920. Modigliani had "caught a severe chill while waiting for friends in the rain". He was taken to his studio where Zborovski and his wife looked after him. Jeanne was heavily pregnant and unable to help. But when on the 22nd January the Chilean artist Ortiz de Zárate, who lived below Modigliani, returned from travelling he found the painter "unconscious in the ice-cold studio". He sent for a doctor who immediately had Modigliani taken to hospital. He died there on the 24th January 1920 without regaining consciousness. His death was ascribed to "meningitis, which had been brought on by a tuberculosis pathogen".

It was left to Moise Kisling and André Salmon to raise funds to provide for a suitable funeral and on the 27th January the funeral procession made its way from Montparnasse to Père Lachaise cemetery. "Numerous artist friends, models, dealers and art lovers followed Modigliani's coffin across the city". The day after the funeral Jeanne jumped from a balcony at her parents' home, killing herself and her unborn child. Her family had disinherited her when she went to live with Modigliani, and even in death they refused to let her be buried near him. She was also denied internment in the family vault because she had committed suicide.

As usual with bohemian tragedies there is the ironic fact that the paintings and other works that Modigliani was paid very little for soon began to accumulate in value. Death is a great stimulator for raising prices in the art world. It's also a fact that it has always been difficult to ascertain how many works of art Modigliani created and what happened to some of them. Drawings he did while sitting in a café with friends were often given away or left on the table. They may not have been major works, but would be sought after now. As a consequence, any number of forgeries may be floating around. His style was so distinctive that it became relatively easy to copy.

It's difficult to separate Modigliani's work from his personal legend. The paintings were an integral part of his life, often chronicling through portraiture the friends and fellow-artists he moved among. They provide a picture of the Parisian bohemia of the first two decades of the twentieth century. Olaf Mextorf has managed to evoke not only Modigliani's life and work in this excellent small book, but has also drawn attention to a lost world of artists and others who, even while the First World War raged just a few miles away, were attempting to preserve ideals of creativity and beauty.

MODIGLIANI

By Olaf Mextorf

Prestel. 110 pages. £9.99. ISBN 978-3-7913-8659-1

THE SCOTTISH COLOURISTS

The Scottish Colourists were four artists – S.J. Peploe, J.D. Fergusson, F.C.B. Cadell, and Leslie Hunter – who, according to James Knox, are now acknowledged as "one of the most talented, experimental and distinctive groups in 20th century British art". It wasn't always that way and, until comparatively recently, you had to travel quite a distance to see even individual selections of their work. Visitors to Edinburgh and Glasgow could find paintings by them in galleries, and the excellent Fleming Collection in London (now sadly closed) helped to bring the Colourists to the attention of viewers outside Scotland. They were never completely forgotten, but it's doubtful if all that many people were aware of them.

The current exhibition in Kendal is drawn from the Fleming Collection, and is a delight to see. The word "colour" really is distinctively applicable in virtually every canvas on display, though that in no way lessens the effects of often skilled applications of the line. A painting by Peploe of Kirkcudbright, known for its established artists' colony, is perhaps illustrative of a successful combination of colour and line.

What is significant about the four painters in question is that, although sharing interests and some experiences, especially of studying and working in France, they each had individually-identifiable styles. Fergusson and Peploe were friends, both born in Scotland, and brought up in comfortable circumstances. After their initial training, they both studied in Paris, where they were initially influenced by Manet and Whistler, but soon fell under the spell of Matisse and the Fauves. Peploe was "reserved by nature", but Fergusson was "a born instigator and propagator, a lover of credos and manifestos, of movements and affiliations". Knox describes him as a "well-built, handsome swagger of a man". Fergusson could perhaps be described as more-intellectual than the others, and likely to analyse what was being done. It's significant that he was connected with the short-lived (1911-1913) but influential magazine, *Rhythm,* just prior to the First World War. The word "rhythm" often crops up in descriptions of the swirling brush strokes of Colourist paintings.

The group was never actually referred to as "Scottish Colourists" until the 1920s, but prior to that Fergusson and Peploe had been joined by F.C.B. Cadell and Leslie Hunter. Hunter, though born in Scotland, had moved with his family to California when he was fifteen. Precociously talented as a draughtsman, he provided illustrations for magazines and books, including those by Jack London. In Knox's words, he was "a striking bohemian figure with an eye for the ladies". He was determined to succeed as a painter, and not just as an illustrator, but his early work was destroyed in the 1906 San Francisco fire. He returned to Scotland, and began to develop "an individual style, rooted in a study of old masters as well as more recent French schools". He had spent some time in Paris.

As for Cadell, he like Peploe, grew up in Edinburgh, and attended Edinburgh Academy, where he was noted for caring only for drawing. When he was sixteen he moved to Paris with his mother, studying at the Acadèmie Julian. He also spent a year in Munich. He was early influenced by the Impressionists, though a visit to Venice in 1910 "loosened his technique and boldness of colour". Back in Edinburgh, he drew attention with "a series of swagger portraits, still-lifes and interiors". Of the four Colourists, Cadell was the only one to serve in the First World War and was wounded twice.

There is no denying that the Colourists had a certain amount of success before and just after the First World War, with their paintings being exhibited in Edinburgh and Glasgow, London and Paris. But not everything ran smoothly after that. Peploe died in 1935 at the age of 64, possibly during a flu epidemic. Hunter had died earlier, in 1931, after suffering "nerve attacks" which led to a "creative block and problems with his dealers". Cadell, "who had never been business-like, fell prey to the collapse of the art market following the 1929 stock market crash, reducing him to penury. He "died destitute" in 1937.

Fergusson was the survivor, and "lived on until the ripe old age of 87" after a lifetime involved with the "Scottish art scene, writing, editing and founding groups and clubs". It has been polnted out that Fergusson never gave up on his attempts to re-create the cafè culture he'd experienced in Paris for a British context: "Fergusson wanted to invest his corner of each city (he lived in) with Parisian–style culture, its accessibility, vitality and intellectual bite". He was probably often disappointed with his attempts to do it in London and Glasgow, but at least he could look back on his own presence in Paris at a time of great ferment in the arts, and genuinely claim that he had been a contributor, not just a spectator, to what had happened in the heady days before the First World War.

It should be noted that the Colourists had contact with, and in some ways were influenced by certain members of the group known as "the Glasgow Boys". Arthur Melville and John Lavery might be cited as two of the artists who had encouraged both Fergusson and Peploe. Lavery had urged them to take an interest in Whistler, and Melville was allied to the Glasgow Boys who, to quote Knox, were "tonal painters relying in gradations of colour to convey a sense of light and depth. Melville was a proto-colourist, using passages of pure colour to convey light and heat. As such he, he anticipated by 30 or so years the later achievements of the Scottish Colourists". It was Melville who persuaded Fergusson and Peploe to go to Paris.

It's obvious that the early deaths of Peploe, Cadell, and Hunter, and Fergusson's decision to settle in Glasgow when he left France in 1939 rather than reside in London, must have played a part in the subsequent neglect of their work outside Scotland. And the events of the 1940s, and the start of new movements such as the Abstract Expressionists, and the rise of St Ives as a location of some importance, would have drawn attention away from other artists. Later Scottish painters like Robert Colquhoun and Robert MacBryde gravitated to London, and Wilhelmina Barns-Graham went to St Ives. It would be some years (the 1980s) before major group exhibitions of the work of the Glasgow Boys and the Scottish Colourists would again begin to revive interest in their work outside Scotland.

The exhibition at Abbot Hall Gallery is well worth seeing. It includes a few paintings by Lavery and Melville to indicate their influence on the Colourists, and a few others (look out for some especially good work by William Crozier) who, in various ways, can be said to have been influenced by the Colourists. But it is their work that is the main attraction, and its vibrancy and variety is still there. The painters were engrossed by colour, and it shows in the brightness coming from their canvases and lighting up the gallery while outside a cold day was darkening down.

A final note. I recently obtained a copy of *The Society of Six Colourists*, by Nancy Boas (Bedford Arts Publishing, San Francisco, 1988), a book about a group known as the "Oakland Six" notably active in California in the 1920s. Looking at the illustrations I was struck by some similarities to the work of the Scottish Colourists. One of the Americans, William Clapp, had been in Paris in the early-1900s when Fergusson and Peploe were there, though there is no indication that he knew them. But, like them, he had been impressed by the work of the Fauves. Another of the Six, Louis Siegriest, encountered the Fauves when their paintings were shown on the West Coast in the 1920s: "I remember thinking how simple (the Fauves) worked. I thought they were grand".

COLOUR AND LIGHT : THE ART AND INFLUENCE OF THE SCOT-
TISH COLOURISTS

An exhibition at Abbot Hall Art Gallery, Kendal, 18th October, 2019 to 1st
February, 2020

THE SCOTTISH COLOURISTS : THEIR STORY, THEIR ART

By James Knox

The Fleming Collection. 65 pages. £9.95. ISBN 978-15272408-8-9

BURNING THE BOOKS : A HISTORY OF KNOWLEDGE UNDER ATTACK

One of the images perhaps best known to those who have seen documentaries about the rise of Nazism in Germany is that of the burning of books in the streets of Berlin in 1933. Jewish authors, left-wing novelists and poets, and any writer, in fact, who didn't adhere to a narrow definition of what could be written about, would have known that his or her publications were probably being hurled into the flames by fanatics with a cause.

It's probably what comes to mind when the word "burning" is used in connection with books. But attacks on knowledge can arrive in a variety of ways, some of them not necessarily evil in intent. The road leading to arrangements to destroy certain books and documents may be paved with good intentions.

When a group of people met in the offices of John Murray in May 1824 it was to decide what to do about Byron's memoirs. They had been given by Byron to his friend, the Irish writer Thomas Moore, and had been read by a close circle of other friends and acquaintances. Not everyone was convinced that, after Byron died, they should be published. His reputation was already scandalous, and it was felt that the memoirs might affect it adversely even further, and reflect badly on his family, his wife's relatives, and Byron's publisher, John Murray. Richard Ovenden quotes William Gifford, editor of the influential *Quarterly Review,* as saying they were "fit only for a brothel and would damn Lord Byron to certain infamy if published".

Among the group gathered with Murray were Thomas Moore, his friend Henry Luttrell, together with Robert Wilmot-Horton and Colonel Frank Doyle, both of them representing Byron's sister and widow. Moore had a financial interest in seeing the memoirs in print, Byron having authorised his impoverished friend to sell them, but as Ovenden puts it: "What exactly happened next is unclear but the manuscript was ultimately torn up and burned in the fire in the drawing room". Depending on one's point of view you can see this as an act of vandalism or a well-meant decision to protect the interests of those who Byron may have named. Either way, later scholars have regretted what took place. If the manuscript had survived, would it have helped throw useful light on Byron's poetry? We can never know.

Byron clearly wanted his memoirs to be published, but other poets have sometimes left instructions that diaries and related material should be destroyed by their executors. Ovenden discusses the case of Philip Larkin. One of his lovers refused to accede to his request that certain materials should be burned after he died, but another shredded "more than thirty volumes of his diaries" on the grounds that it was what he wanted. It might be asked why Larkin didn't destroy them himself? As a poet and librarian he would have known what might happen when a famous writer dies in terms of disputes about whether or not to follow his or her wishes.

There is the well-known case of Franz Kafka whose friend Max Brod decided not to follow his orders that everything should be burned. And Ovenden also looks into the question of what happened following the death of Sylvia Plath when Ted Hughes disposed of certain items, much to the annoyance of feminists and literary critics. Brod's actions can be seen as benefiting readers and scholars, whereas what Hughes did might be viewed as largely designed to protect his own reputation and not deal fairly with Plath's.

So far I've looked at individual cases involving the destruction of what would have been valuable materials for scholars to refer to. The major attacks on knowledge held in libraries, museums, and archives, have usually come about because of wars and religious and social intolerance. When the British attacked Washington during the War of 1812-14 they deliberately burned the library to the ground. It was claimed that it was a retaliatory action following an American attack on York (later renamed Toronto) when the library there was torched. But, as far as the Washington building was concerned, it was clearly aimed at destroying books and documents that served to provide the legal and historical basis for the American Revolution and the foundation of the nation. If you can do that then you can start to deny the existence of both. The British hadn't really got over the fact that they'd lost the American colonies.

When the Germans invaded Belgium at the beginning of the First World War they seemed to have made a point of setting fire to the famous Louvain Library which "held over three hundred thousand volumes in its collection............Its holdings reflected Belgian cultural identity". The Germans claimed that fires were started by individual soldiers reacting to being fired on by civilian sharpshooters, and denied any deliberate intention to destroy the library. But the act caused widespread anger and went towards creating a view of the Huns as barbarians. Was it part of a specific policy to denigrate Belgian culture?

A more-recent demonstration of an attempt to destroy what might be called the intellectual framework of a state took place in Bosnia during the Serbian siege of Sarajevo. The library, which housed many old books and documents relating to the country and its Muslim past, was deliberately targeted by the Serb artillery with snipers placed to pick off anyone attempting to douse the flames or rescue books and artefacts. There is no doubt that there was a carefully planned design to destroy the building and its contents.

I referred at the beginning of this review to the Nazis burning Jewish books in 1933, and their actions were a forerunner to what was to take place during the twelve years of the Third Reich. Heinrich Heine said, "Wherever they burn books, they will also, in the end, burn human beings", and it was a prophecy that came horribly true for the Jews, "the people of the book", as they were known because of their love of learning and books being central to Jewish religion and culture. Both books and people had been burned before, of course, the Catholic Church and the Protestants of the Reformation being inclined to set light to reading material they didn't like and to people who wouldn't conform to their particular ideologies. That some old books and manuscripts did survive as purges got going was largely due to individuals who hid books whenever they could. According to Ovenden, "The European Reformation of the sixteenth century was in many ways one of the worst periods in the history of knowledge", and he adds that "hundreds of thousands of books were destroyed".

The Nazi campaign against the Jews was equally destructive. As the Nazis took over in Germany and then spread their control into other countries, Jewish property was confiscated. Books and other printed matter were shipped to Germany, if they were not destroyed, so that institutes could be established to study Judaism with a view to discrediting it and, eventually, consigning it to just an item on the list of lost communities and cultures. That would accord with the plan to establish Aryan culture as the principal one in the history of civilisation.

Ovenden looks closely at what happened in Lithuania and especially in Vilnius (then called Vilna), which had "a strong culture of libraries", when the Germans arrived in 1941. Jews were recruited to help sort the books into those that the occupiers wanted to send to Germany and those that would be pulped. The Jews weren't willing recruits, but being employed as they were they had the opportunity to smuggle some books out and hide them. Ovenden describes them as "an extraordinary group of courageous scholars and librarians". He also records that the German in charge of the overall operation was a librarian and a more-than-willing member of the Nazi Party. Knowledge is essential but not necessarily a guaranteed route to a liberal state of mind.

I haven't followed Ovenden's chronology of the devastation wreaked on libraries and archives by wars and fanatics of one kind or another. He surveys the early manifestations of libraries in Nineveh and Alexandria, of which "no material evidence survives from the library itself", and describes it as "the archetypal library of the Western imagination". How was it destroyed? Wars certainly had their impact, but neglect played its part. The transition from papyrus to parchment to paper wasn't a smooth one and things inevitably deteriorated. And he takes us to the Middle-East where, in the nineteenth century, British and French archeologists competed to see who could find artefacts to fill museums in London and Paris. There is so much referred to in Ovenden's narrative that I could happily have spent hours picking up leads and investigating them. He remarks: "From Islamic Spain to the Abbasid Kingdom in Iraq libraries sprang up. There were great libraries in Syria and Egypt, over seventy libraries in Islamic Spain, and thirty six in Baghdad alone". I couldn't help wondering what happened to those libraries in Spain as the Moors were forced out of the country?

In a book I read recently it was stated that "San Francisco Library pulped 250,000 forgotten books to make way for computers and reading spaces". It has happened elsewhere, and Ovenden as a librarian (he's the top man at the prestigious Bodleian Library in Oxford) is alert to the problems that libraries face in the modern world. Besides lack of funding they have to accept that they can't possibly keep everything, a dilemma that those of us who love books face in our own lives, though obviously not on the same scale. Decisions need to be made about what to keep, and what to do with what is to be disposed of. And how much can be digitalised before it does disappear? Who makes the decision about which book is worthy of retention and which can be pulped or, though it seems a crime even to simply say it, burned?

In a neat aside, Ovenden points out that, in our daily lives we all dispose of knowledge. He refers to his own experience of sorting out the house of a deceased relative, and having to decide which documents to throw away. In some ways, perhaps all of them might be relevant to a future scholar? I have had this experience myself when dealing with the letters and other paperwork of a friend. I felt I could get rid of most of the material on the grounds that its relevance was limited in the extreme. But I found it difficult to get rid of her few books and in the end absorbed them into my own. But I am one of those people who hates to let books go even though I know I'll never read them again. People tell

161

me that I could tidy up the house and create more shelf-space if I digitalised some of my books, assuming I could afford to do so. But I like the idea of a book in my hand. And I worry about digitalised documents and whose hands they could fall into.

Burning the Books is a fascinating book and has been written by a man who himself clearly loves libraries and literature and everything connected with them. It ought to be read by anyone who cares about what will happen to libraries in the future. They will continue to exist, but possibly only in major cities and centres of learning. Smaller locations may have to form their own voluntary groups, as they have done with cinemas and pubs, to keep them open. As for books, there seems to be a continued demand for them, though specialist items tend to be priced out of the range of most individuals and even some institutions. But technology has meant that it's easier to produce books. This, of course, can lead to problems for libraries if they try to keep up with the constant flow of new publications from around the country. There isn't the space for them, at least not in printed book form. But I'm never going to suggest that there should be restrictions on the availability of books.

BURNING THE BOOKS : A HISTORY OF KNOWLEDGE UNDER ATTACK

By Richard Ovenden

John Murray. 308 pages. £20. ISBN 978-1-529-37875-7

THE SECRET WAR AGAINST THE ARTS : HOW MI5 TARGETED LEFT-WING WRITERS & ARTISTS 1936-1956

We live in a democracy. There may be various interpretations of what that word means, but we generally agree that the rule of law should apply fairly and freely to all, and that we are on the whole at liberty to read what we want, and express our opinions about most things without falling foul of the institutions of the state. We assume that our homes will be respected and not raided, that the police will leave us alone if we don't commit crimes, that we can move around without hindrance, and that we can communicate openly with other people and not be pilloried for doing so.

Well, that's what should happen, and often does for most people. There are always exceptions to any law or matter of understanding, and we'd no doubt accept many of them on the grounds that the general good requires us to make concessions. Only an extreme libertarian would argue that terrorist material should be easily available, that certain kinds of pornography ought not to be censored, or that everyone has the right to own guns and ammunition. It's also necessary to point out that recent events have shown how quickly some of our "rights" can be tinkered with when governments think it necessary.

A difficulty often arises in relation to political aims and ideas. Provided you don't conspire to overthrow the state by force of arms it might be thought that we ought to be able to read and write anything we please. But the state will most likely claim that it needs to keep an eye on what we are doing in case words turn into actions. And this argument was particularly pronounced during the period covered by Richard Knott's book when communism was the bogey word. Writers and artists, few of who were active in a direct sense, were closely watched and reported on. It was a situation which led to moments of some amusement when people found themselves subject to surveillance, but also times of stress when authors and painters were blacklisted and unable to obtain work.

Clive Branson and Paul Hogarth both came under suspicion because of their links to the Communist Party. Branson was born into comfortable surroundings – Knott refers to his parents as "conventional upper middle class" – and had a good education. When he left Bedford School he worked in an insurance office, but nursed ambitions to become an artist. His parents eventually agreed to provide him with a small allowance while he became a student at the Slade. He didn't settle at the Slade, finding the teaching uninspiring, and left to follow what I sup-

163

pose would be called a bohemian lifestyle while pursuing a lone path with his artistic aspirations. An inheritance gave him freedom from financial worries, but his eyes had been opened to the poverty and distress evident around him, and he became radicalised. He had met Noreen Browne, who came from a family with aristocratic connections, but was. like Branson, growing more aware of the social and political problems of the period. A short stay in the Independent Labour Party (ILP) led them to the Communist Party.

Paul Hogarth was also destined to become a Party member, but his background was a world away from that of Branson. Born in Kendal, and brought up in Manchester, his father was a small shopkeeper who frowned on his son's interest in books and art. Hogarth attended the Manchester School of Art but left home when he was seventeen, and took an interest in politics. When the Civil War broke out in Spain in 1936 Hogarth was an early volunteer, along with Clive Branson. It was a decision that heightened the interest taken in them by both local police and MI5.

That interest, with files kept on their involvements and movements, lasted for years in Hogarth's case. With regard to Branson, his death in action in Burma in 1944, while serving in the British Army, brought matters to an end, though Noreen Branson's continued membership in the Party meant that she was always likely to be watched. Likewise with Hogarth, and he was discharged from the army after a few months even though he was keen to carry on serving in its ranks. His "premature anti-fascism" was held against him. He resigned from the Party in 1957, but was still denied entry to the USA in 1991 because of his one-time Communist Party membership, which the Americans probably knew about thanks to MI5. It might be seen that it was "quixotically British" when he was awarded an OBE in 1989, and was elected to full membership of the Royal Academy.

Branson and Hogarth are just two of the artists Knott deals with. Others include the now, I would guess, largely forgotten Ralph Bates, a novelist and short-story writer with involvements in Spain, who "was deemed to be a potential Red following the discovery of a copy of Stendhal's *The Red and the Black* in his luggage". When Bates made an appeal for aid for the Spanish Republic at a meeting in Conway Hall it was reported that "the audience appeared to be made up of Jewish and intellectual types of communists".

Throughout his book Knott points out how "personal idiosyncrasies" were often noted in reports about supposed communists. It was said of the painter Julian Trevelyan that "he sometimes wears sandals". George Orwell's inclination to "dress like a bohemian" was registered.. A red bow-tie, or owning a pair of red silk-stockings was enough to arouse suspicion, as was merely being seen in the presence of a known radical. It does occur to me to wonder if simply being interested in the arts was considered a questionable activity in the eyes of many policemen, and therefore worthy of attention? Contact tracing was in operation long before Covid19 arrived on the scene.

George Orwell, despite his background at public school and in the Colonial police, was looked on as potentially dangerous by the security services. The fact that he was firmly anti-communist may have been recognised, but it didn't stop Special Branch and MI5 keeping files on him. He'd fought in Spain, but with a non-communist Marxist organisation, though that difference probably didn't count for much with the authorities. The nuances of left-wing thought confused many people. And his attitude towards the police was suspicious, especially when he said of a campaign to have the Scotland Yard surveillance files destroyed if it looked like the Germans might invade: "Some hope. The police are the very people who would go over to Hitler once they were certain he had won".

Knott does refer to what some commentators see as a blot on Orwell's record of opposition to authority, his list of communists and fellow-travellers that he handed to MI5 in 1949. Excuses can be made for his action. He was in poor health, he was possibly influenced by the attentions of a female MI5 agent, and he was genuinely concerned about what communists were planning in terms of infiltrating various organisations. It's difficult to now understand what the atmosphere was like in the late-1940s and early-1950s. There was a general hostility to communism, especially because of the Cold War and the Russian activities in Eastern Europe. Naming names is not necessarily a practice to be approved of, particularly when some of the names might belong to people who are not in any way dangerous, but we may want to allow for special circumstances at times.

It would be difficult to ascertain just how many lives were affected by the presence in them of the operatives from MI5 and the police. Knott inevitably focuses on some of the better-known names in the arts. But I suspect that others were also caught up in the dragnet, with Special Branch officers from local police forces, and informants, feeding details to MI5. It's highly likely that some of the details had more to do with the social prejudices of the observers rather than any actual activities on the part of the observed. Dressing a little differently, being in-

165

terested in things most people ignored, and not openly participating in what might be called normal day-to-day involvements, were all possible grounds for comment.

Shopkeepers, postmen, and neighbours, would know which newspapers and magazines were read, where mail came from, and how many curious-looking visitors arrived. The authorities tapped telephones and opened letters to obtain information. It's no secret that Communist Party headquarters in London were bugged and burgled. But what about the provinces where the unusual might be more noticeable than in London? Which painter or poet in Birmingham or Manchester had his ideas and opinions scrutinised? The answers might be in the archives, if they still exist, of local Special Branch units, but accessing them might not be easy. And though Knott can come up with evidence of blacklists which prevented some people from working for the BBC and other organisations, I began to wonder how many others were denied employment with local authorities and private companies because the police or MI5 had advised against them being hired?

Such questions are outside the scope of Knott's book, and his focus is on someone like the poet Randall Swingler. There has been a revival of interest in his life and work in recent years, thanks to the efforts of Andy Croft who has written extensively about him. Swingler had served with some distinction in the British Army in the Second World War, but his continued commitment to communism meant that he found it difficult to obtain suitable employment in the post-war years, and so scuffled to earn a living. He had personal problems, which could have been partly caused by the predicament in which he found himself, and collapsed and died in a Soho street when leaving a pub.

Swingler is a valuable case to study when it comes to how easily a writer can disappear from sight. His writing, and his literary involvements in the 1930s and 1940s, seem impressive, but the onset of the Cold War caused him to be almost "airbrushed" out of history. His radicalism counted against him. It's also true that his poems would probably not have found favour with the Movement poets of the 1950s, nor with the so-called "underground" poets of the 1960s. The majority of poets are fated to be forgotten, but Swingler probably suffered from neglect more than most.

There is a dark humour to be gained from the fact that, while MI5 were harassing writers and artists, most of who were never likely to engage in espionage or other illegal activities, more than a few real spies were escaping its attention. The stories of Blunt, Philby, Burgess, Maclean, and more, are too well-known to need noticing here. While Auden, Spender, the artist James Boswell, the composer Alan Bush, the novelist Doris Lessing, and the theatre activist Joan Littlewood, were all regularly investigated, information of value to the Russians was flowing freely from highly-placed sources.

The Secret War Against the Arts can't possibly tell the whole story of how MI5 and Special Branch harassed writers and artists and what the effects were on their work. Did publishers fight shy of poetry by left-wingers and galleries turn down paintings by artists known to be political radicals? Knott says that the Leicester Galleries, his regular outlet, refused to display Paul Hogarth's drawings from a 1956 trip to Africa, "because of their challenging content". It isn't specified what was "challenging" about the drawings, but it's not unreasonable to assume that what they showed was not in accord with official policy about the colonies. MI5 had informed the police in South Africa and Southern Rhodesia that Hogarth and Lessing were on their way. Knott says that both had their luggage searched before they left England. The authorities presumably knew that funds for the trip, which was in connection with a book Lessing was writing and Hogarth illustrating, had been provided by the Soviet News Agency, TASS.

Richard Knott has written a lively and thought-provoking book. It won't be the last word on the subject. He notes that researchers continue to be denied access to some files, and that those that are made available are often heavily-redacted. "National security" is the usual excuse for limits imposed on allowing access to files or redacting them.. The names of informants are blacked out. The state doesn't want us to know too much about how and why we've been watched. Which makes one think about who is being observed now besides suspected terrorists? Police in recent years have infiltrated a variety of protest groups, and the growth of surveillance equipment means that we're all watched a lot of the time. Technology enables investigators to follow our movements, find out what we buy and who we meet. It's no longer a case of a local policeman sending in a report to say that someone has the appearance of a "bohemian" or sports a red tie. MI5 will now already know much more than that.

THE SECRET WAR AGAINST THE ARTS : HOW MI5 TARGETED
LEFT-WING WRITERS & ARTISTS 1936-1956

By Richard Knott

Pen & Sword Books. 226 pages. £25. ISBN 978-1-52677—031-8

LABOR'S MIND: A HISTORY OF WORKING-CLASS INTELLECTUAL LIFE

I never saw my father read a book. He did read a newspaper, *The Daily Herald*, which was pro-Labour in its political leanings, and each Friday there was *Thomson's Weekly*, a magazine which had been started in the 19th century and was aimed at the artisan class. It published articles and puzzles, and what I remember most, a series of short crime stories featuring Inspector Dandy McLean. They intrigued me because they managed to say everything within the confines of a single page. There were a few books in the house, Sunday School prizes and things like that, but my father never touched them.

I mention this because I think he may have been typical in some ways of many men of his age and background. Along with his lack of interest in books, he didn't have any great devotion to political ideas or ideals. He voted Labour at election time, and had what might be called an underdog's distrust of anyone in authority, which I suspect extended to union leaders almost as much as to politicians. He kept clear of policemen and would have nothing to do with priests. The school of hard knocks (twelve years at sea, jobs as a steeplejack, docker, labourer) had been his education beyond the basics the state had provided before the age of fourteen. I can't say that he imparted any great pearls of wisdom about life or anything else to me beyond the observation, as we passed the local prison, that the really big criminals weren't in there. I inherited that notion from him, along with his misgivings about those with power, and their tendency to be corrupted by it.

The observations about my father's life were triggered by reading Tobias Higbie's *Labor's Mind: A History of Working-Class Intellectual Life*. Leaving aside the obvious fact that Higbie is writing about an American situation, and my father lived in England, I couldn't help thinking about how and why some people might come to social and political activism of one kind or another. My father's experiences could have taught him about the iniquities of the capitalist system, but beyond expressing the underdog resentments I referred to earlier, I doubt that he reflected too much on them. Any militancy he nursed was more likely to come out as a desire for shorter hours and higher pay, or as anger against a bullying foreman, not as a demand for an overhaul of the entire system of exploitation.

The people Higbie discusses did have higher aims when they set out on journeys to improve their minds and use their new-found knowledge for political purposes. Unlike Jonathan Rose's *The Intellectual Life of the British Working Classes* (Yale University Press, New Haven, 2001) which took in a wide range of reading material, much of which wasn't in any way concerned to educate readers in terms of socio-political awareness, *Labor's Mind* focuses on activists and what inspired them. It's true that they may have come to reading through an early encounter with popular fiction, and even comics. Reading a writer like Jack Conroy, author of the autobiographical novel, *The Disinherited* (Seven Seas Books, Berlin,1965), brings home how any kind of printed word was seized on by those with an imaginative bent who thought there might be more to life than the drudgery of the coal camps and industrial towns they grew up in.

They soon turned to books and magazines that could offer them wider intellectual fields to explore, and to works that laid down policies and prescriptions for social change and, perhaps, even revolutionary aims. Higbie is keen to emphasise how so many of those he deals with wanted to rise with their class and not out of it. This could lead to problems as, inevitably, their improved educational status frequently gave them the opportunity to move into areas of employment and social mobility not often open to most working-class people. Becoming a teacher or writer, for example, set one apart from people one may have grown up with and who had inclined towards traditional working-class jobs. But the fact of having intellectual interests, in literature, music, art, could in itself be a barrier that was likely to set up a distancing from fellow workers and even family members. I'm talking in terms of the past, but I wonder if the situation is very different now?

In saying that I'm not intending to doubt the sincerity of the people Higbie is concerned to credit with attempting to widen the scope of working-class life. Reading about how the men and women whose lives he chronicles struggled to find their way through to a deeper involvement in intellectual pursuits, while at the same time participating in social and political activities designed to benefit other people, can be very moving. Whatever we may think of the later involvements of someone like William Z. Foster, who became head of the American Communist Party, his early adventures, as recounted in *Pages From a Worker's Life (*International Publishers, New York, 1970), are a chronicle of hard times on land, and at sea, and the development of a political consciousness that grew out of direct experience and not books.

There are other examples of individual lives in Higbie's book, and they are well worth reading, but what a lot of it concerns is the general outline of intellectual activity, as when he refers to the IWW (the Industrial Workers of the World) as "as much an educational organisation as a union", and points to the variety of newspapers it published, some in languages other than English, and their contents, which covered "reports from rank and file organisers, commentary on current events, theoretical debates about unionism, and book reviews".

There were also several colleges where activists could pursue their interest in political theory, practical organising, and cultural matters which mostly connected with social concerns. Art for art's sake was not a priority in these establishments: "There is no one road to freedom. There are roads to freedom. So workers' education will include elementary classes in English, and entertainment for the crowd. But the road for leaders of the people will be straight and hard. Only a few thousand out of the millions will take it. It is different, a new way of life to which the worker is being called".

That statement by a radical journalist, and circulated widely in the labour movement, according to Higbie, might well have summed up how many activists felt. It might also have raised a few doubts in the minds of the anarchist-inclined when it referred to "leaders of the people". The Wobblies had a term, "pie-card artists", which described those who had become "leaders" and union and other bureaucrats, and no longer earned their bread in the factories and fields.

Brookwood Labor College in New York State was probably the most famous of its kind, though several others, such as the Highlander Folk School and the Pacific Coast Labor School, were also in existence in the 1920s and 1930s. They all came under attack from establishment sources, with Brookwood particularly a target of the American Federation of Labor (AFL) because of its alleged radical programmes. The AFL represented various American craft unions and was seen as conservative in its relationship with business interests, and opposed to socialist and communist involvements in labour organisations. But Brookwood did have an impact and helped prepare some later union leaders for their battles with management. The Reuthers, who became well-known for their determination to unionise the auto industry, are perhaps among the more-famous products of Brookwood. It's of interest to note that Nicholas Ray, who was in due course a well-known director in Hollywood, had briefly worked with the drama department at Brookwood.

Not all working-class education revolved around places like Brookwood, and there were lessons to be learned in more-spontaneous and loosely-organised locations. Chicago's Bug House Square was a kind of open forum where proponents of various ideas and organisations gathered to push their various methods for bringing about change of one kind or another. It wasn't all just economic or political, but encompassed a wide selection of cultural interests. Along with the Dil Pickle Club in Chicago, and with a strong Wobbly influence, the hobohemia centred around Bug House Square represented a free-wheeling American radicalism that attracted its fair share of oddballs and eccentrics along with the "serious" activists. It's worth noting that this tradition has been carried on through publications from the Charles H. Kerr Publishing Company which was founded in 1886 and dedicated to circulating a range of radical literature. There could be some value in having a look at Franklin Rosemont's *Joe Hill, the IWW & the Making of a Revolutionary Workingclass Culture* (Charles H.Kerr, Chicago and PM Press, Oakland, 2015) for an insight into what might be called an "alternative" approach to "working-class intellectual life".

One thing that occurs to me in connection with the whole question of "working-class intellectual life" is what frequently appears to be an assumption that it automatically implies a link to radical politics. It sometimes does, I agree, but it may not be true in the majority of cases. We simply don't hear too much about people who, in their activities outside their working lives, have a serious interest in ornithology, Egyptology, and the Peninsular War (I'm using three examples from my own encounters) but who, though possibly being kindly and liberal in their attitudes, have no desire to participate in effecting major changes in the overall structure of society. They will be criticised by radicals because of this, but it's wrong to assume that they don't have an "intellectual life" of any kind. But they are not self-satisfied, just not dissatisfied. Nor do they want to be academics.

There is an interesting short passage in *Labor's Mind* where Higbie mentions Eric Hoffer, the American longshoreman and philosopher. I read Hoffer some years ago and was intrigued by the fact that he'd worked on the San Francisco waterfront and also established a wide reputation for his observations about life, society, and other subjects. As far as I could tell, he had no leanings towards radicalism and, in fact, condemned systems which were likely to result in tyrannies. It seems obvious that Higbie doesn't approve of Hoffer: "Hoffer's analysis of contemporary politics was a balm for political leaders who were eager to defuse the era's volatile social movements. For many radicals, Hoffer's performance was confirmation that prosperity had drained the unionised working class of its fighting spirit". There is perhaps an irony implicit in that assumption. The "fighting spirit" had been, for most

171

people, essentially aimed at modifying working conditions and achieving prosperity, and surely it was inevitable that it would wane when the required situation was arrived at?

Higbie's summing up of the current situation refers to a time when "Universities were one part of a more diffuse field of educational practice that included popular lectures and home study. It was only after World War II that modern universities sought to claim the field of higher education as their exclusive domain". Prior to that "Higher education was also a more diffuse and less bureaucratised social field", which took in open forums, labour colleges, university extension programmes, not to mention personal reading habits, the school of hard knocks, and much more.

I've raised some questions with regard to aspects of *Labor's Mind*, but in general it strikes me as an extremely informative and stimulating book. For readers outside the United States, and perhaps even inside that country, it provides a fascinating glimpse into the lives and activities of many spirited individuals, as well as details of organisations they were involved with. From the *Appeal to Reason* to Julius Haldeman's "Little Blue Books" in the nineteenth century and on to IWW publications and communist-inspired John Reed Clubs in the twentieth, Higbie provides a broad picture of how numerous "working-class intellectual lives" were supported and shaped.

LABOR'S MIND: A HISTORY OF WORKING-CLASS INTELLECTUAL LIFE

By Tobias Higbie

University of Illinois Press. 213 pages. $25. ISBN 978-0-252-08402-7

THE KING OVER THE WATER: A COMPLETE HISTORY OF THE JACOBITES

I suppose for many people the saga of the Jacobites is largely focused around Bonnie Prince Charlie and the invasion of England in 1745, the retreat back to Scotland, and the disaster at Culloden in 1746. But there is a bigger story that spans many years, and is much more complex.

When James II abandoned his throne after William of Orange was "invited" to bring an army and ensure that Protestantism and not Catholicism was the official religion in Britain, he fled to the Continent following the defeat of his supporters at the battles of the Boyne and Aughrim in Ireland. Desmond Seward puts it succinctly: "For many, the moment when the Henrietta sailed for France with King James on board marked the end of Britain's rule by her ancient, natural and rightful line of sovereigns. It was also the beginning of Jacobitism". And he adds: "For all the talk of 'revolution principles,' the real reason why James lost his throne was England's neurotic terror of Catholicism, a terror exploited by ambitious politicians".

It was a fact that not everyone welcomed William and Mary when they arrived in England. Some people had only wanted James's powers limited. And there were plenty of Catholics who were sympathetic to his situation. As early as 1689 James's standard was raised in Scotland by Viscount Dundee and attempts were made to arouse the clans. But it might give an indication of the problems that arose later when we learn that the forces pursuing Dundee were led by General Hugh Mackay, a Highlander. Despite some Jacobite victories, notably at Killiecrankie, the rising quickly collapsed.

The 1707 Act of Union, which brought Scotland into the United Kingdom, was disliked by many Scots: "But if all classes are taken into account, especially the less privileged, then the majority saw the Union as a shabby conspiracy to deny the Scottish people control of their own destiny". And when Queen Anne died in 1714, and an Act of Settlement called for George, Elector of Hanover, to inherit the throne, the fat was in the fire. In Scotland there was dissatisfaction with changes to taxation and other matters that the Act of Union had brought, and sentiment was increasingly inclined towards a revival of the rights of the "Old Pretender", James, and the Stuart dynasty. James fretted and plotted with his French sympathisers and exiles from Ireland and Britain. It would not be long before anger turned into action.

There were pro-Jacobite riots in some parts of England, and the threat of an armed uprising in the West Country. Swift action on the part of the authorities took the sting out of that. But things were different in Scotland and parts of Northern England. The Earl of Mar was busy raising an army that began by seizing Perth and other towns; "Soon after, Mar's troops overran the entire Kingdom of Fife". Across the border, in Northumberland, Jacobite forces gathered and waited for the expected arrival of James with French troops. There was a problem, however, described by Seward as "England's fear of Popery", Catholic Jacobites rallied to the Cause, but Protestant Jacobites held back, wary of lending their support to a would-be King who might impose the Catholic faith on England.

"Whig Britain's saviour" was, according to Seward, "John Campbell, Duke of Argyll, whose family had been sworn enemies of the Stuarts for generations". He had assembled a relatively small force of around 3,000 men and met Mar's much-superior army (in terms of numbers) at Sheriffmuir, north of Sterling. Argyll did have one advantage. He had experience of warfare, having fought at Malplaquet during the War of the Spanish Succession. In the end the battle petered out, Mar failing to follow up on earlier achievements by his men, and Argyll having to withdraw, though in good order, because his troops had been badly mauled when charged by the Jacobites. Both sides claimed a victory.

Other Jacobites under General Thomas Forster had moved into England and reached Preston in Lancashire, a county known as the most Catholic in England. They had encountered little resistance as they moved down through Carlisle, Kendal, and Lancaster, and they picked up recruits from among the local Catholic population. Seward says that locals almost doubled the Jacobite forces to about 2,500. The difficulty was that they were untrained and poorly armed. When faced with regular troops under Major-General Charles Wills they soon gave way, though the Highlanders put up a stiff resistance. But reinforcements arrived to bolster the Government forces, and Forster, who seems to have lost his nerve when the fighting started, contacted Wills to negotiate a surrender. Many of the Highlanders wanted to battle their way out of the town but were persuaded to lay down their arms. Had they been allowed to fight as they wished to, it's more than probable they could have defeated Wills, who appears to have been an incompetent commander issuing orders that led to heavy casualties among his men.

James had landed in Scotland, but the French troops he had promised to bring with him never materialised. The Jacobite army had shrunk in size, and it didn't endear itself to the local people when it burned down houses, barns, stables, etc., in a "scorched earth" policy designed to deny any kind of succour to advancing Government forces. Houses were looted and animals stolen, while the locals were left to survive as best they could in the bleak, winter landscape. It was the beginning of the end for James and he was soon spirited away on a ship bound for France. As for his army, it disintegrated as men slipped into the hills, or found ways of getting to the Continent. Seward says: "The Fifteen ended in disaster; aborted in the West Country, crushed in Lancashire, broken in Scotland".

It was to be another thirty years before a determined armed attempt to re-establish a Stuart on the throne took place. That isn't to say that there weren't earlier plots and plans to invade, using French, Swedish, and Spanish soldiers to back up the Jacobites in Scotland, Ireland, and England. James established a court in Avignon, which soon grew to "500 people, counting servants, ragged refugees, English, Scots and Irish, who included peers and clan chieftains". In 1719 three hundred Spanish troops landed at Lewis and were billeted in Stornoway. More were supposed to be on the way, but storms had dispersed the fleet carrying them. When a call went out for the clans to gather in support of the Spanish, only 1500 men responded. News then came that Major-General Wightman was marching to confront the Jacobites. After a short fight the clansmen retreated into the mountains and headed for home. The Spanish soldiers remained on the battlefield, but were eventually persuaded to surrender. It was yet another somewhat chaotic end to a scheme designed to promote the Stuart cause.

It's impossible for me to go into detail about all the various Jacobite plots and how they were betrayed, or came to nothing because assured military support never arrived. Seward does a good job of telling the stories in a readable fashion. George continued to be unpopular, and not only in Scotland and Ireland. Seward perhaps betrays his partiality for the Stuarts in his description of him arriving at a theatre: "a line of carriages drew up outside, from the first of which alighted a tubby little man of about sixty, with two remarkably ugly women in late middle-age, one tall and thin, and the other enormously fat. It was George with his concubines".

That George and his supporters continued to be wary of the Jacobites at home and abroad was obvious. They had need to. In 1744 it was reported that 10,000 French troops had assembled and were due to embark for a landing in England which would be accompanied by a rising among the British Jacobites. James's son, Charles, was to leave for London once the invasion was successful, and would be appointed Regent until his father arrived to be crowned King. Unfortunately, the elements intervened once again, and a violent storm damaged many of the ships in the fleet, with the result that the French government called off the invasion. It was, perhaps, not a complete failure, Seward being of the opinion that "it helped to inspire the Forty-Five".

Another event which possibly contributed to instilling a belief that a rising could succeed was the French victory over a combined force of British, Hanoverian and Austrian troops at Fontenoy. The commander of the British soldiers was the Duke of Cumberland, George II's youngest son. Serving on the French side were the men of the Irish Brigade, exiles from their own land who had enlisted with the French. It was their gallantry that won the day at Fontenoy, and it acted as a catalyst, "inspiring Irishmen abroad to make every effort to help the Prince of Wales regain his father's throne".

Charles landed in Scotland on the 23rd July, 1745. There was an initial reluctance on the part of the clans to rally to his flag. The reason was that, as had happened in the past, he had arrived minus the French troops that everyone expected him to bring. But he entered Edinburgh without opposition in September, and soon the Jacobites had a stunning victory to their credit when they decimated a Government army under the command of Lieutenant-General Sir John Cope at Prestonpans. He escaped with some of his cavalry but left the majority of his men either dead (300) or as prisoners (1,500). Seward refers to the popular song, "Hey, Johnny Cope, are ye wauking yet?" which mocked the leader of the Government forces. The Jacobites suffered only thirty killed.

"Prestonpans was the spectacular victory the Cause needed. Recruits flooded in", says Seward. The army soon reached around 13,500, made up of 6,750 Highlanders, 5,400 Lowlanders, 830 Irish, and 300 English. This looks like a healthy figure, but Seward says that the proportion of Scots who came out was less than it was in 1715. Morale among the Jacobites was raised when several French ships turned up with arms and money. A decision was then taken, though not without some argument, to move into England through Carlisle. It was expected that, as the Jacobites came into Carlisle and down through Lancaster, Preston, and Manchester, local sympathisers would join them. But few did. There were expressions of support, but not many volunteers for the Prince's army. People were wary of being seen to be committed to a Cause that might not carry the day. The harsh punishments meted out after the failure of the '15 still lingered in their minds.

The Jacobites reached Derby on the 4th December, 1745, but with their lines of supply and communication over-extended, and the Duke of Cumberland organising forces to move against them, a decision was taken to return to Scotland. Charles wanted to carry on advancing towards London. But some of the clan chiefs were worried about the prospects of having to fight Cumberland and, even if they defeated him, then facing up to the troops defending the English capital. It has always been debated whether or not the Jacobites could have taken London had they carried on.

Once back in Scotland the Jacobites could still function efficiently enough to defeat government forces at Falkirk, but desertions from the ranks, and disagreements among the officers, weakened the army. By the time they faced Cumberland at Culloden they were disorganised, and in bad shape (the troops hadn't been fed properly for several days, and were wet and in generally poor condition). Many of them fought bravely, despite their dismal situation and lack of any sort of inspired leadership, but defeat was inevitable. Seward gives a harrowing account of how the Jacobite wounded were bayoneted and bludgeoned to death as they lay on the battlefield. Later, in the immediate aftermath of the battle, and for months after, there was to be little pity shown to the "rebels" as they were hunted down, their property seized, houses burned, and their owners often driven into exile. I think it's worth noting that Cumberland's army included Scottish regiments. Things were never clearcut in Scotland, nor was it ever a simple case of Highlanders versus Lowlanders.

Charles escaped after adventures that have become the stuff of legend. I grew up knowing stories about Flora MacDonald and the way she helped him get away. But his Cause never again prospered, though various people still attempted to come up with schemes to launch an invasion or foment a rising. Jacobites still gathered in secret and toasted the King over the Water. There is an interesting proposition by Seward that it was not Culloden that finally put paid to hopes of a Stuart revival, but the naval battle of Quiberon Bay when a French fleet that was sailing to provide escorts for an invasion force was soundly beaten by the Royal Navy.

As for Charles, his later years were sad ones. A chronic and abusive alcoholic he drifted around the Continent, looked after by those who could tolerate him. Seward describes him as "the wreck who had once been Europe's hero". He died in 1788.

The King Over the Water tells a fascinating story full of heroes and villains, and colourful characters and spirited ladies. It is "popular history" at its best, which means that it is clearly written and avoids academic jargon. There are ample notes and a useful bibliography. Seward also provides a short guide to novels about Jacobitism by the likes of Sir Walter Scott, Robert Louis Stevenson, John Buchan, and a few others.

THE KING OVER THE WATER: A COMPLETE HISTORY OF THE JACOBITES

By Desmond Seward

Birlinn Limited. 406 pages. £25. ISBN 978-1-78027-606-9

THE IRISH WAR OF INDEPENDENCE AND CIVIL WAR

The first act of the Irish War of Independence occurred on the 21st January 1919, when two members of the Royal Irish Constabulary (RIC) escorting a delivery of gelignite to a quarry were killed by gunmen from the Irish Republican Army (IRA), "the name now applied to the older paramilitary Irish Volunteers (the nationalist militia originally founded in 1913 in support of home rule)". The act was prophetic. Policemen were to become among the main targets during the War, with around 350 being killed and many injured.

The War was inevitable following the events of Easter 1916, and the abandonment of home rule which, prior to 1914, had been widely welcomed in the South, but vigorously opposed in the north. After 1916, support for Sinn Féin grew rapidly, and when elections took place in December 1918, the party won 73 out of Ireland's 105 Westminster Seats. Sinn Féin was the political wing of the IRA. The die was cast because more people were now in favour of independence rather than home rule. And the situation was exacerbated when, in 1920, "Ireland was partitioned into two regions, in a move that primarily catered to Ulster unionists". I'm shortcutting the convoluted politics of Ireland during this period. In effect, they involved three interested groups: the British government, Sinn Féin/IRA, and the new Belfast parliament.

The IRA did not have the manpower or the armaments to conduct a military operation of any size, and consequently adopted a system of guerrilla warfare: "The ambushes and assassinations that were the IRA's stock in trade (as advocated in particular by Michael Collins, another 1916 veteran who became one of the principal leaders of the independence movement) posed problems for British forces accustomed to the open warfare of the 'Great War'".

Sinn Féin also used a form of "guerrilla government" to undermine British rule in Ireland: "They established arbitration courts to defuse local disputes (especially over land) and administer such justice as they could, with the IRA sometimes acting as police. By 1920 Sinn Féin had taken over most of the local authorities in the country and proved remarkably successful at running the machinery of local government themselves". Together with determined activity on the part of the IRA, it caused the British authorities to bring in more and more repressive legislation. When this impacted on local people it increased support for the militants. There is an interesting essay, "Smoking gun? British government policy and RIC reprisals, summer 1920", which discusses the level of official awareness of targeted assassinations of known-IRA members. It includes a reproduction of a letter written by "one of the most senior officers of the RIC and addressed to one of the most influential civil servants in Dublin Castle" which "reveals a disturbing policy of assassination sanctioned by the highest level of the British government in Ireland".

It needs to be pointed out that targeted assassinations were practised by both sides during the conflict. The IRA, in an operation organised by Michael Collins, killed twelve British intelligence officers, identified as such by an informant in Dublin Castle, in a single day in November 1920. And individual policemen, known for their enthusiasm in harassing Republicans, were singled out for killing. "Oh God, what did I do to deserve this?": The Life and death of Detective Sergeant John Barton" is one example, and covered in an essay by Padraig Yeates. Some people, and certainly his assassins at the time, would most likely have said that he got what he deserved. An efficient policeman, Barton, a member of the Dublin Metropolitan Police (DMP), had identified leading rebels among those who surrendered in 1916. And before that he had been especially active in arresting members of Irish Transport and General Workers Union (ITGWU) during the 1913 strike and lockout.

With the police suffering quite heavy losses, many of them resigning as their families were ostracised by the wider community, and recruitment falling, it became necessary to bolster them in some way. The notorious Black and Tans were the answer. I think most people, even those with only a sketchy awareness of Irish history, will have heard the term at one time or another. In actual fact, there were two units formed from recruits who responded to advertisements for men to enrol in support of the police. The Black and Tans were recruited from ex-soldiers who had served in the British Army as non-commissioned officers and other ranks, while the Auxiliaries were recruited from ex-officers. The Black and Tans were so named because their uniforms were a mixture of khaki and the dark bottle-green of the RIC. They were para-militaries and were ostensibly under the control of the police. The Auxiliaries were identifiable because of the tam-o-shanters they wore, and had a greater degree of autonomy. The reputation of both groups was not only low in Irish eyes. In Britain many people, when reports of Black and Tans and Auxiliaries terrorising villagers started to circulate, began to ask questions about what they were doing. My father, who served in the Royal Navy from 1913 to 1925, had encountered them while ashore in Cork, and had nothing good to say on their behalf.

Both units were noted for their harsh methods of arrest and interrogation, and numerous acts of violence were attributed to them. Among the most notorious was the burning of Cork. This was a reprisal raid in response to the ambush of an Auxiliary patrol which left sixteen of them dead. One man who was wounded seems to have escaped. An IRA unit led by a noted commander, Tom Barry (who had previously served in the British Army), was responsible for the ambush, the nature of which has been a matter for argument. There were allegations that some of the Auxiliaries attempted to surrender, but were shot. In response, it was said that the surrender was simply a ruse to draw the IRA men out of their cover and they were then fired on. The IRA volunteers returned fire and killed all the Auxiliaries. A more-complete account of the ambush can be found in Charles Townshend's *The Republic: The Fight for Irish Independence 1918-1923* (Allen Lane, London, 2013).

Peace negotiations between the British government and Sinn Féin/IRA got underway, and an Anglo-Irish Treaty was signed in 1921. It wasn't popular among many IRA activists and Eamon De Valera was especially opposed to certain of its clauses. It allowed for an Irish Free State with Dominion status in the British Empire, and required an oath of allegiance to the Crown. It's a subject that has lent itself to much debate over the years. Michael Collins led the Irish deputation during the negotiations, and he and his team eventually signed the Treaty. It was, they said, the best deal they could get in the circumstances. The alternative was a continuation of the war, with Britain sending even more troops to Ireland. And it was probable that the IRA, with losses of men and arms affecting its operational capabilities, might not have been able to sustain its activities to any effective degree.

It was not a surprise when militant members of the IRA refused to accept the Treaty terms. They occupied buildings in Dublin, in particular the Four Courts. A stand-off ensued until the British Government, concerned that law and order was breaking down in Ireland, threatened to move back in to bring the situation to a conclusion. The new government had to be shown to be capable of acting on its own initiative if it was not to lose credibility. With only a small, poorly equipped army at its disposal it borrowed artillery from the British, and commenced shelling the Four Courts on the 28th June 1922. The Civil War was underway and was to last until April 1923.

The Civil War, like the War of Independence, was largely a matter of small actions involving limited numbers of participants on both sides. Guerrilla warfare was largely the order of the day. Neither side was in a position to field large numbers of well-equipped, trained troops. There were problems with discipline among the Pro-Treaty forces, and even a reluctance to fire on anti-Treaty volunteers. The situation had been simpler when the enemy was obvious, but a Civil War brought up the uncomfortable fact that one might have to kill one's fellow-countrymen, and possibly even people one had fought alongside during the War of Independence.

That didn't stop the new Government acting in a way that outstripped anything the British had done. Its security was threatened and its authority not yet certain. Draconian measures meant that anyone caught with a gun could be executed. There was the case of Erskine Childers who had a miniature pistol (given to him as a present by Michael Collins) in his possession when arrested. He was sentenced to death, a decision many people thought was due to his being a notable anti-Treaty activist, albeit not of the fighting kind. And there were incidents when captured IRA men were given short shrift and executed on the spot. Townshend says that numerous assassinations of known republicans were carried out. An especially savage reprisal took place when four pro-Treaty soldiers were killed by a booby-trap in a dugout they were searching. Nine anti-Treaty prisoners were brought from prison, tied together in a circle, and a mine exploded in their midst. Eight died, and one man escaped with only minor injuries. It all came to an end when the IRA, its men and resources exhausted, laid down its arms.

I've taken certain details from Charles Townshend's book in order to provide some sort of continuity in the story of the War of Independence and the Civil War. The book under review isn't a chronological history of events, and is instead a collection of short essays on different aspects of the two wars. And it explores what might be called several little-known areas of activity. For example, there is the Italian connection. This revolved around the Italian adventurer, Gabriel D'Annunzio, who had led a march on the disputed port of Fiume on the Adriatic coast. He offered to help the IRA during the War of Independence with supplies of arms and ammunition. It all came to nothing when Michael Collins realised that there was little chance of a vessel loaded with guns avoiding the attention of Royal Navy warships patrolling off the coast of Ireland.

There is also an intriguing piece about the 1922 postal strike which was seen by the government as a threat to its authority. Strikebreakers were brought in and both police and army were forceful in their attacks on pickets. There is an irony in the fact that the strikers were treated in a manner reminiscent of what workers experienced during the strike and lockout in 1913. Governments change, but people in power continue to behave in the same way.

Another interesting essay looks at the campaign to close cinemas that the IRA carried out during the Civil War. It was part of their aim to disrupt everyday life. And, as a piece of social history, an intriguing piece looks at "the Templemore Miracles" when a local man claimed to have experienced "Marian apparitions" and religious statues in the area were said to have shed tears of blood. This happened shortly after soldiers from the Northamptonshire Regiment had stormed into the village, looting and burning, following the killing of an RIC officer by the IRA. Thousands of people flocked to Templemore to witness the miracles.

An essay on how the IRA dealt with people they suspected of passing information to the British highllghts the case of Mrs Maria Lyndsay who was executed for allegedly informing the British Army of a planned ambush. Five IRA Volunteers were captured and, after being court martialled, were executed. The IRA had told the British that if the men were executed they would kill her, which they did. An interesting point is raised here. A Catholic priest had also been involved but no action was taken against him: "Although the killing of women was a taboo rarely broken, killing a clergyman of any denomination would have been even more controversial, and although the IRA knew of several clergymen, both Catholic and Protestant, who had gathered intelligence for the British, none of them were executed".

As noted, *The Irish War of Independence and Civil War* does not claim to offer a strict chronological account of those events. But what it does provide are some fascinating short essays on lesser-known situations and personalities arising out of the conflicts. As such, it should be of interest to anyone who wants to know more about what happened in Ireland a hundred or so years ago. The book is illustrated and has a short bibliography.

THE IRISH WAR OF INDEPENDENCE AND CIVIL WAR

Edited by John Gibney

Pen & Sword. 162 pages. £14.99. ISBN 978-152675-798-2

DOWN IN THE VALLEY : SOME WRITERS FROM SOUTH WALES

In 1921 Sir Alfred Zimmerman, writing about his impressions of Wales, thought that there wasn't one Wales but three – "There is Welsh Wales; there is industrial or, as I sometimes think of it, American Wales; and there is upper class or English Wales". He was of the opinion that: "These three represent different types and different traditions". He went on to say that: "Of American Wales, the Wales of the coalfield and the industrial working class......let me only say......for the benefit of those who are apt to sneer at South Wales as a 'storm centre', what a joy it has been to pass a too fleeting and infrequent weekend among men and women who really care for ideas and love the search for truth......"

It's not my intention to discuss what happened in terms of the decline of the coal industry and the resultant effects on South Wales communities. They were obviously devastating. What I'm concerned to do in this essay is to draw attention to several writers who grew up in "American Wales" and reflected aspects of it in their novels and poems. Raymond Williams, writing in *The London Review of Books* in the 1980s, was of the opinion that: "the industrial Welsh by-passed the muted tones of English culture for their version of the brash expansiveness of North Americans....From Welsh-language Wales this was often seen ....as a vulgar, Anglicised betrayal of 'Welshness'. Yet Anglicised, at least, it was not. The work of the English-language writers of industrial South Wales is unmistakeably indigenous; its English in tone and rhythm is not an English literary style......In these writers and in the everyday speech of the valleys.....a distinctive culture is using that diverse and flexible language for its own unmistakeably native writing and speech".

It might be asked why, besides the reference to the "brash expansiveness of North Americans", it was thought that South Wales had some similarities to the United States. I would guess that the rapid industrialisation in South Wales in the late-19th century reminded people of what happened in America when the Civil War ended. Mines and mills developed and towns and villages grew up around them. People moved into these areas, looking for work, and along with them came social problems. Conditions in the coalfields were harsh and class conflict was a part of everyday life. There may not have been violence in South Wales of a kind comparable to American industrial relations, but strikes and other forms of protest were always present. And the mixture fed into the novels and poems that were produced by writers who had direct experience of life in "American Wales".

Lewis Jones wrote two novels before his untimely death in 1939. The first, *Cwmardy*, was published in 1937, and the second, *We Live*, in 1939. Jones was born in 1897 and went to work when he was twelve in the Cambrian Combine Colliery. He was present when there was a strike in 1910/11 which led to a riot in Tonypandy and troops being called in to aid police. A miner died during the riot, possibly from being clubbed on the head by a policeman, but there doesn't appear to be any evidence to support allegations of miners being shot. It's probable that the events in Tonypandy became confused with an incident in Llanelli in 1911 when troops did fire on striking railwaymen, causing two fatalities. Lewis Jones has a riot at the centre of *Cwmardy* in which several miners are shot by soldiers, but it is fiction and has no real basis in fact.

The 1911 strikes took place against a background of the spread of syndicalist ideas, advocating direct action and workers' control, in union circles, and especially among members of the South Wales Miners' Federation (the Fed, as it was popularly known) and activists like Noah Ablett. He was one of the driving forces behind a pamphlet, *The Miners' Next Step,* which circulated in the coalfields and appealed to union activists, if not the great mass of union members. There have always been differing views about how many people actually read the pamphlet. Most miners were more than likely to have been interested in the usual reasons for strikes – shorter hours, better pay, working conditions, and other practical measures - than in theories about syndicalism.

Jones's *We Live* continued the story of life in the valleys and the struggle to survive during the dark days of the Depression. But Jones himself had almost burnt out. He had been blacklisted from the mines, joined the Communist Party in the early-1920s, and involved himself in local politics. He was active in the Unemployed Workers Movement in the 1930s and led several Hunger Marches from South Wales to London. When he died of a heart attack in 1939 it was following a day when he was said to have made around thirty or so speeches in support of the Spanish Republic.

Both of Jones's novels follow a traditional narrative pattern, and there is nothing to indicate that he may have been influenced by any of the shifts in prose styles – Hemingway or James Joyce, to call on two examples - in the 1920s. I would guess that what he had to say was of more importance to him than any stylistic innovations. The narrative drive is straightforward, and when the characters speak they do so in a way that Jones intended to represent the common parlance of the everyday. It may be that contemporary readers would find the writing slow, with its attention to detail, but it has a cumulative power and pulls the reader into the story in an emphatic way.

Jones had lived through the turbulence of the 1920s when, in 1926, the General Strike took place, and after it was called off the miners stayed out for several more months. So had Idris Davies. He was born in 1905 in Rhymney and left school when he was fourteen to go down the pit. He was injured in 1926, losing a finger, and the fact of the strike and his doubtful future prospects as a miner, encouraged him to train to be a teacher. In 1932 he was teaching in a London primary school and publishing poems in magazines. One of them, "The Bells of Rhymney", was set to music and became popular among folk-singers. There are recordings of it by Pete Seeger and others. In the early 1940s he began writing *The Angry Summer: A Poem of 1926*, a book-length work which Faber published in 1943.

It comprises what are, in effect, fifty short but linked poems. A poem-sequence, in other words. The opening lines of the first poem begin to set the scene: "Now it is May among the mountains,/Days for speeches in the valley towns", and it then moves through the various stages of the miners' bitter struggle as their spokesmen "plead and plan and fight/For those who toil without a name/And pass into the night". There isn't what might be called a set scheme to the structure of each poem. Some are longer than others, some have a rhyming pattern, some not. And though the thread running through them all is the strike, and its consequences in terms of poverty and hunger, there is still time for occasional flights of fancy and moments of romance: "Hywel and Olwen lie warm in the fern/With passionate mouth on mouth/And the lights in the valley twinkle and turn/And the moon climbs up from the south".

The strike was lost and the miners driven back to work, apart from those who had been prominent in picketing and general agitation and found that jobs in the mines were no longer available to them. Idris Davies continued to write and publish poetry. His collection, *Tonypandy and Other Poems,* was published by Faber in 1945. It's worth noting that T.S. Eliot, who hardly shared Davies's social and political views, spoke highly of his work, and said that it was: "The best poetic document I know about a particular epoch in a particular place". Sadly, Davies died of cancer in 1953.

The works by Lewis Jones and Idris Davies that I've looked at so far leave one in no doubt that the events of the 1920s and 1930s had a major effect on life in South Wales, particularly among the mining communities. And unemployment and poverty are always present in Gwyn Thomas's two short novels, *The Alone to the Alone* and *The Dark Philosophers*. But there is an element of humour present at all times in the storytelling, The principal characters around which the narratives revolve are survivors and determined to preserve their humanity and individuality come what may.

Thomas was born in 1913, one of twelve children fathered by a miner who was often unemployed. That fact may have been in his mind when it's said of a character in one of his novels who has been out of work for years, but has several daughters, that love-making is just a way of keeping warm in a house without heating of any kind. Thanks to scholarships, one of them from the miners' union, Thomas managed to get to university and to study in Spain, but when he graduated and returned to Wales he was without work for long periods. He eventually obtained employment in the educational system and taught at Barry Grammar School for some years.

It was his wife who pushed him into publishing some of the writings he'd been doing. In 1946 the short novel, *The Dark Philosophers,* appeared in print, to be followed in 1947 by *The Alone to the Alone.* Both feature the same central characters, a group of four unemployed middle-aged men who sit on a wall and exchange ideas about life, politics, and whatever else crops up during their conversations. Their politics are never clearly defined, but all seem to be ex-miners and lean to the left, if not in any clearly-specified fashion. There is some talk of syndicalism, which is interesting because Thomas's novels are both set in the 1930s and, aside from the Labour Party, many activists by then chose to relate to the Communist Party. But direct action, and nationalisation, if not outright workers' control of the mines, were potent factors in the policies of the FED.

The four men are by nature inclined to be sympathetic towards anyone they consider downtrodden, so when they encounter Eurona, whose father Morris is feckless and workshy, they decide to help her break away from the confines of The Terraces, the rows of small houses that wind their up the hillsides near the mine. As one of the men explains: "These terraces were put up so that people could eat and breed in between shifts and working in the pits. They were not put up with any notion of giving the voters a full and happy life".

187

Their efforts are hampered by the fact that Eurona has taken a fancy to Rollo, a young man with prospects. He has a job as a bus conductor so stands out in a world where almost everyone else is unemployed. He also looks down on those without a job and is an admirer of Oswald Mosley's fascist organisation. But the men persevere, guiding Eurona through the pitfalls of dealing with the Assistance Board and local charities which might give her money to buy clothes that will make her presentable to prospective employers. The chaos that ensues as various schemes come unstuck (the men are not against breaking a few rules when necessary) is humorously dealt with. But although humour is used adroitly we are always aware that in the background there lurks hunger. And poverty of both a physical and mental kind.

The slightly shorter *The Dark Philosophers* again has the four men at the centre of the story, with their well-meaning efforts directed towards helping two young people find true love. But standing in the way is the Reverend Emmanuel, a popular preacher who was at one time a radical, but has been seduced by the attentions of civic leaders and mine bosses into speaking out against strikes and social protest generally. The four friends have by this time obtained jobs, though not in the mines. The situation is complicated because the young woman in question admires Emmanuel, and he has obvious designs on her virginity. There is a comic factor at work, but as in *The Alone to the Alone* the stark social conditions are always present. The men are rough-and-ready types, but "sometimes showed the wisdom that springs up in the heart of any man who has seen a lot of hunger and hates it, and has met a lot of oppressive nuisances and despises them".

Gwyn Thomas went on to become a reasonably well-known writer and produced novels, short stories, and plays for the theatre, as well as radio and television. He was also something of a media personality on programmes such as "The Brains Trust" and "Tonight". But he's perhaps best-remembered now as the author of the two books I've referred to, and a historical novel, *All Things Betray Thee*. It might be relevant to quote what he thought about the role of humour when he said that the valley where he grew up had been "flung together in a series of swift, large immigrations and, like that other great creation of multitudes on the move, the East Side of New York, it produced a vivid, bright and often outrageous humour". It might also be worth taking note of his comment that "Places like the Rhondda were parts of America that never managed to get to the boat".

The Welsh academic, Dai Smith, has written perceptively about Gwyn Thomas and rightly pointed out how Americans responded more to

Thomas's work than did English critics who "mostly saw a stage-army of Welsh comic figures". In America, Nelson Algren, Norman Rosten, Howard Fast, and Maxwell Geismar spoke positively about Thomas's fiction in which they acknowledged how the humour was often a form of social criticism. It was like so much Jewish writing, a "survival humour". Thomas died in 1981.

I have obviously been very selective in my choice of Welsh writers. They were out of a time and a place that is now long gone. Others will point to different writers as representative of Welsh literature, and perhaps play down my focus on South Wales and its industrial legacy. But it seems to me that the books I've dealt with have all withstood reprinting in recent year not only because they provide vivid pictures of their society, but also because of the quality of the writing. Fashions in literature come and go, but the genuine will remain.

BIBLIOGRAPHICAL NOTE

Cwmardy by Lewis Jones. Parthian, Cardigan, 2006

We Live by Lewis Jones. Parthian, Cardigan, 2006

The Angry Summer : A Poem of 1926 by Idris Davies. University of Wales Press, Cardiff, 1993

The Alone to the Alone with *The Dark Philosophers* by Gwyn Thomas. Golden Grove Editions, Carmarthen, 1998

Aneurin Bevan and the World of South Wales by Dai Smith. University of Wales Press, Cardiff, 1993

In the Frame : Memory in Society 1910 to 2010 by Dai Smith. Parthian, Cardigan, 2010

Climbing Mount Sinai : Noah Ablett 1883-1935 by Robert Turnbull. Socialist History Society, London, 2017

British Syndicalism 1900-1914 by Bob Holton. Pluto Press, London, 1976

The Fed : History of the South Wales Miners in the Twentieth Century by Hywel Francis and Dai Smith. Lawrence & Wishart, London, 1980

Dockers and Detectives: Popular Reading and Popular Writing by Ken Worpole. Verso, London, 1983

THE STREETS OF EUROPE : THE SIGHTS, SOUNDS & SMELLS THAT SHAPED ITS GREAT CITIES

It was André Breton who said "The street - the only valid field of experience", a debatable proposition, perhaps, but not one that can be easily dismissed. And I think of the man who claimed that two things had destroyed sociability in much of the United States – cars and television, both serving to isolate people from each other by keeping them off the streets. I also recall how, when I was growing up in England in the 1940s, the street was the focal point of activity. It offered a form of freedom from the restrictions imposed by the presence of several others (mother, father, a brother, two sisters) in cramped living conditions. The street was where I met my friends and planned what to do next.

Ladd's survey looks at four major cities – London, Paris, Berlin, Vienna - and it primarily deals with them in the nineteenth century, though he does delve back into the eighteenth, and forward into the twentieth, to indicate how various social, architectural, political and other developments were carried out that now determine how we experience contemporary life. I live near a city that arose out of the industrial revolution. When I visit it I'm aware of its past, despite the changes that have been made over the years.

Ladd says: "The quintessential place of crowds and strangers, of stimulations and surprises, is the city street, especially in the enclosed form it developed up to the nineteenth century. There has been a recent revival of interest in this kind of street, as cities across the world have proclaimed or pursued a resurgence of street life. Civic leaders hope to recover something that was lost during the twentieth century when street life was deliberately impoverished or abandoned". Pedestrianised areas have appeared in many cities and towns, and encourage citizens to stroll and not worry about cars, though they increasingly have to be wary of cyclists.

Sometimes the "destruction" of street life came about because older concentrations of housing were demolished for health and hygiene reasons and people moved into high-rise flats or out to estates away from city centres. And the determination to drive roads of one sort or another through urban areas to facilitate the faster movement of traffic also played its part. To be fair, there may be several suggestions that can be made about why established systems of streets were destroyed. But I suspect that the question of traffic flow will loom large in any objective study. Ladd has a couple of quotes relating to Berlin which seem apt. A 1910 proclamation by the chief of police said "the street is exclusively for traffic". And a later planning document stated: "And the pedestrian? The new street has no place for unreconstructed Neanderthals. Anyone who has a destination should be sitting in a car. Anyone who doesn't is on a stroll and should proceed immediately to the nearest park".

When Robert Moses pushed his freeways through Manhattan it was said that, as well as the need to quicken traffic flow, there was a social aim to drive out the old garment industries. When the working-class women from the sweatshops spilled out to socialise and window-shop at lunchtime it disturbed the shop-owners and the well-to-do who patronised their establishments. It may have been a minor consideration for Moses and his planners, and some people will dispute that it ever became one, but it seems possible in my view. Tidying up towns and cities to make them attractive to visitors and shoppers with money to spend happens everywhere. Like gentrification it's a sign to the impoverished or down-and-out to stay away.

It is stressed by Ladd that the move towards turning streets into highways largely designed for traffic got underway before the nineteenth century. Horse-drawn carriages, often driven to speed, were a fixture in London and Paris in the eighteenth century. As streets then rarely had any form of pavements for pedestrians to make their way from one place to another, they were frequently at risk of being run down or crushed as they huddled against buildings for safety. The idea that streets were places where people could socialise became harder to sustain. In some ways the authorities possibly welcomed methods that helped to disperse people and keep them hurrying. Crowds could be dangerous, and as Ladd puts it, were sources of "vitality or worry". Everyone has heard that Haussmann designed his boulevards partly to give troops and police easier access for crowd control.

Streets, of course, were never free of danger from other sources besides coaches, or cars when the latter started to appear. Criminals thrived in crowds, where the opportunities for pick-pocketing, selling poorly-produced goods, and operating crooked deals of one kind or another, were more likely to prosper than in quieter locations. Cities after dark were, and still are, prone to violence, whether from opportunistic individuals looking for the lone pedestrian to rob, or from street gangs intent not only on robbery but also a chance to indulge in their taste for rough-handling of anyone they encountered. And worse when it came to women.

The founding of police forces in major urban centres was meant to act as a curb on crime. Prior to their existence it was often left to poorly-paid night-watchmen and the like to try to prevent the excesses of both criminals and high-spirited and usually drunken young men who thought it good fun to vandalise street furniture, such as it existed. Eighteenth and nineteenth century cities were not noted for the provision of waste bins and too many street lights. Pierce Egan's 1821 *Life in London* chronicled the "rambles and sprees" of Jerry Hawthorn, Corinthian Tom, and Bob Logic the Oxonian, as they toured the city, looking for adventures among high and low society.

Improvements in public hygiene did begin to change the sights and smells of cities. The "Great Stink" of 1858 when a hot summer almost caused the River Thames to dry up is a case in point. It had long been used as a dumping ground for all kinds of waste, and that, combined with "the outflow from the growing number of new water closets", produced a smell that was so strong that politicians in Parliament "suddenly proved eager to expedite the construction of a comprehensive sewer system". Other cities such as Berlin and Vienna soon followed with improved drainage facilities.

Public toilets were "a rarity in every city in 1800", though "makeshift urinals" could be found in parts of London. Without them, people living or working on the streets were forced to urinate or defecate in an alleyway or any other suitable spot. Ladd suggests that "new standards of privacy and public hygiene" were largely responsible for the provision of public toilets, though some people spoke against them because they were seen as "places of gay male sexual encounters". Was there substance in such allegations? Ladd says that "anti-gay hysteria" may have been partly responsible, but adds that "scholars who have combed through nineteenth-century police records confirm that the nexus was a real one".

The closure of so many public toilets in more-recent years may have had something to do with their being used for male assignations, but from my own observations working in a local authority environmental health department for a time, economics mainly brought about decisions to shut them down. The money just wasn't available to employ staff to inspect and clean them. Whatever the reason they are now often sadly lacking in most towns and cities. There may be some humour in the fact that a man might have to revert to the old practice of finding a quiet back-alley if he's caught short on the street. As for women, as usual they are sure to be disadvantaged even more than the men.

Organised and comprehensive public transport systems were largely an invention of the nineteenth-century, whether with private or public funding. And, at least in cities and major towns, they seem to continue to function reasonably efficiently for the most part. My personal experiences of visiting different European cities convince me that one can get around quite well without a car. There are opponents of public transport, those who claim that anyone on a bus or tram is probably some sort of failure who can't afford a car. And someone with that kind of attitude would no doubt resent having to share a seat with a stranger who might not be wearing very clean clothes. Ladd uses illustrations by Daumier in his book, one of which shows people on an omnibus. One of them appears to be nodding off and leaning towards his neighbour who has a disdainful look on her face.

Public transport might be a good example of the democratisation of urban life, but the lessons from it could be that not everyone is as democratic as they claim to be if they are pushed into too close a contact with their fellow-citizens. Cars are not only meant to get us from one place to another in quick fashion. But, as an acquaintance of mine who regularly makes a busy bus journey connecting two northern cities told me, it's a form of theatre as different characters get on and off, greet friends, address the bus generally, sometimes argue, and occasionally even sing. Daumier would have understood what he was talking about.

Ladd makes the interesting observation that: "Most historians who write about 'the crowd' mean only the kind that posed a political threat". There is truth in what he says and it perhaps points to some wishful thinking on the part of armchair radicals who like to dream of the working-class or the masses, whichever term is preferred, as almost always on the brink of revolution. But, as he goes on to say: "Yet the nineteenth-century saw more orderly urban crowds in their daily routines, less prone to random violence and bloodshed in the streets". He ascribes it to more-professional policing, less tolerant attitudes on the part of the authorities to rowdy behaviour, and "changing standards of decorum". This isn't to say that crowds didn't still assemble for reasons other than a celebration, a sporting fixture, or some other largely-peaceful purpose. They did and we have plenty of examples from history to remind us of how crowds can quickly get out of control. But the streets were probably less likely to explode in sudden acts of rebellious violence than they were a hundred or so years before.

And what of the noise in the streets? It was complained of in the eighteenth-century where the cacophony of street cries, organ grinders, disputes, traffic noise, children playing, and other distractions in the then-narrow streets, inclined people to protest and call for bans on at least some of the sounds. There is an amusing Hogarth illustration, "The Enraged Musician", which shows a despairing man, his hands clapped over his ears, staring out in dismay at the crowded street and the makers of the offending din. The later nineteenth-century saw a decline in the amount of street activity in terms of the numbers of entertainers and purveyors of goods for sale as they increasingly required licences to be on the streets. A little of it lingered on into the twentieth-century, and I can recall a fish-seller and a rag-and-bone man calling out their trades in the 1940s. But the noise now mostly comes from cars and loud-speakers blaring out the music that few people seem unable to live without in the modern world.

By exploring who originated the sounds in the streets, where the smells came from, and what could be seen, Ladd creates a picture of different cities in various stages of their developments. Not everyone liked to live in urban centres, though the opportunities and experiences they offered, both good and bad, were seen by some as far superior to what could be found in rural situations. Ladd quotes part of a letter from Charles Lamb to William Wordsworth in which Lamb pokes fun at the poet's rhapsodising over mountain scenery, and exercises his preference for life on the Strand: "I have lived all my days in London, until I have formed as many and intense local attachments, as any of you mountaineers can have done with dead nature". And he goes on to enthuse about the "the lighted shops of the Strand and Fleet Street.....the innumerable trades......all the bustle and wickedness around Covent Garden, the very women of the Town, the Watchmen, drunken scenes, rattles....", and more. I was reminded of a wonderful essay, "Ramblings in Cheapside", by Samuel Butler, dating from later in the nineteenth-century, but which is just as vivid a picture of urban life.

The Streets of Europe is an informative and entertaining book by a well-read writer. Ladd directs us to the ways in which city life was changed over the years. No-one can regret the passing of the kinds of violence and poverty he describes, though we can refer to how both survive in the contemporary urban landscape. But could it be that, as the cities were cleaned up and life became more-ordered and behaviour less varied, something essential was lost somewhere along the way in terms of human contact? I'm not one to sink into nostalgia for times I never knew, but in an increasingly authoritarian society, in which we all seem to be under constant surveillance when outside our homes, I find myself wondering how cities can now thrive on street life? Ladd acknowledges that streets have not always been "orderly", but "they have often been diverse and vibrant places, and as such, they sustain possibilities of encounter and inclusion". Are the streets only to be locations for people to shop or can they offer something else? And do the authorities, and particularly the police, like the idea of people lingering in the streets?

THE STREETS OF EUROPE : THE SIGHTS, SOUNDS & SMELLS THAT SHAPED ITS GREAT CITIES

By Brian Ladd

Chicago University Press. 303 pages. $30. ISBN 978-0-226-67794-1

FIGHTING FOR SPAIN : THE INTERNATIONAL BRIGADES IN THE CIVIL WAR 1936-1939

I'm not sure how many books have been written about the International Brigades and their role in the Spanish Civil War. My own familiarity with them is limited to English-language publications, and I can't claim to have read all those that have appeared in print. But I seem to have accumulated quite a few histories, memoirs, novels, and other items which relate to why people volunteered to go to Spain and what they did there.

And there have been films (documentary and fictional) and plays which have touched on the exploits of Brigaders both during and after the War. One of the examples that come to mind is *Scorpio*, a 1973 film, directed by Michael Winner and starring Burt Lancaster as a CIA operative who fought in Spain but is suspected of spying for the communists and has been marked for assassination. He flees and makes his way across Europe aided by the only people he can trust – ex-members of the International Brigades. And there is a play, *Castles in Spain*, by Edward Boyd, originally broadcast on the BBC in 1986, and which again involves veterans aiding each other in a tricky situation.

The point I'm making by mentioning these things is that a certain legendary, even romantic quality surrounds the men and women of the International Brigades. Over the years I met a few of them and freely admit to having felt humble in their presence. They seemed very ordinary, but I knew that they had done something remarkable by going to Spain and could feel proud of their actions. One of those I was introduced to bore the marks of his experiences all those years before. And I used to see the quiet old lady who lived around the corner from me slowly making her way to the local shops, and wonder how many people knew that she had been a nurse with the Brigades in Spain?

Alexander Clifford has written about Spain previously in his *The People's Army in the Spanish Civil War* (see my NRB review, February, 2020) and it did have material about the International Brigades. I was tempted to say that his new book focuses solely on the Brigades, but that would be misleading in some ways. They were part of the Republican army and it's difficult to completely separate them from what other units did.

Likewise, it's almost impossible to look at the activities of the Brigades without considering the politics of the Spanish Civil War. Clifford's endeavour is to consider the military aspects of the Brigades' achievements and failures, but as both were affected by political decisions regarding command, tactics, and supplies, the overall political situation inevitably keeps surfacing. The Brigades were a Communist Party invention and were largely controlled by members of the Party, whether in military or political terms. Not everyone who enlisted was a communist, though most were, but being a Party member certainly helped when it came to promotion. This was sometimes a drawback from the point of view of political awareness not necessarily leading to battlefield capability. Marxist theory was not a useful guide to commanding troops under fire.

When the war broke out in July 1936, the advantages in terms of military effectiveness were with the Nationalist generals led by Franco. They had a basic force of around 30,000 members of the Spanish Foreign Legion and Moroccan troops known as Regulares. They were the best-equipped and trained units in the Spanish Army and had experience fighting in colonial wars in the 1920s. The Foreign Legion, though modelled on the French Foreign Legion, was largely Spanish and allegedly recruited from the criminal classes and other social misfits. Both they and the Moroccans had reputations as hard fighters but were also known for their brutality.

As mentioned earlier, the Brigades were effectively formed under communist tutelage, even if the Left in general supported the idea of their creation. The plan was that they would help to boost the Republican forces which, in the early days of the war, comprised some loyal units of the army and the para-military police, together with various militias often formed from union members and small political parties like the anarchists and POUM, a non-communist Marxist group. It was often referred to as Trotskyist by the communists when they wanted to disparage support for it. Membership of the Brigades has often been disputed when it comes to the numbers involved. It was sometimes suggested that as many as 45,000 volunteers came forward, but Alexander proposes a lower figure of approximately 32,000. They did not all arrive at the same time.

There were five main Brigades, numbered 11 to 15, and theoretically they were each formed around a language categorisation. The 11th Brigade was German-speaking, the 12th Italian, the 13th Eastern European including Polish, the14th French, the 15th English. The largest contingent came from France and Belgium (10,000), Poland (3,100), Germany and Austria (3,000), Italy (3,000), USA and Canada (3,000), UK and Ireland (2,400), with smaller groups from a wide range of countries. It needs to be noted that the language demarcations were fluid, and units were often amalgamated in times of crisis. The figures quoted for na-tionalities are approximations. And, contrary to popular belief, Span-iards served in the International Brigades almost from the beginning of the war and not just towards its end when the input of non-Spanish vol-unteers had more or less dried up.

Franco's forces had a reasonable supply of arms and ammunition, and could soon rely on a regular flow of the same from Germany and Italy. The Republic, by contrast, lacked any kind of standard armaments in sufficient quantity to outfit the militia units that were essential for its survival in the early days of the conflict. Consequently, a wide range of rifles, revolvers, machine guns and artillery pieces needed varieties of ammunition to keep it functioning, The International Brigades were faced with the same problems once they began to go into action. They didn't even have a regular uniform, and the photos interspersed among Alexander's text display a bewildering array of jackets, hats and hel-mets, shoes and boots, and other apparel.

Some of the senior officers (often Russians or East Europeans, whatev-er else they claimed to be), were usually better dressed. An exception to the rag-tag-and-bobtail look of groups of the British volunteers was the strange George Nathan. He had served in the British Army in the First World War and gained promotion from the ranks to officer status. He later appeared in Ireland as an Auxiliary, a group which had as notori-ous a reputation as the Black and Tans, and then turned up in Spain. He was noted not only for his spick-and-span appearance with shiny black boots and a swagger stick, but also for his bravery. He was later killed in action.

It seems that Nathan was originally from a working-class background, despite his turn-out and clipped speech. And this brings us to the fact that eighty per cent of the volunteers were from the working-classes and had no pretensions to being otherwise. The great majority of them, those who survived the war and its aftermath, just returned to the rou-tines of their previous lives, when they could, and left the writing of memoirs, novels and poems to others. An assumption was born that Spain was awash with poets, painters, novelists, and many more mid-dle-class men and women putting their lives on the line for the Repub-lic. It may have been true that authors and intellectuals flocked to Spain, but it was mostly to observe and not fight. We now remember Hemingway and Stephen Spender rather than Sam Wild ("a tough Mancunian") and Bill Bailey ("the kid from Hoboken"). I'm not ques-tioning the sincerity of many of those who went to help in their various ways (though I suspect that some individuals may have been guilty of "war tourism" and a few of radical chic), nor dismissing the sacrifices of those like Jason Gurney, a talented sculptor who lost an arm, and John Cornford, who lost his life. It's just a fact that most of the dead and wounded, and those who survived, were from the mines and mills and docksides of their respective countries.

A Non-Intervention Agreement supposedly obliged all the signatories to stay out of the Spanish conflict, but was openly ignored by Germany, Italy, and Russia. Germany sent planes and pilots to Franco, and the Italians provided thousands of troops, together with tanks, planes, and ships to blockade Republican ports. Russia eventually began to deliver tanks, planes and their pilots, and supplies of rifles and ammunition, though they were sometimes old stock, The lack of up-to-date and reliable armaments was a problem that the Republic never satisfactorily resolved, any more than it solved the chaotic position with regard to supplies generally. Clothes, food, medical equipment and medicines were frequently never there when needed.

Alexander's military history provides detailed narratives of the various battles – Jarama, Brunete, Teruel, the Ebro are among the main ones – indicating which Brigade units were involved, and how they performed. I haven't the space to analyse his accounts, but the overall picture is often one of brave men attempting to follow orders given from a distance and which ignored advice from those on the ground who pointed out the flaws in the plans. The Brigades were used as shock troops. They led the attacks that were launched on Nationalist defences, and were expected to offer the stoutest resistance when Franco's forces, including the feared Foreign Legion and the Moors, approached the Republican lines. There were Spanish units with good fighting reputations, especially those commanded by Enrique Lister and Juan Modesto, but if the others were mostly comprised of badly-led and poorly-trained conscripts, they could easily break under pressure. Because of their ideological commitments the Brigaders were seen as more likely to stand and fight,

They did, most of the time, and considering how they were frequently not given enough efficient artillery back-up, and couldn't rely on sufficient air support, it's surprising that they functioned as well as they did. This doesn't suggest that all was satisfactory with the Brigades. Discipline could be a problem and desertions were numerous enough to warrant harsh punishments as a means of dissuading those thinking of sneaking away. It was said that André Marty, the martinet commander of the Brigade base at Albacete, had around five hundred men shot for disciplinary infringements. And there were stories, sometimes disputed, that more than one deserter or malingerer had been quickly and quietly disposed of at the front.

The nature of the Brigades, their reason for existence, and why people volunteered to join them, all need to be taken into account when considering why discipline could break down, and people deserted or refused to obey orders. The Brigaders were not professional soldiers, apart from a few officers. Some of the British and European Brigaders had experienced wartime conditions during the Great War. Very few of the Americans had. But, generally speaking, most of the Brigaders had not signed on for a specific period and, as volunteers, many of them thought that they should not be held to staying in Spain indefinitely. Added to which, the ramshackle conduct of the war by the Republican government was not going to make them think that it could lead to a victorious outcome. Their ideological commitment may have helped them put up with unfavourable conditions, but even devotion to a cause can have its limits if the cause seems increasingly hopeless.

The performance of the various Brigades could vary according to the conditions at the particular location where they were in action. As referred to earlier, they often didn't get the artillery or air support necessary to bring a situation to a definite conclusion. The last major Republican offensive took place in the summer of 1938 when its forces made a successful crossing of the Ebro and initially appeared to be breaking through the Nationalist lines. But the advances eventually slowed and halted as supplies failed to reach the front lines. In addition, Franco was able to bring in fresh troops, something the Republican government was unable to do. Its resources in men and materials were exhausted. When the Nationalists started to counter-attack the Republican defences cracked and there was a rush to retreat back across the Ebro.

It was clear by this time (Autumn, 1938) that the writing was on the wall and the Republic was doomed. Internal divisions were evident in the government, the Russians had more or less withdrawn from Spain, and behind the scenes approaches were being made to Franco with a view to bringing the war to an end. As a gesture towards a withdrawal of all foreign troops from the country it was announced that the International Brigades were to be disbanded. It has been suggested that their effectiveness as a fighting force had, in any case, virtually collapsed. With high levels of death, injury, sickness, desertions, and other factors, the battalions of the Brigades had been depleted. There were far more Spanish soldiers than foreigners in their ranks. Clifford gives some figures. The Lincoln-Washington Battalion of the 15th International Brigade had 200 Americans to 500 Spaniards, and about two-thirds of the British Battalion were Spanish.

The Brigades had a final parade in Barcelona on the 28th October, 1938, and left Spain in December of that year and in January, 1939. It would not be true to say that they all went home. Some did, but German, Austrian, Italian, and other volunteers who came from countries that were now right-wing dictatorships mostly went into internment in France. Even when some men could openly return to their countries of origin they were viewed with suspicion by the authorities. American volunteers, for example, were still being hounded by the FBI well into the 1950s. Alvah Bessie, who wrote a book called *Men in Battle* about his experiences in the International Brigades, later became a screenwriter and went to prison as one of the Hollywood Ten. James Yates, a black volunteer who I had the honour of meeting in Paris thirty or so years ago, wrote in his memoir, *Mississippi to Madrid,* that he "was harassed by the FBI and rejected for every job for which I applied".

Clifford in his conclusion says: "Historians are right to point out that the International Brigades suffered from poor leadership, mismanagement, overtly oppressive and bureaucratic command structures, haphazard communication and coordination with other units, high levels of demoralisation and desertion, poor tactics and shoddy equipment". But he points out that "all these issues were systemic flaws in the People's Army more widely". And it's true to say that although Brigaders usually received better training than most Spanish recruits, and when it was available they were allocated the best equipment, they were still poorly equipped for warfare. They were not Gods, and could not be expected to bring about miracles.

Their performances in action were variable, and Clifford considers the 11th and 15th Brigades as the most efficient in the circumstances, and the 14th the worst as the war progressed. The 11th and 15th could experience the same demoralisation in defeat that others did, but usually recovered more quickly. And, as for their overall effect, Clifford probably gets it right when he says: "Despite it all, they fought and died for Spain and on the whole fought remarkably well. This is how the International Brigades should be remembered – as ideologically committed soldiers who made up for their lack of training and equipment with heroism and a readiness to sacrifice".

Fighting for Spain should be read by those wanting a balanced picture of the International Brigades. Alexander Clifford doesn't attempt to make heroes out of people who were imperfect in many ways and yet often behaved heroically. He paints them as ordinary men who rose above the ordinary by participating in a war they could easily have ignored but chose not to. His book is a fitting tribute to their courage. It is well-illustrated with maps and photographs, and has a useful bibliography.

FIGHTING FOR SPAIN : THE INTERNATIONAL BRIGADES IN THE CIVIL WAR 1936-1939

By Alexander Clifford

Pen & Sword Books. 251 pages. £25. ISBN 978-1-52677-438-5

WOODY GUTHRIE/JOE HILL

There is a peculiarly American mixture of rumbustious political activity, travelling, and singing that stretches back to the legendary Wobblies, and is, perhaps, typified in a popular sense by Woody Guthrie's life and music.

Guthrie was never a member of the IWW, though he knew about its ideas and carried a copy of the famous *Little Red Songbook*. But I would guess that, had he seen the light of day a few years earlier, he may well have played a part in the organisation's history.

As it was, Woodrow Wilson Guthrie was born in 1912, just at the time when the Wobblies were in their heyday and singing Joe Hill's songs on street corners around the country. His family wasn't working-class, but it had its share of ups and downs, and the young Woody was reared on a diet of varied experiences.

An erratic scholar, he nonetheless read a great deal and gave early evidence of some idiosyncratic skills. At the beginning of the 1930s he made a living of sorts by playing music, doing odd jobs, and dabbling at commercial art. The first days of the Depression do not seem to have affected him a great deal, either personally or politically.

But he began to drift, hitching his way from one place to another, riding freight trains, mixing with hoboes, migrants, the unemployed. And with old Wobblies, many of them still proudly bearing their battle scars and preaching the gospel of the class war. It was through them that he started to become radicalised.

It wouldn't be true to say that he picked up his politics in the hard school of experience. A lot of his ideas came from books, and from talking with people like the left-wing actor/activist Will Geer, and with Communist Party intellectuals. Guthrie was impressed by their courage and determination in the face of often brutal opposition.

Once established as a singer, he worked on radio, supported radical causes, recorded extensively, and helped out by performing in union halls and on picket lines. He served in the merchant navy during the war, and came out of it to face up to the growing anti-communist mood of the late-1940s. He might have coped with McCarthyism and blacklisting, but his personal behaviour was often affected by heavy drinking and the onset of Huntington's Chorea, which ran in the family blood.

His final years were sad ones and he died in 1967, more of an influence than a performer of any consequence. A man of many moods, there is little point in denying that he could be disturbingly unpredictable, though the disease may have had a lot to do with that. But he generally stood by his friends and his politics. The best of his music will continue to live on record and capture the mood of an era.

Joe Klein's account of Guthrie's life is well-documented, and he doesn't try to gloss over the inconsistencies in his character. I suspect he found it hard to understand Woody's liking for the communists. In this he misses the point that the Thirties were a special time in America, and that it often seemed as if only the Communist Party was willing to put up a fight against poverty and injustice. But, that apart, it's a fair and accurate book.

Guthrie had a talent for taking old tunes and adding new lyrics to them, and it was something he shared with Joe Hill, the enigmatic Wobbly whose words were in the *Little Red Songbook.* But Hill usually got his inspiration from popular songs and hymns rather than from folk ballads. He was, unlike Guthrie, an immigrant, relatively new to America and its traditions.

It would be almost impossible to write a biography of Hill. He seems to have made an art out of hiding his real identity. Whether this was, as some old Wobblies suggested, because he wasn't always particular about how he got his money, is something that can never be known for sure. And Wallace Stegner leaves the question open in his novel.

First published thirty years ago under the title, *The Preacher and the Slave,* it's a vigorous and often moving attempt to get to grips with Hill's character, and the possible reasons for his strange behaviour during his trial in 1916 for the murder of a Salt Lake City shopkeeper.

Hill wasn't an activist in the sense of participating openly in strikes and free speech fights. He came and went in his own way, and the standard histories of the IWW say little about him, other than that he wrote some of its best-known songs. The only time he ever drew attention to himself was at his trial – and if he had a past he didn't disclose it to the police, or even to his friends and lawyers. He died in front of a firing squad as defiant as he'd been in court.

Stegner brilliantly suggests the strangeness of the man, and sets it against the social conditions of the period. Hard times were all around, and it could have been that Hill wasn't averse to appropriating money from those he thought had a little too much of it. But could a small-time thief have had the interest and commitment to produce the witty and pointed songs that Hill wrote? If he did he wouldn't have been alone in

those days in seeking a common link between some forms of criminali-
ty and revolutionary acts.

Joe Hill is a splendid book, immensely readable, and evoking both the
individual and the spirited movement he was connected with. It's good
to have it in print again.

WOODY GUTHRIE : A LIFE by Joe Klein. Faber, 1981

JOE HILL by Wallace Stegner. Nebraska University Press, 1980

SACCO AND VANZETTI

The case of Sacco and Vanzetti continues to intrigue investigators, and to arouse emotional reactions. Brian Jackson visited Boston in connection with his book, and he describes how politicians and others took sides when, in 1977, it was decided to issue an official proclamation acknowledging that the two Italian anarchists did not receive a fair trial over fifty years before when they were accused of taking part in a pay-roll robbery.

It is important to note that the proclamation merely stated that the conduct of the trial was less than satisfactory. It did not make any comment on the guilt or otherwise of the accused.

In this it paralleled some informed opinion in the 1920s in believing that, whatever the truth, the evidence offered against Sacco and Vanzetti should never have been considered sufficient to justify conviction. If this was so, why were they sentenced to death and eventually executed?

When the robbery and murder they allegedly committed took place in 1919 America was in the grip of anti-radical hysteria. Anarchists, socialists, and other activists were being rounded up and either imprisoned or deported. A mass trial of Wobblies was getting under way in Chicago and around the country generally a campaign of often-violent harassment was being conducted against dissidents of any kind. To openly espouse anarchist ideas in this kind of atmosphere was to invite immediate condemnation.

Jackson sketches in the post-1918 mood in America and also provides a potted history of anarchism to help explain the beliefs that Sacco and Vanzetti held. But these pages are the weakest part of the book. It's a pity he didn't pay more attention to them.

Inevitably, though, the central question is whether or not Sacco and Vanzetti did participate in the robbery. Over the years it has been suggested that Sacco was probably involved, but Vanzetti not. Some shaky evidence derived from tests in recent times of the gun supposedly carried by Sacco points to his guilt.

So do various statements by people connected with the defence committee who might be said to have been in the know, such as the veteran anarchist Carlo Tresca. Incidentally, Jackson might check his assertion that the outspokenly anti-fascist Tresca was assassinated by a Soviet agent because of his attacks on communism. A more likely version is that he was murdered by the Mafia as a favour to Mussolini.

One examination of the Sacco and Vanzetti case trial was called *The Case That Will Not Die*, and Brian Jackson demonstrates how true that is. His book is not the best account of the strange and moving account of "the good shoemaker and the poor fish pedlar", who were eventually put to death in 1927, but it could be useful to anyone wanting to obtain some initial information about their story.

THE BLACK FLAG by Brian Jackson. Routledge, 1981.

BRITISH MUSIC HALL : AN ILLUSTRATED HISTORY

I grew up in the 1940s and 1950s with so many of the songs referred to in this book seeming to still be part of the almost common musical language of the period, even though they mostly dated from before the First World War. But, unless my memory is faulty, the best of them could sometimes be heard on the radio, and in old films that were circulating in the small cinemas that survived in towns and cities in the austerity-hit years after the Second World War. And little pubs in the side-streets didn't have piped music, and instead relied on a pianist to get a sing-song going on a Saturday night. The songs were often those that nearly everybody knew, like "Lily of Laguna", "On Mother Kelly's Doorstep", and "Dear Old Pals". And the one that drunks bawled out, "Nellie Dean".

Perhaps I'm being selective with my memories, and I was just an individual who happened to be interested in the old songs, so now remember them as being more available than they actually were? In the 1940s and early-1950s dance-bands were popular and the Top Twenty (though continuing to be based on sheet-music sales) attracted attention on the radio. And if you had asked me in 1950, when I was fourteen, what my prime musical concerns were, I would have immediately said, modern jazz. But I still liked to hear those old music hall songs.

What might be called the "sociology" of the music halls is fascinating. If it's necessary to place some sort of framework on it then I'd suggest the years from 1850 to 1914 might be suitable. It shouldn't be necessary to stress that there were developments that led up to 1850 and others that took place after 1914. Strict boundaries don't apply in a case like this. On the other hand, it does seem to me that the most-significant events and songs associated with British music halls probably did occur in the time-frame referred to. The peak period could be 1880 to 1910.

Richard Anthony Baker sketches in the broad social background to the late-nineteenth century, with its poverty and slums and vast disparities of privilege and wealth. He also shows how the music halls grew out of a tradition of "free-and-easies", rough-and-ready places of working-class entertainment, and pubs with "singing rooms" where professional or semi-professional performers might be hired to pull in customers. Needless to say, such locations were not looked on kindly by middle-class moralists: "The epidemic of vocal music has more particularly spread its contagious and devastating influence amongst the youth of the Metropolis, the London apprentice boys". The writer went on to say that the "free-and-easies" were designed for the "advancement of drunkenness and profligacy".

Purpose-built music halls soon appeared, and Baker pays attention to Canterbury Hall and other establishments built by Charles Morton, the so-called "father of the halls". He initially hired Sam Cowell, a popular "character singer", as a star attraction, but he also aimed to draw in a wider audience than had frequented the free-and-easies" and "singing rooms" of earlier days. There were ways around copyright laws and Morton had an orchestra which played selections from Verdi, Donizetti, and Gounod. Baker notes that Thackeray and Dickens both visited the Canterbury.

With music halls spreading around London and in the provinces there was a demand for singers, comedians and other artists to fill the bills. And the singers required songs, so there was a rise in the number of song writers able to supply them. I think it's often forgotten that, with few exceptions, the performers didn't write their own material. There were thousands of songs produced during the lifetime of the music halls. Most songs came and went within weeks, unless one caught the public's fancy, so there was a constant demand for them. Joe Tabrar claimed to have written 17,000 by 1894. Baker seems a little suspicious, but does acknowledge that the evidence points to at least 7,000. He adds that "He should have been rich, but he was yet another music hall writer who ended his days with scarcely a penny to his name". It's not surprising when we know that he sold "Daddy Wouldn't Buy Me a Bow-Wow" to Vesta Victoria for two guineas. She had a hit with it, and the song became popular world-wide, but Tabrar had parted with it outright and no royalties were involved. And perhaps Tabrar's personal attitudes played a part when he recalled that he'd made thousands for other people, but not for himself, and said: "I am the most Bohemian of all the Bohemians you ever met. I don't value money. I never valued money".

It's probably impossible now to understand why particular songs became popular if one looks closely at the melodies and lyrics in a detached manner. They're mostly mundane, and what gave them any kind of individuality or interest was the way in which they were delivered. Performers knew this and worked to perfect their acts accordingly. It was a case of "It's not what you do it's the way that you do it". There were some recorded examples of music hall songs, but though they can give an indication of how a song was sung in terms of phrasing (and what wonderful, clear diction most of the performers displayed), they can't tell us how they were presented from the point of view of body movements, etc. There are very few early filmed examples from the days of the music halls.

There were exceptions to the generally routine nature of much music hall material. A memorable tune and amusing or appropriate words might help a song to endure. A personal favourite is the delightful, "The Boy in the Gallery", originally written for Nellie Power but made famous by the Queen of the Music Hall, Marie Lloyd. When she sang it to the gallery, where the working-class customers gathered, she was singing to her own (see Walter Sickert's paintings of the gallery at the Old Bedford Music Hall in Camden Town). Like many of the music hall artists she never forgot where she came from. It's a song that has lasted, its simple melody and lyrics having an appealing quality that cuts across the years. Even before a song like "The Boy in the Gallery" played on the working-class setting for at least part of its appeal, Harry Clifton had a hit with "Pretty Polly Perkins of Paddington Green" in 1863.

Many performers were associated with a particular song, though it would be misleading to suggest that Marie Lloyd was only ever known for "The Boy in the Gallery". She could be lively, and even a little bawdy, as in "A Little of What you Fancy Does you Good", where, as can be imagined, a few glances and gestures would quickly add meaning to what is fancied. Lloyd probably earned a reputation for slightly-salacious material more from rumour than actual experience, and a number of anecdotes grew up around her. But, as Baker makes clear, "she sang saucy songs, made saucier by a wink, a naughty look, a flick of her dress". One anecdote that I recall, and my memory may not have all the details right, is of her singing the polite, parlour song, "Come into the Garden, Maude" (based on a Tennyson poem), and with just a few inflections of the voice, and minor movements of the body, making it evident what Maude went into the garden for. When she died 50,000 people lined the route of her funeral procession. T.S. Eliot wrote: "No other comedian succeeded so well in giving expression to the life of (an) audience – in raising it to a kind of art".

Lloyd was one of what Baker calls "music hall's three greatest enter-tainers", the other two being Dan Leno and Little Tich. Leno was a great favourite in pantomimes, as well as on stage at the music-halls. He appeared in the guise of a "wide range of comic characters: the railway guard, the detective, the County Councillor, the holiday-maker, and many more". He doesn't seem to have had any songs he was noted for, and his acts contained a great deal of comic patter "in which he lovingly satirised whichever character he was playing". There is a story

210

about the great classical actor, Henry Irving, appearing at a matinee performance with Leno. Irving expected that he would follow Leno and top the bill, but was advised against it. When he stood in the wings and watched Leno's hold on the audience, he understood why. It would have been a great mistake to have tried to follow him.

Sadly, Leno, like quite a few other entertainers of the time, developed a drink problem which began to affect his performances. He died in 1904, and someone who knew him said, "Leno was killed by his friends. He paid the penalty of genius by becoming a continual show".

Little Tich, the stage persona of Harry Relph, was rightly named, or nick-named (PC wouldn't allow it now), being only 4'6" high. On stage he "performed a highly-individual routine in shoes that were just half that length, managing, at one point, to stand on tiptoe". He eventually terminated the act because of the pain and discomfort it caused him. But before that he'd toured around Europe, and in Paris became a friend of the equally-diminutive artist, Toulouse-Lautrec. He continued well into the 1920s, hardly varying his act – "a song, some patter, a dance in character" – but had a stroke in 1927 and died. J.B.Priestley spoke highly of his talents and described him as "a star of the first magnitude".

Neither Leno nor Little Tich seemed to have relied on notable songs to enhance their performances, but many other music hall entertainers are now often remembered, when they are, for a specific number, sometimes more than one. Gus Elen, who dressed as a cockney coster, had two popular hits, "If it Wasn't for the Houses in Between" and "It's a Great Big Shame", both of which cleverly exploited the kind of circumstances that the working-class component of his audiences would be able to recognise from their own experiences. One mocked the practicalities of urban living where there might be a nice view, "if it wasn't for the houses in between", and the other the sight of a henpecked husband, six foot three, being nagged by a woman only four foot two.

Vesta Victoria was noted for the provocative, "Daddy, wouldn't buy me a bow-wow" (the provocation might stem from how it was performed), and the humorous "Waiting at the Church", where the would-be bride receives a note reading, "Can't get away to marry you to-day/My wife won't let me". Ella Shields sang "Burlington Bertie from Bow", a marvellous send-up of a broken-down Toff who walks "down the Strand with my gloves on my hands/And then walks down again with them off". Vesta Tilley, "the greatest male impersonator in music hall", had "After the Ball", and "Jolly good luck to the girl who loves a soldier". Both had immediately recognisable melodies as well as easy-to-memorise words. Audience participation was often an integral part of a music hall performance.

There were so many other singers and songs. Harry Champion with "Boiled Beef and Carrots", "I'm Henery the Eighth, I am", and "Any Old Iron", George Robey, known as "The Prime Minister of Mirth", sang the lilting "If You Were the Only Girl in the World" and the more-boisterous, "Another little Drink/Wouldn't Do Us Any Harm". The latter title might seem apt when we are aware that Robey's career stretched into the cinema and he played the role of Falstaff in the 1945 film of *Henry the Fifth*. And G.H. Elliott, one of those who specialised in black-faced performances, popular in their day but unwelcome now. Still, one or two of the songs associated with him deserve to be re-called. "I Used to Sigh for the Silvery Moon" has a pleasant tune. And "Lily of Laguna" lasted the years, though some of the words might need altering if the song is sung today. It wasn't really Elliott's song and was originally written for Eugene Stratton. Both of their recorded versions can be found on YouTube.

I could go on – "The Man who Broke the Bank at Monte Carlo" (based on a real event), "The Man on the Flying Trapeze" (another with its basis in a real life character), "Champagne Charlie", "Oh, Mr Porter", "My Old Dutch", "Down at the Old Bull and Bush" ("an archetypal British song, though written by three Americans"), "The Miner's Dream of Home" ("For the bells were ringing the old year out/And the new year in"), the only hit for Leo Dryden, whose career faded to the point where he ended up singing in the streets. There are also a couple of songs forever associated with the First World War. Florrie Forde sang "Pack up Your Troubles in Your Old Kit Bag", with its "philosophy" of "What's the use of Worrying/It Never was Worthwhile", which has always made more sense to me than many other approaches to life. And there was "It's a Long Way to Tipperary", which was actually written a couple of years before the war started but thrived when it did.

The music halls were not always happy places, and those who worked in them didn't always lead happy lives. More than a few succumbed to the attractions of alcohol, often used as a prop to conquer stage fright. Audiences were likely to respond with cat-calls, boos, and missiles if they thought an artist wasn't up to scratch. Early deaths from stress and overwork were common. Artists whose careers never took off, or faded after a brief period of fame, lived out their days in obscurity and poverty. Some who did make money soon found it all slipping away. They were expected to be generous and were. And the women often took up with unreliable husbands and managers.

What brought about the end of the music halls? Baker refers to a combination of "cinema, ragtime, revue and radio", of which I'd suggest that cinema and radio were the most significant. Some music hall performers did manage to adapt to the changed circumstances and moved into broadcasting. But there's no doubt that things had changed. A few of the old songs survived in pubs and seaside variety shows, and lingered on through the 1940s and into the 1950s. And old performers came out of retirement to appear on stage. I recall going to the London Palladium in 1958 or 1959 for a show which featured a number of elderly music hall artists, though I can no longer say who they were. Later, there were TV shows which revived the songs, but they required both artists and audiences to dress up and pretend they were back in the Edwardian era. Still, they did help to keep the songs alive.

The British Music Hall is a fascinating book and mixes facts, anecdotes and reminiscences to good advantage. It is well-illustrated, has ample notes, and a useful bibliography, though I did observe that it doesn't include Colin MacInnes's excellent *Sweet Saturday Night*. But that's a minor quibble, and Baker's book is well worth reading. It is entertaining and informative, and can be dipped into or read at length. Either way, it fulfils a prime function by keeping the reader interested.

A final comment about something that intrigued me. Although I've concentrated on singers and their songs, the music halls provided a variety of entertainment, including jugglers, trapeze artists, illusionists, and escapologists like the great Harry Houdini. Baker tells the story of an appearance of his at the Palace Theatre in Blackburn. It was one of Houdini's gimmicks to offer £25 to anyone who could manacle him with "regulation handcuffs" from which he couldn't escape. Baker says that "a young man named Hodgson, who in time opened a school of physical culture, accepted the challenge", and came up with various chains, padlocks, and other pieces of equipment. There was some discussion about whether or not they were what Houdini had stipulated with his challenge, but he eventually agreed to go ahead. He did manage to free himself, but only after taking longer than usual and with some difficulty.

It occurs to me that the "young man named Hodgson" was probably William Hope Hodgson who was in Blackburn when Houdini appeared there, and did open a "school of physical culture" in the town. He was also a writer whose novels and short-stories are still in circulation. His stories, *Carnacki, the Ghost Finder* are classics of their kind, and his novel, *The House on the Borderland* can always bring a shiver or two when read late at night. The late-Victorian and Edwardian years were productive ones for music hall performances and tales of mystery and imagination. In some ways Hodgson was typical of his generation. He died at Ypres in 1918.

BRITISH MUSIC HALL : AN ILLUSTRATED HISTORY

By Richard Anthony Baker

Pen & Sword Books. 292 pages. £16.99. ISBN 978-1-78383-1180

DAVE BRUBECK : A LIFE IN TIME

Dave Brubeck aroused a variety of responses when his group came to the fore in jazz in the 1950s. Looking through an old scrapbook in which I pasted cuttings from the *Melody Maker* and other weekly music papers during my army days between 1954 and 1957, I came across an interview with clarinettist and saxophone player Tony Scott in which he stated that "He just doesn't swing. Just now I said a musician must build. Brubeck, his music is like a box and he's caught inside it. I don't think he's a jazzman and I think he's a poor musician even in what he plays. I've studied modern music for years and had an education in classical music. Believe me, Brubeck is childish. In classical music he's childish, and it's the same in what he calls his jazz".

Philip Clark doesn't refer to Scott's dismissal of Brubeck, though he mentions some other negative comments about his music by saxophonist Billy Root and critic Ira Gitler. But after reading his book it's plain that he'd have strongly objected to what Scott said, had he seen it at the time. Clark is an unabashed and enthusiastic advocate for the pianist's achievements, ranging from his earliest trio, quartet and octet recordings in the late-1940s and early-1950s to his later extended compositions using larger groups of musicians. He isn't blind to certain Brubeck performances on record that he sees as below par, but at the same time he places them in a context that considers them as minor failings in a generally high level of musical accomplishment.

Dave Brubeck was born in 1920 in California. His mother was a talented pianist and his father a rancher. He grew up with classical music in his consciousness and combined it with practical work on the ranch his father managed. It's interesting to note that Brubeck had difficulty reading music throughout his career: "I can write music, but I am not a good reader. I got used to using my ears from such an early age, through listening to records (and) then trying to work out what I had heard by going to the piano, and listening in to the piano lessons my mother gave, that reading kind of passed me by. But my mother did teach me the basics of notating music on paper and harmony, so that by the time I went to College of Pacific I had enough to go on. But I could never, even now, play a piece of Beethoven or Milhaud from the sheet music".

It's clear that Brubeck's poor reading skills probably limited his opportunities to follow a conventional path by working in groups, and especially big-bands, as most aspiring young musicians did at the time. He needed his own groups so that he could, in a sense, dominate in order to fulfil his potential as a soloist. Improvisation was of key importance in his thinking, even though in the mid-1940s he experimented with a group that utilised a fair amount of arranged music. And he needed sympathetic musicians to achieve the sort of sounds he wanted. Trumpeter Dick Collins and tenor-saxophonist Dave Van Kriedt were vital components of the Octet, just as alto-saxophonist Paul Desmond played a key part in the classic Brubeck Quartet of the 1950s.

It is the Brubeck/Desmond partnership that most people will think of whenever the pianist's name crops up, and especially the group with Gene Wright on bass and drummer Joe Morello. There had been other bassists and drummers present as Brubeck began to establish a reputation in the early and mid-1950s, but for various reasons none of them ever settled into the format that the pianist devised as his experiments with time signatures began to occupy his thinking. Clark is particularly keen on these and devotes a fair amount of space to investigating their use in the Quartet's performances. "Take Five" is the best-known example, and became a popular hit.

Before the days of fame when Brubeck toured the world, there were periods when he and his musicians, always including Paul Desmond but with several different bassists and drummers, appeared in jazz clubs across America. Life wasn't easy for them, and there were the usual problems relating to travelling, accommodation, and facing up to the fact that the clubs were often controlled by the Mafia. Brubeck was always a clean-living person, but some of his musicians succumbed to the lure of the drugs scene that was seemingly an integral part of the early-1950s jazz world. At one point he lost the services of bassist Ron Crotty and drummer Lloyd Davis.

Another problem that Brubeck had to face when the black bassist Eugene Wright joined his group was that of racial prejudice while working in the South. Clark has a couple of anecdotes which highlight the kind of situations that could arise. When they arrived to play a concert in 1958 at East Carolina College in Greenville, North Carolina, Brubeck was informed that it wasn't acceptable for Eugene Wright to appear on stage. His response was that if Wright couldn't be there then neither could the other musicians. The college authorities backed down and the concert went ahead successfully. An even more telling story is of Brubeck rejecting what would have been a financially beneficial tour of the Southern States when he was asked to replace Wright with a white bassist.

216

DAVE BRUBECK

I have to say that Clark doesn't place a lot of emphasis on a close biographical analysis of Brubeck's life. A reader looking for lots of anecdotes about incidents and personalities will have to search hard for
them. They're there, but the book doesn't follow a conventional pattern
of biographical studies with a clear chronological narrative. Where personal details do occur, whether of Brubeck or his fellow-musicians,
they mostly do so in relation to the music they produced. And it's the
music that concerns Clark most of all.

I mentioned earlier about his partiality for what he refers to as polytonality and polyrhythm. He defines them in this way:

"Polytonality – music sounding in two or more keys simultaneously –
and polyrhythms – overlays of different rhythmic impulses and grooves
– were, like the attitude he took towards life, techniques that allowed
obsessions and tics to coexist. Brubeck plied his music with overlaps
between musical cultures in "Blue Rondo a la Turk", which combined
an indigenous Turkish rhythm with the blues, and in "Three to Get
Ready", which squared the circles of a waltz by inserting bars of 4/4;
between different time signatures, like his version of "Someday My
Prince Will Come", which managed to be in 4/4 and 3/4 at the same
time; between the radically diverse range of musical styles through
which he waded in his improvised solos - no sweat as Liszt flowed into
James P. Johnson".

I suppose it could be asked if most of the audiences hearing and enjoy-
ing Brubeck's group in performance would have been aware of what
was taking place rhythmically other than in a general sense? Let me
make a personal confession at this point. I was familiar with early Brubeck recordings like "Frenesi", "Mamselle", and "Crazy Chris", which
had been issued on 78s before I went into the army in 1954. And I'd
started to buy a few Brubeck LPs as they appeared later in the decade.
Tracks like the exciting "Le Souk" and the attractive "Laura" caught
my attention. I also saw the Quartet live at concerts when I got back
into civilian circulation after 1957. My main pre-occupation was admittedly with the alto playing of Paul Desmond. And though I no doubt
tapped my feet in time to the tricky rhythms I was hearing, I couldn't
have identified them beyond the straight 4/4. That's not completely true
because I could recognise a waltz rhythm. But along with many others
in the audience I was just responding to the overall musical experience.
It may offend musicians to say it, but listeners on the whole don't need
to identify which notes are being played, any more than they do the
rhythms, in order to enjoy what they're hearing.

217

As I said earlier, it was always Paul Desmond who was, for me, the main attraction whenever I attended a concert or bought a Brubeck LP. His feather-light tone, and his melodic improvisations seemed to be the epitome of "cool". I was primarily a fan of the more-intense playing of Charlie Parker, Ernie Henry, and East Coast altoists like Phil Woods, Gene Quill and Charlie Mariano, and Desmond provided a contrast to them that was impossible to ignore. I think that what persuaded me to pay attention to his work, as opposed to that of Brubeck as a soloist, is that I could place Desmond in a tradition of jazz that the pianist didn't seem to easily fit into. I'm talking about my impressions of the music I was hearing in the 1950s, and I have to say that Clark does a good job of analysing Brubeck's solos and demonstrating how, as well as incorporating classical references, they indicated that he had a sound awareness of jazz traditions. He wasn't a bebop improviser in the style of Bud Powell, and the numerous pianists who followed him, such as Wynton Kelly, Sonny Clark, Barry Harris, and Hampton Hawes, and that may have worked against him in the minds of critics and fans. They expected to hear bebop-influenced music and were confused when they didn't get it. I include myself in that category.

Clark mentions Hampton Hawes when, discussing how different pianists played, he describes how bop practitioners functioned: "the left hand outlined the rapidly unfolding harmonic patterns, a secure grounding over which the right hand launched busy, athletic lines". If I can don my nerdish cap for a moment, he also refers to Hawes making "his debut record in 1955". But Hawes had recorded under his own name several times in the early-1950s, as well as with altoist Sonny Criss in 1949. And he was one of the two young pianists (the other was Russ Freeman) who took part in the legendary 1947 recordings from a concert at the Elk's Club, Los Angeles.

Paul Desmond's behaviour had become erratic by the early-1960s and he was reputed to be drinking heavily. There is a story of him disappearing part-way through a concert tour of Germany, and eventually being found a couple of days later in a Hamburg bar. It wasn't perhaps surprising when the Quartet broke up in 1967. Clark provides a thorough survey of how Brubeck carried on with other musicians added, including some from his own family. He didn't just restrict himself to the conventions of the Quartet, and moved into what some jazz enthusiasts might have regarded as the dubious territory of classical music. However, I suspect that when his name crops up in conversation or elsewhere it will be in connection with the Quartet recordings of the 1950s and early-1960s.

Philip Clark has written an informative and informed book. He knew Dave Brubeck and talked to him on many occasions about his life and music. His biography of the pianist does rely a great deal on pages of close analysis of recorded material, and anyone looking for colourful descriptions of personally outlandish behaviour will be disappointed. Brubeck was a dedicated family man and married to the same woman for 70 years, didn't smoke or use drugs, drank little, and paid close attention to business as well as musical matters. It's difficult to imagine Hollywood ever making a biopic about his life. Desmond with his drinking, womanising, frustrations about wanting recognition as a writer as well as a musician, and other personal foibles, might make a better candidate. It's to Clark's credit that he manages to blend the personal details in with the music. Writing about music for a general audience that might not want to know all about the intricacies of polyrhythms and polytonality isn't easy. I just applied my own test to Clark's book – did it make me want to listen to the music? It did, and I was soon hunting for those old Brubeck tracks from the 1950s.

DAVE BRUBECK : A LIFE IN TIME

By Philip Clark

Headline Publishing. 445 pages. £25. ISBN 978-1-4722-7247-8

JAZZ FROM DETROIT

It's inevitable, I suppose, that mentioning music from Detroit will cause most people to think of Tamla-Motown and its associated singers. But prior to the so-called Tamla Motown Sound the city had a well-established jazz scene. It's "golden age" was, according to Mark Stryker, between 1940 and 1960. It's a classification I'd be inclined to agree with and, in fact, I'd propose that it was a particularly fertile period generally for modern jazz. This isn't to suggest that jazz hadn't attracted a degree of popularity before that – many of the swing era bigbands of the 1930s blended jazz and dance music – but from the point of view of invention and experimentation the 1940s and 1950s seem to have been especially active. What happened after 1960 is a matter for debate, but there was a decline in interest in jazz. Jazz musicians had a hard time surviving as pop music came to the fore. In Warren Leight's play, *Side Man,* a small group of New York musicians gather in front of a TV to watch Elvis Presley's first appearance on the Ed Sullivan Show in 1956. As the singer gyrates with his guitar, one of them remarks: "That kid will do to horn players what talkies did to Buster Keaton".

There was an earlier book about jazz in Detroit (*Before Motown: A History of Jazz in Detroit, 1920-1960,* by Lars Bjorn with Jim Gallert, University of Michigan Press, Ann Arbor, 2001), and Stryker is keen to point out that his narrative takes a different direction: "This book is not meant to account for every significant jazz musician from Detroit.......it carries the story of Detroit jazz from the 1940s into the 21st century, digging deeper into the lives of key musicians and the influence of the Detroit diaspora, while also keeping up with the action on the home front". The diaspora" referred to is the fact that most musicians, once they had established a reputation in Detroit, moved on to New York. This seems to have been impressively true in "the hard bop era from about 1955 to 1965". Detroit was a hard-working industrial city and the music played predominantly by black musicians reflected the tough times that many of them experienced as they grew up in an atmosphere of segregation, police harassment, and violence.

Detroit's population had expanded rapidly as the automobile industry developed, and there was a continual demand for labour. Along with the growth in the numbers of people, both black and white, there was a corresponding increase in the demand for entertainment. Clubs, theatres and bars flourished, and offered work for musicians and entertainers. They could hone their skills playing in such premises, but it's also of importance to note that Detroit had a programme of "exceptional music education in the public schools". There were, too, influential individuals who helped train many younger jazzmen to become more proficient in their chosen art form. Stryker singles out the fine pianist, Barry Harris, for praise, and it's notable that his name runs throughout the book. Harris was always keen to carry forward the message of bebop, a jazz form that made its mark on the city: "Beyond New York, Detroit was one of the first cities where bebop took root". And it's further pointed out that, as the 1960s got underway, the "free jazz" movement never really established a firm foothold among Detroit's jazz community.

It's difficult to know how advanced some of the local musicians in Detroit were in terms of their allegiance to bebop. Certainly a musician like the vibraphone-player, Milt Jackson, born in Detroit in 1923, was proficient enough to work in the clubs of New York and record with Dizzy Gillespie in the mid-1940s. There is an interesting small-group session for the short-lived Detroit-based record label, Sensation in 1948. Led by saxophonist Sonny Stitt (listed as "Lord Nelson", presumably for contractual reasons), the group included trumpeter Willie Wells, Jackson, pianist Will Davis, bassist Jimmy Glover, and drummer Dave Heard. Wells, Davis, Glover, and Heard were all Detroit jazzmen. It's perhaps of interest to note that, as an indication of how difficult it was to earn a living playing jazz alone, Wells can be heard on several tracks by Gene Nero's Sextet (featuring vocalist Tina Dixon) recorded in Detroit around 1947/48. Nero's group, if the scant recorded evidence is anything to go by, leaned more to rhythm and blues than jazz, which was probably a necessity when performing for a broad audience. Titles such as "Blow Mr Bebop" and "Parrot Bar Boogie" give an indication of the sort of music Nero's group played. The Parrot Lounge was a popular club in Detroit.

If most of the others, excluding Stitt, never established reputations in the jazz world outside Detroit, Milt Jackson, of course, went on to become a member of the Modern Jazz Quartet, a group in which pianist John Lewis was the dominant voice in terms of its overall approach. But in my experience of hearing it at concerts and on records, it only really came alive when Jackson soloed. And even then he often appeared constrained by the format of the music, polite and tightly-arranged as it was. To gain a true picture of the vibraphonist at his most scintillating and forceful, I'd suggest that it's best to turn to the recordings he made with his own groups. There are some splendid collaborations with the tenor-saxophonist Lucky Thompson from the 1950s that have stood the test of time.

One of the most prolific jazzmen to step out of the Detroit scene was trumpeter Donald Byrd, though some people might challenge the view that the material he recorded later in his career can truthfully be called jazz. I very much preferred the records that Byrd made in the 1950s. A concert in Detroit in 1955 had him alongside local jazzmen like tenor-man Yusef Lateef and pianist Barry Harris, and playing in a bright boppish manner. He had a good tone and a fund of ideas. There are so many albums from the late-1950s and early-1960s that it's difficult to select some to recommend, but a personal choice would include sides with Hank Mobley and Gigi Gryce. And the gritty tracks he recorded with someone else from the testing ground of the Detroit jazz scene, baritone saxophonist Pepper Adams.

I think it's true to say that the Detroit jazz scene was predominantly black, but there were several white jazzmen who, when they left the city, achieved some prominence on a national level. I mentioned Pep-per Adams, and trombonist Frank Rosolino also spent his early days in Detroit. Like many Detroit musicians he was musically educated at Cass Technical High School. The city's schools had been racially inte-grated for many years, and it's worth noting that the Musician' Union in Detroit was one of the few in the country to be fully integrated in the 1950s. Rosolino is often linked to West Coast jazz, and he did indeed work and record a great deal in Los Angeles. But before that he had played in Gene Krupa's band in the late-1940s (he can be heard chant-ing an amusing bebop "vocal" and playing a solo on the drummer's 1949 recording of "Lemon Drop"), and he was a featured soloist with Stan Kenton's orchestra in the early-1950s. I recall seeing him playing agile and inventive solos at a 1953 Kenton concert in Dublin. Among his earliest appearances on records were the four tracks recorded for the Dee Gee label in 1953, with Barry Harris on piano.

I should perhaps draw attention to drummer Art Mardigan, described by Stryker as "the top bebop jazz drummer in Detroit". Mardigan had made the New York jazz scene and recorded with Dexter Gordon in 1946. He was the drummer with Georgie Auld's big-band in the mid-1940s, and along the way worked and/or recorded with Charlie Parker, Allen Eager, Wardell Gray, Fats Navarro, Nick Travis, and others. He clearly had impeccable bebop credentials, but seems to have fallen vic-tim to the problem that affected so many of the pioneer bop musicians – heroin addiction. He was in the group that Parker took to Montreal in October 1953 for an ill-fated appearance at the Latin Quarter club. Supposedly for seven nights, the booking was terminated after the first night because of the general condition of the musicians. Mardigan had arrived without his drum kit, the pianist Harry Biss was said to be "always in a fog", and the way they generally conducted themselves on stage was questioned.

There are so many other musicians with a Detroit connection that Stryker discusses that I can't do much more than mention them in this review. Trombonist Curtis Fuller, saxophonist Yusef Lateef, drummer Louis Hayes, altoist Charles McPherson, guitarist Kenny Burrell, trumpeter and arranger Gerald Wilson. And the Jones Brothers – Hank, Thad, and Elvin. All three of them became stalwarts of the 1950s jazz scene. Hank Jones appeared on numerous record sessions, both as a soloist and as an accompanist to many of the leading jazz performers. Thad Jones was also a prolific recording artist, both with his own groups and as a member of other units. And he had a featured solo role with Count Basie's band (I caught it a couple of times just after I came out of the army in 1957, and I'm certain Jones, Frank Foster, and Joe Newman were all there), and, later, formed the exuberant Thad Jones-Mel Lewis orchestra. Elvin Jones became famous for his role in the John Coltrane group of the early-1960s. It was around that time I saw him in concert in London with Coltrane. I have to admit that, having grown up with bebop and cool jazz ringing in my ears (I started collecting jazz records around 1950), it took me a little time to adjust to the music that Coltrane played. A saxophonist such as Hank Mobley was more to my taste.

I'm conscious of the fact that I've focused on the "Golden Era" 1940-1960 that Stryker writes about. It's my own favourite period for my listening pleasure. But it's only fair to point out that he does give a fair amount of space to what happened in Detroit after1960. The city itself went into decline as the automobile industry virtually collapsed. Poverty and crime increased. People left Detroit to search for work elsewhere.

When it came to music, there was an effect in terms of a reduction in the number of jobs available in clubs and theatres. The rise of pop music affected jazz musicians, in particular, though some adjusted enough to obtain work backing singers and in the recording studios. There was an impact, too, on what had been a fertile musical education programme in schools. Cutbacks meant that many music departments were closed.

It wasn't all bad, and musicians carried on getting together. I was quite intrigued when I read what Stryker writes about the Detroit Artists Workshop and John Sinclair. I was in touch with him in the 1960s and had poems in a couple of issues of a magazine called *Work* that Sinclair edited. Stryker doesn't mention it, but he does refer to another of Sinclair's publications, the jazz-oriented *Change*. I have a vague memory that I may have also contributed to it, though I don't think that I did more than pick up some notes from jazz magazines about developments in Britain and pass them to Sinclair. I still have my copies of *Work,* but not of *Change*. Stryker says that John Sinclair was harassed by the Detroit police and went to prison on drugs charges. I recall that he sent me the envelope from one of my letters to him to show me that it had been opened by the U.S. Postal Service because it was believed to contain subversive material, or something like that. It's not easy to remember exactly what happened more than fifty years ago.

Jazz From Detroit provided me with a great deal of reading pleasure, as well as an opportunity to dig out a variety of records by some of the jazzmen it refers to. I'd recommend it to anyone interested in the music. The fact that it is often about jazz located somewhere other than New York or Los Angeles gives it added value. I don't think Mark Stryker will be offended if I suggest that it could be useful to read it alongside the book I mentioned earlier – *Before Motown: A History of Jazz in Detroit 1920-1960*. Taken together, the two books offer a vivid portrait of a city, and the lives and music of the jazz musicians who were born, or were resident there at one time or another.

JAZZ FROM DETROIT

By Mark Stryker

University of Michigan Press. 342 pages. £33.95. ISBN 978-0-472-07426-6

FOOLNG AROUND

When Tom opened his eyes it took him a couple of seconds to realise where he was. Then he became conscious of the girl beside him, and he raised himself on one arm and looked down at her. She was still asleep, hair spread out on the pillow, mouth slightly open, and head turned to one side. He pulled the sheet down below her breasts and ran a finger lightly over her nipples. She murmured softly and moved towards him, but when he took away his hand she relaxed and her breathing settled into a steady pattern again.

Tom slid out of the bed, pulled on his pyjama pants, and walked over to the window. He drew the curtains partly open, taking care that the light entering the room didn't disturb the girl, and looked down into the street. The shopkeepers were carrying boxes and baskets onto the pavement, and old women, clutching shopping bags and purses, moved slowly among them and occasionally stopped to gossip.

A well-dressed woman getting out of a car attracted Tom's attention. The car had stopped just below the window and the woman sensed that someone was watching her. Her skirt had pulled back high on her thighs as she slid her legs onto the pavement. She glanced each way along the street and then took off her dark glasses and looked up at Tom. When she saw him, his hair tousled, one hand scratching his bare chest, she smiled and made a motion with her hands. Tom shook his head and pointed back over his shoulder into the room. He held his hands together and rested his head on them. The woman seemed to understand and shrugged her shoulders. She waved to Tom and he waved back.

"Who's there, Tom?" the girl said in German, and when he turned he saw she was sitting up in bed. She had his pyjama jacket around her shoulders, but he walked over and pulled it off. He kissed her breasts. "Who was it?" she asked, this time in English.

"A kid", he answered, "I was fooling around with a kid". He pressed her against the pillow and kissed her. When he lowered himself onto her she tensed a little, but soon began thrusting her thighs against his.

When they'd finished Tom lay beside her and they talked about having to leave the place that day.

"Oh, I wish we could stay another night", she said, speaking in German as she invariably did when she was emotionally involved with something. Tom didn't say anything in answer to this, but when she asked him if he loved her, he said "Of course", and stood up and started dressing.

The girl lay on the bed, watching him, and she suddenly said, "You'll leave me soon". It wasn't an accusation, or a question, but a statement of fact she'd obviously decided to believe in. When Tom looked at her she laughed and made a funny face at him.

"You don't know", he told her, but she shook her head and laughed again. She got off the bed and walked over to the wash-basin. As she was filling it with water she hummed the tune of "The Faithful Hussar" and smiled at Tom a mocking manner.

"You don't know", he insisted, and she giggled and flicked some water at him. "Alright", he said, "I will leave you soon. Now, does that make you any happier?".

"Who was outside, Tom?" she asked quietly.

"I told you. A kid. I was fooling around." He was tying his shoe-laces as he said this, and when he looked up he saw the tears in her eyes. She stood facing him, fists clenched and mouth trembling.

"You're always fooling around, aren't you?" she said.

THE GIRL

She was small and blonde, and Tom thought her attractive, though in actual fact her mouth was too wide, and her profile somehow out of proportion to the rest of her. He could always tell who it was from behind, because of the way she had of walking with her head thrown back, as if she was determined not to take any notice of the men who looked at her. She also had well-shaped legs.

He ought to have known after the first few conversations that he would have trouble with her. She sometimes read poetry and she had a few bohemian friends and enjoyed talking about them. One was a writer who lived in a shabby flat, and didn't work. He didn't publish, either, but it was hard for a dedicated writer to be published, she said. It always made Tom feel uncomfortable as he stood, neatly dressed and obviously not starving, listening to her talk about someone like that. She had read Tom's poems and given him his books back with a smile and the comment, "They're nice and simple, but I prefer poetry which is more subtle, if you know what I mean". Tom felt he ought to apologise for dressing tidily and not writing obscure poetry.

Another of her tricks – he was convinced they were tricks – was the way in which she rubbed it in about how she'd travelled a lot. Tom hadn't but felt forced to improvise. Yes, he'd been to Ireland (he didn't tell her he was only there a couple of days) and he'd spent two years in Germany (in the army) and Paris (eight days) and Holland (briefly passing through). Then she asked him if he spoke French. No, he muttered, and she turned away and looked at the sunset across the park. "Doesn't it just make you feel like dashing off somewhere?" she said. Tom thought about the nearest pub and agreed.

So it went on. Tom enjoyed seeing her, although she nearly always upset him when they were together. When she found out that he'd written quite a few articles and reviews for various magazines and newspapers, she asked if he'd read a certain novel. No, he replied, and she arched her eyebrows in surprise. It was one of her writer friend's favourite books, she told Tom. It would be, he thought, and felt like asking if he was supposed to have read every bloody book published?

One day she didn't turn up at work, and when Tom asked where she was, someone said, "Oh, didn't you know, she's marrying someone who works for one of the local papers – a reporter, or something".

Tom didn't know, but he thought, Oh, what the hell, and figured he'd at least get a poem out of it. She came out on top right to the end, though. It was rejected by every publication he sent it to, usually with the comment that it was far too obscure.

THE SALESMEN

They all wore their best suits to the meeting, and they had their hair cut short, not that it was ever really long. Most of them arrived early and stood around talking about business, what this customer was like, the competition they were facing at the moment, how prices were these days. They called each other by their Christian names, but when the managers came through the hallway the salesmen said, "Good morning, Mr......." or "Nasty weather, sir", and laughed loudly at the weak jokes they got in return.

During the meeting they were all very attentive and asked questions at appropriate moments. One manager had an aloof attitude and spoke to them as if briefing junior officers before an attack. Another thumped the table and told them, "Gentlemen, sales promotion does work, we have proved it does. Now let's see you apply it to your particular areas". A third favoured a witty and slightly friendly approach. When the General Manager spoke, however, he was blunt and to the point. The company was cutting down on costs, it was more than likely there would soon be a reduction in staff, this sales campaign counted, and the results would be studied closely when certain decisions were made.

They broke up for lunch and drifted into the bar for a drink. They again talked about business, about what had been said that morning. When they sat down to eat their meal, though, they spoke of cars, holidays abroad, the quality of the food at this restaurant or that, which wine to have with certain dishes, and all the other things they knew everything about.

The meeting finished at four in the afternoon and, with the exception of a couple who'd been asked to stay behind, they all said, "Cheerio, sir", or "Good afternoon, Mr....." to the managers. In the car park they made notes in their diaries, exchanged last-minute snippets of information, and showed each other samples and papers out of the back seats of their cars. The managers were in a group in the hotel, laughing and talking. The two salesmen who had to have an interview with the General Manager were very quiet.

LUNCHTIME O'BOOZE

He was in the long room of the hotel, perched on a stool, his back against the bar and a glass in his hand. "In this job", he said, "I say you're more or less self-employed. I mean you're on your own. Now what would be the use of a union to someone like me?. And don't get me wrong, I'm not against unions when they're responsible, you understand. I mean, don't think I'm condemning working people just because I've managed to rise a bit in the.....well, you know what I mean, how would you say it? Because I've worked towards the position I'm in". He broke off, and glanced around the room, nodding to a couple of men a few feet away, and winking at a girl.

It was Friday lunchtime and the bar was quite full. The girls were in groups, or with their boyfriends, and the men, if not with women, were huddled together, their eyes intense, hands on each other's arms or maybe gesturing, glasses half empty.

"Now take me", he continued, "Can I complain?". He half-turned and rattled his glass on the bar. "A half of bitter for me, dear, and......he waved his hand in my direction. I shook my head.

When his drink came he sat on a stool again, belched, and lit a cigarette. His eyes were wandering around the room. Suddenly, he slid off the stool, and said, "Excuse me". He stepped out into the middle of the floor and said "Hello" to a couple of men who'd just walked in. "Won't you have a drink, Mr.....?", I heard him say, "And your friend, too, of course". As the three of them moved towards the other end of the bar, I could hear him talking briskly about some samples.

When he came back he was smiling broadly. "Another order there, old boy" he said. He bought me a beer, ordered a whisky for himself, and took two more drinks across to the men. They smiled and nodded, and he bent lower over them. A moment later they all burst into laughter, the kind of laughter you hear when someone has just told a dirty joke.

"Well", he continued when he returned. "Just like I was telling you, a man's free in this job. He's not tied to anyone really. I mean, I feel sorry for those people in factories and offices, you know, having to clock on and all that. I couldn't live if I didn't have my independence". His eyes were on the two men in the corner, watching their glasses, waiting for them to finish.

THE SWINGER
(A sketch from the Sixties)

I was looking along the shelves of poetry books when this character came in. He wore a coloured shirt and jeans, and also had on a kind of fur coat whuch hung below his knees. He said, "Hi, kids" to everyone and walked over to the telephone. Then he turned back to the counter. "Like, has anyone from Tony been in for me?" he asked the girl. His accent was a mixture of South London and TV American. She shook her head and he went back to the phone, picked it up, and dialled a number.

I was near enough to hear it stop ringing at the other end. "Hey, Tony". he said, "Like, I'm here, man, at the bookshop and there hasn't anyone shown to lay the bread on me". He paused, listening. "Well, like all right, man", he carried on, "But that ain't cool". Another pause. "Yes, man, I know, but when you fuck up my scene too, man, well, you know". He listened again, clicking his fingers and shuffling his feet. "Well, all right. Now, look, man, you just can't say you don't want the things. I mean, I've had people working on this, man, and it costs money. OK, baby, it's a bad world, but we're all cool down here, man, and it's staying that way. Now, come on, man, stop fucking up, and how about the bread?"

I glanced around the shop. Two girls were standing in a corner, whispering, and a couple of bearded types in scruffy clothes were flicking through a pile of magazines. No-one was taking any notice of the character on the phone, apart from me, and I was pretending not to listen. He was still talking about the money, but by now his voice had a nasty edge to it. "Man, you asked for them, we've delivered, but there ain't no bread. Now, come on, like, you know, I'm not putting any of mine in. I've been caught that way before. These people want paying, and, like, man, you've got the bread". He clicked his fingers and waved to a couple who had just walked in. A pause, "Like, if I don't get it then I'm going to have to give your address to these people. I mean, they want paying, man". His mouth had a thin, exasperated look about it as he listened to what was being said on the other end of the line. "OK, I'll be over in twenty". He slammed down the phone and "Shit".

When he went towards the door the bearded boys smiled and said something to him. "Hi", he replied, and went across to the people who'd come in when he was on the phone. He kissed the girl and put his arm around the boy. They talked for a few minutes and then he said

231

he had to leave. At the door he turned and looked around the shop. "God bless everyone", he said, "Peace and love", and they all said, "Yeah, Mike" and "See you, Mike" and "Later, Mike" until the door closed.

Contents of Jim Burns' previous essay collections

Beats, Bohemians and Intellectuals *Trent Books 2000*

Radicals, Beats and Beboppers *PPP (2011)*

Brits, Beats & Outsiders *PPP (2012)*

Bohemians, Beats and Blues People *PPP* (2013)

Artists, Beats and Cool Cats *PPP* (2014)

Rebels, Beats and Poets *PPP* (2015)

PREVIOUS COLLECTIONS

Anarchists, Beats & Dadaists *PPP* (2016)

Paris, Painters, Poets *PPP* (2017)

Painting, Poetry, Politics (*PPP* 2018)

Books, Artists, Beats (PPP 2019)

Militants, Artists Poets (PPP 2020)